International Cooperation:
The Extents and Limits of Multilateralism

A number of new approaches to the subject of international cooperation were developed in the 1980s. As a result, further questions have arisen, particularly with regard to the methods and limits of cooperation and the relationship between cooperation and the debate over multilateralism. *International Cooperation* considers these questions, identifies further areas for research, and pushes the analysis of this fundamental concept in international relations in new directions. Its two parts address the historic roots and modern development of the notion of cooperation, and the strategies used to achieve it, with a conclusion that reaches beyond international relations into new disciplinary avenues. This edited collection incorporates historical research, social and economic analysis, and political and evolutionary game theory.

I. William Zartman is the Jacob Blaustein Distinguished Professor Emeritus of International Organization and Conflict Resolution at the Paul H. Nitze School of Advanced International Studies of the Johns Hopkins University. He is the author of a number of books, including *Cowardly Lions: Missed Opportunities for Preventing Deadly Conflict and State Collapse* (2005) and *Negotiation and Conflict Management: Essays on Theory and Practice* (2008), and editor of *Imbalance of Power: US Hegemony and International Order* (2009) and *Peacemaking in International Conflict: Methods and Techniques* (2005). He is recipient of the Lifetime Achievement Award of the International Association for Conflict Management.

The late Saadia Touval, former professor and Dean at Tel Aviv University, taught at Johns Hopkins University's Paul H. Nitze School of Advanced International Studies from 1994 to 2007. He was the author of a number of books including *The Peace Brokers: Mediation in the Arab–Israeli Conflict, 1948–1979* (1982) and *Mediation in the Yugoslav Wars* (2001).

International Cooperation: The Extents and Limits of Multilateralism

Edited by

I. William Zartman

and

Saadia Touval

The Nitze School of Advanced International Studies,
The Johns Hopkins University

CAMBRIDGE UNIVERSITY PRESS
Cambridge, New York, Melbourne, Madrid, Cape Town, Singapore,
São Paulo, Delhi, Dubai, Tokyo

Cambridge University Press
The Edinburgh Building, Cambridge CB2 8RU, UK

Published in the United States of America by Cambridge University Press,
New York

www.cambridge.org
Information on this title: www.cambridge.org/9780521191296

First published 2010

Printed in the United Kingdom at the University Press, Cambridge

A catalogue record for this publication is available from the British Library

Library of Congress Cataloguing in Publication data
International cooperation : the extents and limits of multilateralism / edited by
I. William Zartman, Saadia Touval.
    p.   cm.
ISBN 978-0-521-19129-6 (hardback)
1. International cooperation.   I. Zartman,   I. William.   II. Touval, Saadia.
III. Title.
JZ1318.I568   2010
327.1′7–dc22

                                                        2009045830

ISBN 978-0-521-19129-6 Hardback
ISBN 978-0-521-13865-9 Paperback

To the late Saadia Touval,
warm friend, close colleague, twin

Contents

Figures

Tables

Contributors

JEAN-CLAUDE BERTHÉLEMY is Professor of Economics at the University of Paris 1 Panthéon-Sorbonne, where he received his PhD in 1984. He was Director of the CEPIII (*Centre d'Etudes Prospectives et d'Informations Internationales*), the leading French think tank specializing in international economics, from 1998 to 2000. Before holding that position he had worked for about seven years for the Organization of Economic Cooperation and Development, where he was Head of Division at the Development Centre. He has also collaborated with other international organizations such as the World Bank, the International Monetary Fund, the African Development Bank, the United Nations Development Programme, and The World Institute for Development Economics Research. He has published numerous articles on development economics in referred journals, as well as eleven books, related to a variety of subjects such as economic growth analysis, development finance, and peace economics. Among other professional affiliations, he is a member of the European Development Research Network, of which he was elected vice-president in 2004. In recognition of his significant contributions to development economics, he was in November 2003 awarded the Luc Durand-Réville prize by the French Académie des sciences morales et politiques.

CHARLES DORAN is Andrew W. Mellon Professor of International Relations and Director of the Global Theory and History and Canadian Studies Programs at the Paul H. Nitze School of Advanced International Studies, The Johns Hopkins University. His recent books are *Power Cycle Theory and Global Politics* (2003, special issue of *International Political Science Review*), *Democratic Pluralism at Risk: Why Canadian Unity Matters and Why Americans Care* (2001) and *Systems in Crisis: Imperatives of High Politics at the Century's End* (1991). His doctorate is from The Johns Hopkins University. charles.doran@att.net

JOSHUA S. GOLDSTEIN is Professor Emeritus of International Relations at the American University in Washington. He is author of *International*

Relations (9th ed., 2010), *How Gender Shapes the War System and Vice Versa* (2001), and *Long Cycles: Prosperity and War in the Modern Age* (1988). His doctorate is from the Massachusetts Institute of Technology. jg@joshuagoldstein.com

FEN OSLER HAMPSON is Chancellor's Professor and Director of the Norman Paterson School of International Affairs, Carleton University, Ottawa. His recent works are *Nurturing Peace: Why Peace Settlements Succeed or Fail* (1996) and *Multilateral Negotiations: Lessons From Arms Control, Trade, and the Environment* (1999). He holds a PhD from Harvard. fen_hampson@carleton.ca

P. TERRENCE HOPMANN is Professor of International Relations and Director of the Conflict Management Program at the Paul H. Nitze School of Advanced International Studies, The Johns Hopkins University. He is Professor Emeritus of Political Science at Brown University, where he also served as Director of the Global Security Program in the Thomas J. Watson Jr. Institute of International Studies. His recent research has focused on conflict management by regional security institutions, especially the Organization for Security and Cooperation in Europe. His major book is *The Negotiation Process and the Resolution of International Conflicts* (1996). His doctorate is from Stanford. pthopmann@jhu.edu

ALEXIS KELLER is Professor of History of Legal and Political Thought at the University of Geneva. He is a former fellow of the Carr Center for Human Rights Policy at the Kennedy School of Government, Harvard University. Most recently, he has edited *What is a Just Peace?* (2006) and *Counterterrorism: Democracy's Challenge* (2008). He is currently working on a book entitled *Defending Justice among Nations (1650–1850)*. His doctorate is from the University of Geneva. Alexis. Keller@droit.unige.ch

DEBORAH WELCH LARSON is Professor of Political Science at the University of California, Los Angeles. Her research draws on cognitive social psychology to explain foreign-policy decision making, as in *Origins of Containment: A Psychological Explanation* (1985). She is the author most recently of *Anatomy of Mistrust: U.S.–Soviet Relations during the Cold War* (1997) and *Good Judgment in Foreign Policy: Theory and Application* (2003, with Stanley Renshon). She holds a Stanford PhD. dlarson@polisci.ucla.edu

ALEXEI V. SHEVCHENKO is Assistant Professor at the Department of Political Science, California State University Fullerton. His research interests include international relations theory and the foreign policies of China and Russia. His previous work appeared in *No More States? Globalization, National Self-Determination, and Terrorism*, ed. Richard N. Rosecrance and Arthur A. Stein (2006), *Communist and Post-Communist Studies*, and *International Organization*. His doctorate is from UCLA. ashevchenko@fullerton.edu

ALLISON STANGER is the Russell Leng Professor of International Politics and Economics, chair of the Political Science Department, and Director of the Rohatyn Center for International Affairs at Middlebury College. Her most recent book is *One Nation Under Contract: The Outsourcing of American Power and the Future of Foreign Policy* (2009). A mathematics major as an undergraduate, she received her PhD in political science from Harvard University. stanger@middlebury.edu

The late SAADIA TOUVAL was Adjunct Professor and Associate Director of the Conflict Management Program at the Paul H. Nitze School of Advanced International Studies, The Johns Hopkins University. He was former Professor and Political Science Department Chair and Dean at Tel Aviv University. He is the author of *The Peace Brokers* (1982) and *Mediation in the Yugoslav Wars* (2002) among others. His doctorate is from Harvard.

I. WILLIAM ZARTMAN is the Jacob Blaustein Distinguished Professor Emeritus at the Nitze School of Advanced International Studies (SAIS) of The Johns Hopkins University, and member of the Steering Committee of the Processes of International Negotiation (PIN) Program at the International Institute of Applied Systems Analysis (IIASA) in Vienna. He is author of *Cowardly Lions: Missed Opportunities to Prevent Deadly Conflict and State Collapse* (2005) and *Negotiation and Conflict Management: Essays on Theory and Practice* (2007) among others. His doctorate is from Yale and his honorary doctorate from the Catholic University of Louvain. zartman@jhu.edu

Acknowledgements

I am grateful to SAIS and the US Institute of Peace for their generous support for this project and to Isabelle Talpain-Long for carefully shepherding the manuscript through to completion. Thanks too to Julia Lendorfer for indexing. I am above all grateful for the chance to work with my friend, colleague, and twin Saadia Touval on this work, our last and lasting of a long list of collaboration.

1 Introduction: return to the theories of cooperation

I. William Zartman and Saadia Touval

Cooperation among states is much more common than war. Yet there is much less conceptualization about cooperation than there is about the causes of and behavior in war, and the study of international cooperation – attempts to understand the phenomenon – has produced much debate. "Conflict seems very natural, and it is easy to understand, ... Cooperation, however, appears as a phenomenon that requires subtle explanations" (Hammerstein 2003, pp. 1–2).

Cooperation is defined here as a situation where parties agree to work together to produce new gains for each of the participants unavailable to them by unilateral action, at some cost. Its constituent elements are working together, agreement to do so (not just coincidence), cost, and new gains for all parties. (This definition is not too far from, but a bit more specific than, *Webster's*: "an association of parties for their common benefit; collective action in pursuit of common well-being." Cf. Smith 2003; Clements and Stephens 1995; Dugatkin 1997). By "gains" we mean not only material gains, but also perception of progress toward goals, such as improved security, status, or freedom of action for oneself and the imposition of constraints on other actors, and so on. Thus, cooperation is used here to mean more than simply the opposite or absence of conflict, as some binary codings indicate. It is a conscious, specific, positive action.

Some definitions require that at least one party in the cooperating group be worse off, at least in the short run, by cooperating than by not cooperating (Bowles and Gintis 2003; Richerson et al. 2003), but this definition is illogical. The party in question would only cooperate if its calculations are other than material and/or short run; it must get either (non-material) satisfaction or long-run gains of some sort to make cooperation worthwhile. The opposite of this condition of cost without gain is the free-rider problem of gain without cost. But this in its turn depends on the establishment of cooperation by those who both pay and gain.

Conflicts in meaning

But differences in the use of the term in reference to the dynamics of cooperation and its reflection in multilateralism still abound, and are reflected in some of the following chapters. Both terms – "cooperation" and "multilateral" – carry pairs of meanings in popular usage, developing different implications from different meanings. They raise new questions and suggest areas for further inquiry.

Cooperation sometimes refers to actors' strategy aimed at resolving particular issues, and sometimes to a pattern of interactions – in other words, to a relationship, as explored in the chapters by Doran and Hampson. The first, resolving specific issues, can take place between states that are antagonistic, even hostile to each other. Like the United States and the Soviet Union during the Cold War or Israel and Hizbollah in their prisoner exchange, antagonists, even enemies, cooperate on occasions to resolve specific concerns, without addressing the broader conflict – in other words, to manage but not to resolve their conflict (George, Farley, and Dallin 1988; Kanet and Kolodziej 1991). Descriptions of strategies available to competing players in various game theory models often use the term "cooperation" in the same sense of agreement to resolve particular issues.

The second meaning of the term, describing a relationship, refers not only to specific interactions but also implies a desire on the part of the actors to maintain and foster those interactions through joint problem solving. It also implies a certain basic empathy between them, and a mutual sense that each party's well-being depends on the well-being of the other. It does not preclude occasional conflict, or competition between the parties. But it presupposes a security community, where a resort to violence and war is unthinkable (e.g. United States–Britain, United States–Canada, the European Union, NATO).

"Multilateral," too, has two forms, developed in the following chapters. One is the noun, "multilateral*ism*", in the sense of a diplomatic strategy employed by states in order to coordinate policy among three or more actors or cooperation in its second meaning (Ruggie 1993). It is sometimes described as a pattern of behavior that contributes to world peace, and therefore is intrinsically moral. The other, "multilateral" as an adjective, without the "ism", is often used to refer to an ad hoc tactic (or strategy) adopted by a state or group of states in pursuit of a defined objective, in the first definition of cooperation. Such a strategy may be aimed at resolving or reducing conflict among the participating parties, but it may also be used to compete against others who are excluded from the group, to put pressure on them, even to fight them.

Multilateralism as a foreign policy principle has been attributed by Ruggie and Ikenberry to the United States in certain historical periods, primarily the latter half of the twentieth century, as discussed in the Larson and Shevchenko chapter. The other, a multilateral strategy, has been attributed to coalitions, such as military alliances and trade blocs, and to great power concerts, as discussed in the chapter by Zartman. The first is inclusive, and tends toward universal membership; the second is exclusive. It is sometimes called "minilateralism," "plurilateralism," or "bilateralism" – a strategy of coordinating with single or small numbers of partners, through separate arrangements with each of them, as Touval notes. Since mutilateral strategies are exclusive,they can have contradictory purposes – multilateral cooperation to act and multilateral cooperation to block action. Hampson and Doran in their chapters refer to further variations in the meaning of the term.

Such different meanings attached to terms can hinder communication and hamper effective research. Mere recognition that terms can mean different things is a step forward. Rather than invent new terms, the following discussion will explore differences while trying to keep the different uses and their implications explicit.

Conflict and cooperation

While there is conflict without cooperation, it appears that there is no cooperation without conflict. Cooperation is dependent on these being conflict to overcome. Indeed, attempts at cooperation may create conflict (to be overcome), since the parties' attempt to work together brings out differing interests to be tailored to fit – the costs of cooperation. By "conflict" we do not mean war or violence, but rather perceptions of incompatibilities. Cooperating nations generally perceive both common and conflicting interests. They may thus disagree about some of their goals, their respective contributions, the burdens they carry, and the benefits they derive in the common enterprise. This produces a rich field for inquiry on why states cooperate, how they arrive at cooperation, how they practice cooperation, and how cooperation is sustained.

If so, then the first step in understanding cooperation is to take stock of the current understanding of "conflict." While the term is frequently used as shorthand for "violent conflict," the violent form of conflict cannot be understood without addressing first its broader form, which is simply an incompatibility of goals (Bernard 1949; 1957, p. 38; Coser 1956, p. 8). Of course, incompatibility is scarcely significant if it is taken lying down; it is when value incompatibility leads to some escalation of action or conflict behavior that it becomes an object of concern, both practical and analytical. A focused form of this notion sees frustration over the inability to attain blocked goals as the source of conflict, based on a clear understanding of the component incompatibilities.

However, recent studies have focused on the misperception and fear of conflict behavior as the basis of perceived incompatibilities, rather than on the substance of the incompatibilities themselves. Conflict comes from the security dilemma, where a party seeking to assure even minimal security is perceived as acting threateningly toward another party, who takes measures to assure its own security and thereby threatens the other even more (Jervis 1978; Posner 1993). The current focus of analysis is on information, bypassing the substance of the incompatibility. If parties could accurately communicate both their intentions and their capabilities, they would not venture into conflict, which would be either unnecessary or unwise (Fearon 1995).

On this basis cooperation is achieved by overcoming the tendency toward conflict, whether that tendency is based on objective incompatibilities or on erroneous information about them. However, the remedy is different in the two views of conflict sources. If the conflict lies in real goal incompatibility, that clash must be dealt with by lowering the incompatibility or at least its salience. Various means are available: one party can bow to the other, the two can negotiate concessions or compensation or can construct a new set of goals that reframes them in such a way that they become compatible or are subsumed under superordinate values, or, finally, the parties can agree that the incompatible goals are unimportant and table them without actually dropping them. More importantly, these means of reducing the conflict borne of incompatibilities can be exercised on a case-by-case basis or extended more lengthily and generically. Even ad hoc resolution builds norms and precedents that influence future cooperative settlements, whereas longer-term or more institutionalized measures and mechanisms address generic elements explicitly.

If unreliable information is the problem, the answer is easier in concept: get it right! But because it is suspicion about information that is the difficulty, more information is as suspect as less; cooperation comes with the installation of trust. (Yet mechanisms for inducing trust, such as provisions for verification and punishment or for third parties as trustholders, usually require cooperation in order to produce cooperation: a circular argument.)

Nature and cooperation

The analytical questions then become, why, when and how do parties agree to pay the cost of working together to produce new gains? and how do they then apportion the gains so as to maintain their cooperation? A common reason for cooperation is interdependence. States are not politically or economically autarkic; they are not alone. They need the active or passive help of others in order to achieve their goals. They need others as allies to help assure their security, they need them for establishing rules of international behavior, they need them for commerce and as partners in managing international economic relations, and they need them to help protect from public bads such as environmental risks. Calculations of efficiency accompany the needs generated by interdependence: states may believe that it would cost them less to achieve their goals by cooperating with others than to act alone.

Social scientists debate whether cooperation is innate or learned, whether it is genetic or social, related to fairness ("what's best for all of us") as opposed to justice ("what's best for me, and what you deserve"), hence whether it is based in inherent tendencies toward unselfish or selfish behavior. Some scholars believe that states are defensive, self-identifying, and self-interested entities, whose leaders are responsible only for their population's security and welfare, and are therefore in competitive or conflictual relation with other states. They must have done something, however, to overcome this natural condition of conflict and produce the prevailing cooperation. This action is extraordinarily successful, given the pervasiveness of cooperation over conflict, yet relatively little is known about it conceptually. This work aims at expanding that knowledge.

Notions of inherently selfish behavior or "cooperation for me" include elements of acquisition, effectiveness, and efficiency (Lax and Sebenius 1986). "Acquisition" refers to the need to create value where the desired ends are unavailable to the individual party. "Effectiveness" refers to the need to work with other parties to create that value and accomplish certain goals, when parties cannot achieve their ends unilaterally. "Efficiency" refers to the need to reduce costs – primarily transaction costs – in working with other parties, so that the wheel of concerted action does not need to be reinvented each time. These three needs – elusive ends, scarce means, reducible costs – drive parties to work together over a short or longer time, depending in turn on their estimates of the other parties' proclivities to do the same thing.

Other scholars, however, question the view that interstate relations are characterized by a Hobbesian "state of nature" and are inherently conflictual. The notion of innate sociability runs through Grotius, Pufendorf, and Montesquieu to Adam Smith, where it forms the basis of mutual regulation and gains through trade, as Keller discusses in the next chapter. Notions of inherently unselfish behavior or "cooperation in me" include expectations such as requitement, reputation, and fairness (Vogel 2004;

de Waal 1992; Sober and Wilson 1998). Requitement is the expectation of reciprocity, negative and/or positive, an inherent quality in social relations and in most ethical systems. Reputation refers to the expectations parties create about themselves, operating in two directions in support of cooperation: as images that parties tend for purposes of self-esteem, and as bases for others' actions. Fairness, a loose form of justice, involves the expectation and behavioral norm that parties are due to receive treatment corresponding to some universal notion of equality, either as numerical individuals or as deserving actors (Zartman et al. 1996; Albin 2001). These three qualities, and perhaps others in support, provide a network that lies at the base of claims of inherency in the tendency to cooperate.

Since the debate continues over whether cooperative behavior is innate or learned, the search for the etiology and the means of cooperation must take both into account. But the difference between the two assumptions is not as great as is often assumed. For those who see cooperation as innate it is the avoidance of conflict, whereas for those for whom it must be learned it is a defense against conflict. Either way, cooperation is the antidote to conflict. The two approaches differ, however, on the durability of cooperation.

Schools and cooperation

The key to cooperation is reciprocity, that is, an assurance of similar, beneficial return behavior in the future. Selfish states bury conflict if (as long as) the other party does so too, and unselfish states bury conflict because the other party does so too; again, the grave is shallower for the first than for the second. Thus the various schools of international relations (IR) differ only in their perspective: Realists take a short-term and Liberals a long-term view. The former believe that cooperation is not sustainable but occurs only on a momentary basis, as long as benefits are present and up to date. Parties have a tendency to cheat and free-ride as soon as they can gain greater benefits from doing so than from cooperating. Problems of information cannot be overcome reliably, since states will cheat when it is in their interest to do so; all that can be done is to understand when cheating is likely and to take appropriate safeguards. Indeed, Realism, by its short-term "rational" tendency to defect, actually reduces the benefits of cooperation, by enhancing fear of defection (Bowles and Gintis 2003, p. 433, implicitly equate Realists with sociopaths).

Liberals believe that states cooperate in the expectation of benefits from future cooperation, as well as current payoffs. In addition they hold that anticipated reciprocity provides benefits from reputation and relationship that are not only less precise but tie states into patterns of behavior. Information can play a role in sustaining this expectation, since the greater the reliable information on future reciprocity, the greater the chances of cooperation lasting. Since it is inefficient to negotiate the terms of reciprocity each time, states institutionalize their cooperation through regimes, laws, and organizations. Thus Realists take measures to guard against foreseeable defection, whereas Liberals emphasize measures to prolong foreseeable cooperation.

Yet cooperation is more than just about defection and reciprocity, despite much of the current focus; it is about benefits – their creation and their allocation. The mechanisms by which cooperation is established carry high transaction costs; it is always quicker to act by oneself and, beyond that, costs rise in proportion to the number of parties, as discussed by Touval below. Theoretically, however, costs should fall in relation to the number of issues, since more issues provide more trade-offs and a greater chance to attain "comparative advantage" deals at the Nash Point according to Homans' Maxim (1960) – "The more the items at stake can be divided into goods valued more by one party than they cost to the other and [the reverse], the greater the chances of a successful outcome." These negotiations deal with the twin aspects of cooperation, value-making and value taking, referring to integrative and distributive negotiations. Cooperation, as noted, occurs to create beneficial outcomes that the parties cannot create alone, but it is also needed to allocate those benefits; there is always a distributive as well as an integrative aspect to cooperation.

Beyond creation and allocation of costs and benefits, cooperation is also about underlying or overarching values as an element that separates Realists from Liberals. For cooperation to be more than a single engagement, as Realists see it, it must rest on and contribute to a community of values, as Hampson discusses. Thus negotiations on cooperation relate not only to the specific stakes and measures of the encounter but also to the pact-building relationship and reiteration – that is, to shared decision-making.

These two aspects of cooperation can be dealt with instance by instance or on a more prolonged basis through the establishment of regimes, both through negotiation (Spector and Zartman 2003). The advantages of each are straightforward: successive, essentially ad hoc negotiations are less efficient, since the wheel of cooperation has to be reinvented each time, whereas regimes are established and corrected by negotiated principles that do not have to concern themselves with the immediate details of individual cases. Essentially, regimes establish formulas for cooperation, leaving the details to their application, while "reinvented" cooperation needs to negotiate both formula and details. In reality, the two necessarily overlap, since even ad hoc cooperation in an area not governed by pre-viously negotiated regimes does not occur in a vacuum, but in a context of norms, expectations, and precedents that act as a proto-regime. The philosophy of multilateral cooperation, termed "multilateralism," confers legitimacy as one of its benefits, more so than unilateralism or bilateral-ism, although it does so at the expense of efficiency and possibly even of effectiveness.

There is also an external problem to cooperation: how to legitimize it to those outside, whether those rejecting the action or those not invited to join it. Cooperation has an outside shell, involving cooperation with those who are not enemies but nonetheless are external to the cooperating core. It is in the interest of the cooperators not to arouse conflict with those left out, lest they make common cause with the conflictors. This area lies outside the normal conceptual concerns of cooperation but is of crucial importance to practitioners. Bilateral cooperation is also a means to deal with other states that are not involved in the core multilateral cooperative enterprise, but it may compound the problem. An alliance between two may be perceived by others as impacting on their security, bilateral trade affects the commercial prospects of others, and so on. This is why coop-eration requires consideration of its wider impact, and why it often assumes multilateral form. Again, Liberals handle the problem better than Realists, who seem to assume conflict in any case. For Liberals, regimes and extended, forward-looking, even institutionalized coopera-tion sets the stage for at least substantive, if not procedural, inclusion of the outer shell, leaving them free to join later or to approve without direct involvement. Yet handling that gray area of cooperation, the subject of Zartman's chapter, is a major practical as well as conceptual challenge.

As in so many aspects of international relations (and probably other) theory, error lies in an insistence on exclusivity. It is important both to prolong foreseeable cooperation and to protect against defection, since the latter fosters the former. Cooperation is not self-implementing; one has to work at it, because of the danger of conflict. Even the proponents of inherently unselfish behavior would agree. On this basis, this book turns toward an examination of ways of accomplishing these two goals of cooperation.

New understandings of cooperation

The contributions to this book address these questions, harking back to central issues in these debates and to the group of seminal works that launched the subject over a ten-year period beginning two decades ago (Axelrod 1984; Taylor 1987; Young 1989; Stein 1990; Stein and Pauly

1993). As much as possible, this collection seeks to fill holes left by the initial studies, often where the holes were explicitly acknowledged.

One group of essays deals with the various ambiguities and implications inherent in the meanings of cooperation itself. The historic basis of the debate is developed by Alexis Keller, following on the philosophical side of the argument developed by Taylor in 1987. He shows how an alternative understanding of interstate relations, contrasted to the post-Westphalian view of formal and hierarchical legal relations – law – grew up grounded in commerce as cooperation. The approach replaced the model of international anarchy with a model of the market, which, though self-ordered, implies norms of cooperation and specific actions to maintain it. Charles Doran discusses the question of how many it takes to cooperate. Both bilateral and multilateral arrangements take a state – particularly a hegemonic state – away from unconstrained unilateralism but with very different implications, the two being conflicting alternatives to each other. Cooperation provides resources, legitimacy, and approval, to create value or benefits. It raises problems, however, over the allocation of those benefits and the appropriate size to claim that legitimacy, as well as problems arising from transaction time.

Fen Osler Hampson develops further subdivisions with the typology of multilateral cooperation. In a second level of debate beyond the initial questions about cooperation itself, institutionalized cooperation raises procedural questions about the allocation of role as well as substantive questions about the allocation of payoffs and benefits. Saadia Touval examines many of these characteristics from the angle of multilateral negotiation, in both symmetrical and asymmetrical situations, a subject left over from Young's study of regime formation. Multilateral cooperation requires negotiation because parties have to come together to establish the norms and principles they wish to institute and to coordinate their policies. However, cooperation among unequal parties can work two ways – to lock in norms and principles that either assure the compliance of the weaker parties and/or promise the compliance of the stronger party were it later to lose its hegemony.

A second group of essays addresses strategies of cooperation and their implications. P. Terrence Hopmann examines structural and motivational factors that lead to negotiation and cooperation; negotiation as a cooperative process that creates the terms of a more prolonged cooperation has not received the attention its importance merits from theorization over international politics. Focusing on the process of negotiating cooperation, he reaches beyond the Realist–Liberal debate to link cooperation to the constructivist approach and to IR theory more broadly. Picking up on the game theoretic images in the previous chapter, Joshua Goldstein develops the unsung side of the classical dilemmas, the Chicken Dilemma Game (CDG) discussed by Taylor (1987), which receives less attention than its Prisoner (PDG) cousin. Yet CDG is a much more frequent image of interstate problems of cooperation, its two equilibria posing a coordination rather than a collaboration problem. While double defection – the Prisoner's second worst, but the Chicken's worst, outcome – is avoided, it takes strategies of creativity to arrive at cooperation. Chicken shows the perception of the situation that pushes the parties to create a new game reflecting such strategies. Allison Stanger, starting off from Axelrod's 1984 study on the evolution of cooperation, examines the impact of past experience upon learning to cooperate through interaction. To the Shadow of the Future, she adds the Shadow of the Past and to these "vertical shadows" she adds the "horizontal shadows" of current relations. Taking up a topic that Stein (1990, pp. 188–98) left as context-dependent, I. William Zartman examines the relation between cooperation and two different types of conflict management – cooperation as a strategy of dealing with conflict with another party, and cooperation as a strategy for managers of conflict among third parties. While the first represents a major shift in policy, it is found that it depends on the second, termed the "playback effect" or the "alliance dilemma" (Stein 1990, p. 188) and not just on estimates of success and of cost-benefits.

At the end, two contributions use specific case studies to examine the role of asymmetry in multilateral cooperation. Deborah Larson and Alexi Shevchenko employ social psychology to look at asymmetrical cooperation in a hegemonic system, by examining ways by which the United States can persuade states that are not allies to cooperate. By addressing status concerns, the greater power can lessen the attraction of competition and conflict strategies and attitudes on the part of second-level powers. This means avoiding conflict and competition strategies on the part of the hegemon, and making cooperation rather than convergence a basis of policy. The analysis focuses on functional identity enhancement as a basis for building cooperation in place of conflict. Jean-Claude Berthélemy examines the effects of asymmetric cooperation through the angle of development aid policies. Allocation favors the stronger party's proximate interests in bilateral aid relations, and tends to be more altruistic (i.e., favoring more distant interests) in the case of multilateral aid. But since the chosen recipients of self-interested bilateral cooperation tend to be open economies that are favored by the underlying trade linkages between the two sides, the ostensibly one-sided interest is rebalanced. On the other hand, weaker economies, which cannot attract self-interested bilateral cooperation, benefit from multilateral cooperation, however asymmetrical.

The concluding chapter brings in an additional literature that was present but not as salient during previous work on cooperation – the study of cooperation and related altruism in evolutionary studies. While much of this work dates from previous decades (Hamilton 1964; Trivers 1971), it has not been applied to international relations or used as a guide for research. The final chapter will do so, in drawing out of the previous chapters their answers to the initial question, why (and when) do states cooperate? and how do these answers relate to related theoretical work? These contributions do not aspire to end the debate over cooperation, so badly needed conceptually and practically, as the editors' conclusion emphasizes, but they will open further discussion, patch holes in the previous analyses, and carry on the debate to create better understandings of the complexities of cooperation.

Part 1

Multilateral meanings of cooperation

2 Debating cooperation in Europe from Grotius to Adam Smith

Alexis Keller

Following the irrevocable success of the Reformation in northern Europe, a new, secular theory on war and interstate relations was needed at the dawn of the seventeenth century. In many ways, it was the Peace of Westphalia (1648) that ushered in what Carl Schmitt (1950) termed the *Jus Publicum Europaeum*. The treaties introduced a secular notion of relations between states and reinvigorated the law of nations (*jus gentium*). They also enshrined the principle of state sovereignty, which had been gradually gaining force since the fourteenth century (Skinner 1978).[1] The law of war, treaties and embassies was all part of the practical and theoretical response to new political challenges. Diplomacy was shaped by the growing need for enduring relations among states. The "balance of power" idea was built as a counterweight to state sovereignty, to rein in the dangers inherent in universal monarchy.

The nature of international society since 1648 has been the subject of an extensive literature. However, international relations theorists have often strayed on a number of key issues. First, their use of terms such as "Westphalian system", "Grotian tradition," and "society of states" is based on a narrow interpretation of thinking on the advent of an international political and legal order.[2] In many ways, their interpretation is ahistorical. Hugo Grotius is thus more renowned for having advocated the existence of an international society than actually analysing its make-up and elucidating how it works.[3] As explained by Edward Keene,

---

[1] The Peace of Westphalia, also known as the Treaties of Münster and Osnabrück, refers to the series of treaties that ended the Thirty Years War. They officially recognized the United Provinces and the Swiss Confederation. The idea of the Holy Roman Empire dominating the entire Christian world was definitely broken, thus giving the sovereigns the right to choose the religion of their state. Recent works have disputed the very existence of a "Westphalian system," or have at least highlighted its limits within the context of international relations. See, e.g. Brown 2002; Strange, 1999; Kegley and Raymond 2002; Lyons and Mastanduno 2001.

[2] For a recent discussion of the problems that flow from conceptualizing modern world history in terms of the idea of a states-system, see the very inspiring study of Edward Keene (2002).

[3] In general, historians of legal and political thought have avoided this oversimplification. For an excellent analysis of Grotius, see Tuck (1977, 1999); see also David Kennedy, (1986, vol. 27, pp. 1–98).

[O]ver the last thirty years or so, the historical analysis of Grotianism by theorists of international relations has moved away from debates about the sources, content and scope of international law within a *societas gentium*, and has instead concentrated on debates about the nature of international politics within a states-system. (Keene 2002, p. 40)

Furthermore, their blinkered interpretation has led these theorists to categorize conflicting views on international politics. Hedley Bull, for example, drew on Martin Wight to suggest what has become a classic distinction between three rival intellectual traditions: the Hobbesian or realist tradition, which sees international politics as a state of war; the Grotian or internationalist tradition, which presents international politics as a cornerstone of international society; and the Kantian or universalist tradition, which argues that international politics has the potential to embrace humanity as a whole (Wight 1991, especially ch. 2; Bull 1977). Similarly, other authors have referred to the Machiavellian or Hobbesian anthropological pessimism, or Kant's optimism (Boucher 1998).[4] While these categories are useful and valid in their own right, they provide an incomplete picture of early modern international legal thought. They squeeze Grotius's, Hobbes's, or Kant's extremely eclectic account of the law of nations into a small box that was historically constructed in the early nineteenth century for the specific purpose of defending the independence of dynastic monarchs against the French Revolution and Napoleonic imperialism.[5]

Moreover, these categories offer a historical narrative of the development of the legal and political order in the modern world that excludes one of the eighteenth century's flagship approaches to analyzing interstate relations: the idea of the market.[6] Throughout the seventeenth century, the legal notion of "contract" was central to political and legal theories. It accounted for the very existence of society, which was founded on a political pact. The fundamental question at the time was how to think about the development of society and politics without resorting to external

---

[4] David Boucher organizes his book around three traditions of thought, which he terms "empirical realism", "universal moral order", and "historical reason".

[5] Hedley Bull himself recognizes that, in practice, Kant advocates a society of states rather than a World state. Conversely, he contends that even within what he calls the "Grotian tradition," Grotius has a "solidarist" vision heavily influenced by the medieval or Christian idea of universal community, rather than the strictly interstate approach described by Vattel and his successors. For an attempt at moving beyond such classification, see Pangle and Ahrensdorf 1999.

[6] There is a notable exception in the work of Kenneth N. Waltz. In his *Theory of International Politics* (1979), he uses an analogy with microeconomic theory, and especially with the two concepts of economic units and of the market, to conceive an order where formal organization is lacking. Nevertheless, it seems to me that the role of the market in Waltz's theory is purely analogical.

props, primarily from religious circles. However, natural law theorists, including Hobbes, Locke, and Rousseau, came up against a series of theoretical hurdles, one of which is particularly relevant here. Although social contract theories posited the principle of civil peace, they were somewhat disappointing in their analysis of war and peace between states. Social contract in society fitted the definition of a non-zero-sum game (improved security and civil peace make everybody a "winner"), but dealings between states were stuck in a zero-sum loop (one party wins what the other loses).

In the eighteenth century, the idea of depicting civil society as a market offered some theorists a way over that hurdle. A theory of exchange made it possible to grasp that, unlike military interaction, economic relations between states constituted a win–win situation. It also paved the way for interstate cooperation to be analyzed in non-legal terms, outside the language of rights. This new understanding of international relations came into its own in France and, above all, in Scotland through the work of Adam Smith. It broadened the idea of the market beyond that of a mere technical mechanism structuring economic activity, and embraced a deeper sociological and political purpose. As such, Adam Smith was not so much the father of political economy as the proponent of a new interpretation of politics proper. Instead of being an economist tinkering with philosophy, he was a philosopher who described his approach to politics as "political economy."[7]

In the first part of my chapter, I shall explore how natural law theorists such as Grotius, Hobbes, Pufendorf, and Locke addressed the issue of the society of nations (*societas gentium*). I will concentrate on their conceptions of the law of nations (*jus gentium*), with its roots in natural law, and take a close look at their attempts to codify the norms governing a new international order. The legal nature of this order will be flagged as well as the importance of the concept of the state of nature in defining interstate relations.[8] Ultimately, diverging from the classifications suggested by many international relations scholars, I shall argue that Grotius and Hobbes were thinking along very similar lines. In the second part of my chapter, I shall seek to show how a number of eighteenth-century

---

[7] For an excellent treatment of Adam Smith's conception of politics, see Winch 1991, 1992; see also Winch 1996, parts I and II.

[8] It must be underlined that, in early modern Europe, the expression "law of nations" was given various meanings. Broadly speaking, it applied to the "relations between human societies." The law of nations was not solely limited to public international law, as it also dealt with the issues of trade, colonies, and the status of foreigners. To limit its scope solely to the relations between states is to misunderstand an entire philosophical movement, which in the eighteenth century argued against this very restriction.

philosophers, using arguments from the natural law theorists, furnished an alternative analysis of interstate relations. Building on the ideas of commerce and market, they posited a *political* model, which broke with both the formal and hierarchical structures of authority and the topics expounded in civic humanism and republicanism (Pocock 1975, 1985; also Hont and Ignatieff 1983). The idea of the market enabled them to depict a new type of international order based on free trade among nations.

Constructing the modern law of nations: Grotius and his successors

In the seventeenth century, there were several attempts at crafting a system of international relations that reflected Europe's religious divide and the new balance of power between states. Theory at last caught up with fact, as Europe was no longer deemed a "Christian republic." Although the dream of universal peace lived on, states merely coexisted and, if necessary, resorted to war to enforce their claims.[9] In the eyes of his contemporaries, Hugo Grotius played a crucial role in redrawing the picture. He viewed the legal relations between nations as a reflection of man's innate sociability. "Man is, to be sure, an animal, but an animal of a superior kind," Grotius wrote in his *De Jure Belli ac Pacis* (1625).

Among the traits characteristic of man is an impelling desire for society, that is, for the social life – not of any and every sort, but peaceful, and organized according to the measure of his intelligence, with those who are of his own kind; this social trend the *Stoics* called "sociableness". . . . The mature man in fact has knowledge, which prompts him to similar actions under similar conditions, together with an impelling desire for society, for the gratification of which he alone among animals possesses a special instrument, speech. He has also been endowed with the faculty of knowing and of acting in accordance with general principles. Whatever accords with that faculty is not common to all animals, but peculiar to the nature of man. (Grotius 1925, II, pp. 11–12).

By championing man's intrinsic sociability, Grotius counters the arguments of the Greek philosopher Carneades and, through him, the Skeptics (Tuck 1983, 1987).[10] It is with this in mind that he alludes to the Stoics in his writing. His faith in sociability enables him to assert that our behavior is not solely driven by self-preservation (*amor sui*). Concern for others is possible. The Grotian rule of sociability is also extrapolated to the

---

[9] The "discovery" of the American continent in 1492 had a significant impact in redefining the rights of war and peace (Tuck 1999; Pagden 1995).

[10] This view has recently been challenged by Thomas Mautner (2005).

international arena provided there are a number of states linked by more than war. Where a state seeks sole dominion, Grotius shares Carneades's view that universal justice is nothing more than window dressing for power. States on an equal footing, however, can get along. This was the line that Grotius held in *De Jure Praedae Commentarius* (1604) in a bid to win Spanish support for unfettered access to the seas.

Sociability implies that war does not lead to the cutting of all legal ties between states. But it leads to the idea that the law of nations is *forged*. Unlike natural law, it is a compendium of "human" rules and conventions shaped through human will. As such, our understanding of it is not preordained, but rather gleaned through jurisprudence. It is with this in mind that Grotius uses historical and biblical illustrations to substantiate his arguments. Drawing on an analogy involving the individual, Grotius describes states as the sole guardians enforcing the law of nations (Grotius 1625, book I, ch. 3, 7, 1–2). Natural law applies to all beings, but although it stems from human reason, men baulk at it deep down in the absence of a *public* facet.[11] Like men, it is the willingness of states to subjugate their will to pacts that lies behind all contracts, pledges, and duties. Pacts signed between states are just as binding on them as promises made between individuals. The law of nations has a moral core which is binding on individual parties and can be summed up in one formal requirement: *pacta sunt servanda*, treaties must be respected.[12]

The linchpin here is the principle of good faith, *fides*, which is center stage in the final six chapters of *De Jure Belli ac Pacis*. The first of those chapters – Chapter 19 of Book 3 – bears the telling title of *De fide inter hostes* and expounds the central theme of the sanctity of agreements between enemies: *fides et hosti servanda est.*[13] It makes no difference whether enemies are heretics or infidels, they are all human beings. Likewise, it does not matter if they violate the agreement (they are *perfidus*) or even if they are pirates, brigands, tyrants or usurpers.

---

[11] On Grotius's conceptions of natural law, see Dufour 1984, pp. 15–41.

[12] The origin of the principle can be traced back to the expression in Ulpian in D. 2, 14, 7, 7: "Ait praetor: Pacta conventa [...] servabo," turned into a general maxim by the canon lawyers, for example in the Decretals of Gregor IX: "Pacta quantumcunque nuda servanda sunt" (Decretales Gregorii P.IX, Lib. 1, Tit. 35, Cap. 1), and thus making informal contractual agreements enforceable. See Zimmermann 1990, esp. pp. 543–44, 576–77. See also Lesaffer 2000. Randall Lesaffer rightly stresses that "until the seventeenth or even eighteenth centuries, treaties have more to be considered as private *pacta* or *conventiones* between rulers than as public *foedera* between political entities" (Lesaffer 2000, p. 182). For an overview see also Wehberg 1959.

[13] Grotius, extensively quoting Roman contract law and Roman moralists, considers *fides* as the basis of justice (1925, book II, ch. 11, 4–5). A similar bond between faith, justice and treaties is also to be found a few years earlier in Bodin (1576, book V, ch. 6, on treaties between princes). On the idea of *bona fides* in international law see Kolb 2000.

A pledge made to them should always be upheld, even in the face of fear or constraint. Like international order in general, the Grotian law of nations is rooted in good faith, the vital ingredient in all human relations. It is the very crux of the society of men and states. Grotius was well aware that this society was often plunged into anarchy, but he still maintained that states and people were united by shared norms and cultural ties.[14]

Thomas Hobbes incorporated many of Grotius's arguments on the law of nations (Tuck 1999). His theoretical starting point on the "state of nature" was, however, very different. In his major work *Leviathan* (1651), he describes the state of nature as one of perpetual war between all.[15] It offers no refuge and, since all men are driven by the same goals, they seek to attack first and thereby protect their own interests and reputation. Hobbes compares interstate relations to dealings between men in a state of nature. Among states, each "republic" is free to act in its own best interests (Hobbes 1996, ch. 17). While men can discard the state of nature to embrace a new social contract, states cannot. Hobbes is firm on this point. No higher authority or political mechanism ranks above states. Anarchy is at the heart of international relations and is very difficult to shake off. Each state acts as it sees fit and casts a suspicious eye on the doings of others. Whenever power is yielded in return for specific pledges on the conduct of others, it is on a self-serving, transient, and fickle basis.[16]

Hobbes has often been accused of putting conflict at the heart of international politics. According to this viewpoint, states are always think-ing about defence or attack. His thinking should, however, be analyzed carefully. While it is true that Hobbes sees states as fundamentally selfish, they do not exist in a vacuum and without any form of relationship between them. The Hobbesian state of nature is one in which interaction is necessary, frequent, chaotic, and, at times, violent. States need each other and may even end up joining forces to serve their own short-term interests. Hobbes may have presented international society as anarchical,

---

[14] It is hardly surprising that Hugo Grotius's theory of the laws of nations gained its colossal popularity. His account was practically tailor-made for the main Protestant powers in the Thirty Years War, in the sense that it justified their prosecution of the war against Spain and the Habsburgs without providing their own subjects with a rationale for rebellion.

[15] "Hereby it is manifest," writes Hobbes, "that during the time men live without a common Power to keep them all in awe, there are in that condition which is called Warre; and such a warre, as is of every man, against every man." (Hobbes 1996, p. 88).

[16] "In all times," Hobbes said in 1651, "Kings, and persons of Soveraigne authority, because of their Independency, are in continuall jealousies, and in the state and posture of Gladiators; having their weapons pointing, and their eyes fixed on one another; that is, their Forts, Garrisons, and Guns upon the Frontiers of their Kingdomes; and continuall Spyes upon their neighbours, which is a posture of War" (Hobbes 1996, p. 90).

but his actual message was that there is no such thing as morality between states. Each of them has an intellectual and emotional identity, which steers its action. With a nod to the Skeptics, Hobbes agrees that there are no moral absolutes enabling us to determine right and wrong for all, which means that we cannot break out of the cycle of war through a better understanding of the situation at hand.

Grotius had envisaged the possibility of an international community responsible for enforcing agreements. Hobbes, on the other hand, sees sovereignty as uncompromising independence from outside influence and, as such, questions the very existence of such an international community. The idea of "international order" is meaningless and all eyes are on states and their internal affairs. Hobbes's reasoning is watertight, uncontested even by Rousseau. It was Hobbes's views on passions and the state of nature that were reworked and which became a lightning rod for the dissenting premises of both Pufendorf and Locke, albeit in very different historical contexts.

Pufendorf drew on Grotius's arguments to posit sociability as the keystone of any society of men and states. He differed, however, in his exposition of it in his *De Jure Naturae et Gentium* (1934 [1672], II, pp. 207–08). Grotius had mapped a link between justice (*justum*) and utility (*utile*), but Pufendorf went much further, making sociability and utility almost indistinguishable. He does not refute the inconsistency found in Hobbes's thinking, since conflict is inevitable once utility is pitted against equality. He does, however, question the robustness of a theory rooted solely in self-interest or self-preservation, one which disregards the ultimate usefulness of personal motives. Sociability opens that door. Man's inherent sociability is not based on altruism alone, but also stems from the fact that it is in his interest to be sociable (Pufendorf 1934, II, p. 214). Pufendorf rates interest as a positive side effect of man's desire for preservation, something that Hobbes sees as largely negative. Society, the precursor to government, is therefore driven by interest rather than fear. In *socialitas*, self-regarding and other regarding motives are not in opposition but form a distinctive combination.

According to Pufendorf, states are legal entities and, as such, enjoy the same rights as individuals in the state of nature. The principle of sociability is circumscribed by the right to act in one's own best interests in the absence of a mutual sovereign arbitrator. The international order is therefore powered by the interests of the states. No nation is irrevocably bound by international agreements if they clash with that state's interests. The overarching principle is absolute and indivisible sovereignty. Pufendorf develops his theory in his historical works, in particular in his *Introduction to the History of the Principal Realms and States as they currently exist in*

Europe (1682). He distinguishes between several types of interests, amongst which are "imaginary" and "real" interests. The nature of the "imaginary" interests is such that they must only be pursued in cases of serious wrong or in pursuit of a legitimate universal claim. "Real" interests pertain to what is specific to a country: its constitutional history, its national character, or its situation. Paradoxically, although this element is the basis for the absolute autonomy of the sovereign, it also opens the door to a vision of the law of nations, which is less aggressively interventionist. Colonization and imperialist ambitions are thus viewed as contrary to the morality of modern nations involved in commerce – a view that would be endorsed by Kant later on (Tuck 1999, pp. 140–65).

John Locke later broke with Hobbes and Pufendorf to resurrect some Grotian arguments on the purpose of the law of nations. Like his contemporaries, the author of *Two Treatises of Government* (1690) had to grapple with the territorial acquisitions of European states. He sought to rework Grotian rationale on international society and contribute towards the debate on the appropriation of "unoccupied" land.

Locke's vision of the law of nations rests upon a fresh take on the state of nature, which is characterized by equality and freedom, with natural law prevailing. As such, the state of nature is not all that different from the civil society, in that it already has a social dimension. Natural law and reason provide a moral compass, rooted in self-preservation (Locke 1988, p. 271). The state of nature is, however, constantly poised on the brink of war, as there is no recognized judge to stamp out violence. In other words, Locke's state of nature is unstable, oscillating between war and peace. Since everyone is his own judge, everyone is in danger, given man's propensity to let passion override reason. Civil society emerges when men surrender their executive right and adopt a constitution based on the declaration of their natural rights and assigning the job of safeguarding those rights to society alone.

Locke's views on the state of nature include a new historical account of the rise of property. By describing property as the product of labour, Locke defines property as an extension of the individual. Property exists in the state of nature because labor does (*Second Treatise*, Chapter V, §44). Locke turns property into something autonomous, private, and personal. Consequently, he makes no distinction between self-preservation and the preservation of property. Clearly, society is formed to uphold civil peace *and* safeguard property.

Locke maintains that the state of nature exists among nations because there is no higher authority to which states can yield their executive powers. He advocates a law of nations that binds nations in the same way that the declaration of natural rights binds individuals in society, by providing a legal bond to uphold peace. As such, his conception of international society is not at all different from that of his predecessors. However, his account of individuals' property rights leads him to develop one core proposition: since civil societies are established to foster an unmitigated defence of natural rights, the law of nations is equally bound by the need to protect property and should be construed as a means of safeguarding the state's possessions. Locke goes even further to work out a set of arguments that paves the way for the colonial settlement of "vacant" lands and that endorses the English expansion.[17] He builds the Grotian idea of *occupatio* into a theory of appropriation that stresses the importance of making "improvements" to the land as a necessary condition for ownership.[18] Therefore dealings between states boil down to cooperation between *European* states and allow for the appropriation of the "great tracts of ground to be found" and which "lie in common" (Locke 1988, ch. 5, §45).

Despite their theoretical variances, Grotius and his successors analyzed the foundations of the international order by drawing a distinction between the state of nature and civil society. Nations signed treaties for the same reason men turned their backs on the state of nature. The society of nations, the social contract binding nations, was a work in progress.

By the eighteenth century, the building blocks of international society were no longer being called into question. Instead, attention was focused on how best to regulate such a society. The Treaty of Utrecht (1713) marked the end of the Spanish war of succession and sparked widespread debate on how to bring peace to Europe and where the limits of the society of nations lay. The challenge was to analyze harmony between nations and espouse a vision of solidarity in international affairs. This was the background to the economic conception of society which emerged in the writings of several authors around 1730. This new idea of the market provided a fresh insight into international relations, especially concerning the issue of war and peace. Most of the natural law theorists had found that the concepts used to describe civil society could not be stretched enough to include cooperation among states. The idea of social contract offered

---

[17] For example, according to Locke, the indigenous people have property rights that are limited to the result of their labor. They own the fruit and nuts they collect, the wild wheat that they harvest, the meat they hunt, but in *no way* do they own the land on which they live. Conversely, people who belong to civilization live under a *government* and farm the land are entitled to "wage war against the Indians" and to impose severe peace conditions in retribution for damages incurred (Locke 1998, ch. 5, § 37–38, 41–43, and ch. 16).

[18] Several scholars have underlined the affinities between Grotius's thinking here and the subsequent arguments of Locke and other liberal political theorists (Arneil 1996, pp. 46–54; also Tully 1993a, pp. 137–78; 1993b, pp. 253–82).

no guarantee of peace among nations. War was averted through agreements and mutual pledges, as exemplified in Abbé Saint-Pierre's famous *Mémoire pour rendre la paix perpétuelle en Europe* (Project to bring perpetual peace in Europe) (1712), in which he set out his doctrine on collective security.

By 1730, many authors had subscribed to the view that economics could replace politics to create a new international order. France's "egalitarian liberals" went up against mercantilist forces and the absolute rule of Louis XIV, using economic rationale to reinvigorate the State and champion their vision of solidarity between nations (Meyssonnier 1989). The Physiocrats (Quesnay, Dupont de Nemours, Mercier de la Rivière, and Gournay), who drew heavily on natural law theorists, pushed to its limits the boundaries of this new perception of political dealings between nations (Larrère 1992). Similarly, in Scotland, David Hume and the Scottish historical school (Adam Ferguson, William Robertson, and John Millar) building on Mandeville's social theory all agreed that international relations needed a fresh start, with zero-sum (power play) rationale giving way to a win–win philosophy based on commerce. Two authors take centre stage in this debate: Montesquieu and Adam Smith.

Rethinking international order in eighteenth-century Europe: Montesquieu and Adam Smith

When addressing the issue of relations between states, Montesquieu unequivocally acknowledges his intellectual debt to natural law theorists. In his *Pensées*, he explicitly says that he is "[paying] tribute to Messrs Grotius and Pufendorf for having accomplished in exemplary fashion something that part of this work [*The Spirit of the Laws*] required of me, with a touch of genius to which I could never have aspired (Montesquieu 1991, *Pensées* no. 1537 and no. 1863 (my translation))." In keeping with this debt, he levels fierce criticism against the Hobbesian view of the state of nature in *The Spirit of the Laws* (Book I, Chap. 2), drawing on Pufendorf's arguments on inherent sociability and the Stoic perception of justice espoused by Cicero.[19]

A man in the state of nature would have the faculty of knowing rather than knowledge. It is clear that his first ideas would not be speculative ones; he would think of the preservation of his being before seeking the origin of his being. Such a man would at first feel only his weakness; his timidity would be extreme: and as for

---

[19] On the relations between Montesquieu and Stoicism see Larrère 1999.

evidence, if it is needed on this point, savages have been found in forests; every-thing makes them tremble, everything makes them flee. In this state, each feels himself inferior; he scarcely feels himself an equal. Such men would not seek to attack one another, and peace would be the first natural law. Hobbes gives men first the desire to subjugate one another, but this is not reasonable. The idea of empire and domination is so complex and depends on so many other ideas, that it would not be the one they would first have. ... Besides feelings, which belong to men from the outset, they also succeed in gaining knowledge; thus they have a second bond, which other animals do not have. Therefore, they have another motive for uniting, and the desire to live in society is a fourth natural law. (Montesquieu 1989, book I, ch. 2, pp. 6–7)

His belief in man's innate sociability in the state of nature did not stop Montesquieu from recognizing that nations are prone to war when men form societies. On that score, he moved closer to Hobbes. The thirst for strength and power puts states at loggerheads. International politics is all about war – moving on from past wars and facing up to impending wars and efforts to forestall war (Montesquieu 1989, book I, ch. 3). Nevertheless, Montesquieu rejects out of hand the solutions furnished by his contemporaries. While he shares their distaste for "universal monarchy," with its anarchical, power-hungry bent, he refutes their conclusions. International order should not be forged through a system of balance of power, and sustaining the balance does not safeguard peace among nations.

This view guided Montesquieu when, in 1724, he wrote his *Réflexions sur la Monarchie universelle en Europe* (Reflections on universal monarchy in Europe).[20] The term "balance" only appears in one footnote (Montesquieu 1951, II, p. 37, note a), and is referred to in the body of the text as "sum of all against all [cet état d'effort de tous contre tous]," a paraphrase which leaves the reader in no doubt that it refers to the flux of war rather than the stability of peace. Efforts to maintain the balance spark an arms race, keeping the risk of conflict alive and ultimately wreaking just as much havoc as actual warfare. The mix of universal monarchy and balance is not enough to check the downward spiral into war or forge a genuine relationship between states.[21] What makes Montesquieu's ideas groundbreaking is that his answer to military conquest is not balance of power, but commerce. Like Melon, who published his *Essai politique sur le commerce* (Political essay upon commerce) in 1734, Montesquieu sees

---

[20] This thirty-one page document remained unpublished until 1891, although Montesquieu did incorporate most of the text in his *(The) Spirit of the Laws*.

[21] Montesquieu's critique of the Abbé de Saint-Pierre's vision for peace and of Liebniz's "European republic" must be viewed in this context. For Montesquieu's critique of the ideas of Leibniz see Montesquieu, 1998, n°352.

commerce as more than a means to power, something that Colbert, Leibniz, and many others before him had clearly grasped. Commerce is a different type of power, a counterweight rather than a mainstay of conquest.[22]

The thesis Montesquieu began outlining in his *Reflections* is fleshed out in full in *The Spirit of the Laws* (1748) (Larrère 2001, pp. 335–73). The work's fourth section (Books 20–23) specifically addresses the issues of commerce, currency, and population. While the first nineteen books also refer to trade, the comments are more focused on the activities of "merchants" and their role as private individuals. Book 20 marks the start of an extensive study of the international dimension to commerce. Montesquieu does not seek merely to counter the advocates of mercantilism or the French egalitarian liberals. If that were all, he would have expounded a full-blooded economic theory in *The Spirit of the Laws*, like Quesnay or Adam Smith. Instead, he was more interested in showing commerce in a political light, portraying it as the new bedrock of cooperation between trading nations, a point he himself stresses at the start of Book 20 (ch. 4), "commerce is related to the constitution."

The passage in Book 20 (ch. 2) setting out his thinking has gone down in history:

The natural effect of commerce is to lead to peace. Two nations that trade with each other become reciprocally dependent; if one has an interest in buying, the other has an interest in selling, and all unions are founded on mutual needs. (Montesquieu 1989, p. 338)

It was not a new idea in Europe. The entire eighteenth century was a standoff between the opposing views of commerce as a civilizing force and as a craven, warmongering venture, between age-old virtues and modern-day corruption (Pocock 1975, 1985).[23] Merchants gradually came to represent the values of sociability which the Enlightenment movement

---

[22] During the eighteenth century the term "commerce" applied to more than the exchange of merchandise. Besides referring to the exchange of goods, Daniel Roche explains that it also referred "in the broadest general sense ... to the agent of the reciprocal relationship between men, a key element of sociability" (Roche 1993, p. 39). This coincides with the definition found in the 1694 edition of the *Dictionnaire de l'Académie française*: "Commerce signifie aussi communication et correspondance ordinaires avec quelqu'un, soit pour la société seulement, soit aussi pour quelques affaires." Decades later, the physiocrat Véron de Forbonnais will similarly state in his article on "commerce" of the *Encyclopédie* (1753), "On entend par ce mot, dans le sens général, une communication réciproque. Il s'applique plus particulièrement à la communication que les hommes se font entre eux des productions de leur terre et de leur industrie."

[23] We should, however, point out that eigtheenth-century French political thought does not feature prominently in the analysis put forth by Pocock. Rousseau and Mably are scarcely mentioned, as well as Montesquieu, whose seminal work *The Spirit of the Laws* is proof

in France in particular held up as an antithesis to the blue-blooded veneration of warfare. Commerce put morality into perspective and helped overcome prejudice.

Although it was not new, Montesquieu's vision of commerce had by no means garnered broad consensus. At the time, foreign trade was perceived almost exclusively as leverage used by governments in their dealings with other states. The *Réflexions politiques sur les finances et le commerce* (Political reflections upon finance and commerce) (1738), by Charles-Henri Dutot, is a perfect example of the wave of writing that portrayed war and commerce as two sides of the same political coin. Montesquieu does not just underscore the inter-reliance of states, but also their shared interests:

Europe is now a nation of nations; France and England need the prosperity of Poland and Muscovy just as their own provinces need each other. Similarly, states seeking to consolidate power by destroying their neighbours tend to weaken their own position in the process. (Montesquieu 1951, II, p. 34 (my translation))

Since a country can only sell its produce to others if they too are in a position to sell and thus acquire wealth, one state's prosperity cannot be built on others' poverty. A country's trading system can only be sustainable if commerce is balanced (Montesquieu 1989, book 20, ch. 23). Commerce cannot remain unilateral. Factories in other countries produce the resources needed to satisfy the demand that domestic output cannot meet (Montesquieu 1991, *Pensées*, no. 343).

The logical conclusion of recognizing that states need each other to acquire wealth is an acceptance of free trade, albeit subject to conditions. Montesquieu does not countenance unbridled freedom of trade, all clearly demonstrated by his detailed views on border taxes:

Where there is commerce there are customs houses. The object of commerce is to export and import commodities in favor of the state, and the object of the customs houses is a certain duty on that same exporting, also in favor of the state. Therefore, the state must be neutral between its customs houses and its commerce and must arrange that these two things never thwart one another; then one enjoys the liberty of commerce there. (Montesquieu 1989, book 20, ch. 13)

On this score, commerce is unmistakably subject to a measured degree of state control. To ensure that customs and commerce "never thwart one another," states must resign themselves to adopting prudent policies that do not ultimately sap this source of income. Free trade is indeed the norm, but it remains connected to a higher imperative, that of the state's interests.

that the future of modern societies was the object of extensive debates in France. For more on these debates in France see Spitz 1995. More generally, on the benefits beyond peace that commerce brings in the eighteenth century, see Neff 1990.

While rejoicing in the fact that rising commerce brought nations together, Montesquieu was aware of the pitfalls. Despite their shared interests rooted in trade, states still desired power and this exacerbated economic rivalry. In his own words, "the avarice of nations disputes the movables of the whole universe" (Montesquieu 1989, book 20, ch. 23). Hence his reservations about the English model, set out in Chapter 27 of Book 19. The entire chapter focuses on the "general spirit" of the English nation and is written in the conditional tense, as if Montesquieu were describing a unique, fragile, and inimitable model, which did not match any of the forms of government he had outlined (Baker 1990, ch. 8). He dwelt on the power of this nation, which could "assert against its enemies an immense fictional wealth that the trust and the nature of its government would make real" (Montesquieu 1989, book 19, ch. 27, p. 327), yet he used the example of England to undermine the idea of "doux commerce":

A commercial nation has a prodigious number of small, particular interests; therefore, it can offend in an infinity of ways. This nation would become sovereignly jealous and would find more distress in the prosperity of others than enjoyment in its own. And its laws, otherwise gentle and easy, might be so rigid in regard to the commerce and navigation carried on with it that it would seem to negotiate only with enemies. (Montesquieu 1989, book 19, ch. 27, p. 328)

Basically, Montesquieu is torn. Although trade should in theory bring nations together around shared interests, the lack of any checks on human passions such as "hatred, envy and jealousy" and the increase in prosperity spark fresh conflict. States still crave glory and seek to dominate other countries. The only difference is that their methods have changed: wealth, not arms, is their leverage.

Furthermore, although the spread of commerce tended to ease the power play between "civilized" nations, Montesquieu recognized that the struggle was merely shifted to dealings between European powers and their colonies. Interdependence gave way to full-blown reliance, and commerce reserved its benefits for European nations alone (Montesquieu 1989, book 21, ch. 21). This view shaped his critique of imperial ideology. In his *Considérations sur les causes de la grandeur des Romains et de leur décadence* (Considerations on the causes of the greatness and decadence of the Romans) (1734), Montesquieu expands on the well-known tale of the conquering Romans shedding their civic virtues as they built their empire. He rejects the idea of turning armies into a Praetorian Guard following victory and questions the deployment of occupying forces when troops are needed to protect home territory. Let there be no mistake, however. His criticism of empires or what David Hume named "enormous monarchies" (Hume 1985, p. 340) is driven by economic rationale, the pioneering vision of social relations based on commerce (Pagden 1995, especially pp. 156–77). His censure of the colonial system stems from its perversion of the true "spirit of commerce" which should be rooted in mutual recognition and gain.

Montesquieu never equated this true "spirit of commerce" with mere trade in goods. He viewed it chiefly as a relationship between people. As commerce spread, so too did knowledge, not least knowledge of the world around us. Mindful of this fact, Montesquieu did not share the disdain of merchants' travel writings shown by many of his contemporaries, including Diderot and Rousseau. The infinite spread of commercial networks creates an arena in which "nations come together" without erasing political borders. Montesquieu is categorical on this point. Any move to focus on commercial ties to the exclusion of state borders would once again raise the spectre of universalism. Complementarity is the byword. Hence Montesquieu was fundamentally opposed to the idea of completely cutting all ties between commerce and state, which became the holy grail of political economy after 1750. His rationale did, however, help to pave the way for the market to be perceived as a mechanism regulating relations between states. Instead of marking a transition from one reference system to another, *The Spirit of the Laws* tackled a fresh subject, one later taken up and finalized by Adam Smith when he merged the political concept of nation with the economic idea of the market.

Even more strikingly than in France, the eighteenth century heralded a return to brass tacks in Britain. In a sense, the Act of Union with Scotland in 1707 ushered in an era of extensive debate on the inner workings of civil society.[24] Scotland embraced a historical and comparative approach to philosophy putting into broader perspective the hardcore Whiggism spawned by England's 1689 revolution (Hont and Ignatieff 1983; Pocock 1993, especially part III).[25] Constitutional advances were deemed part and parcel of progress in society. Civil freedom was equated with commercial success and civic virtue or public-mindedness, inextricably linked to a series of favorable social and economic conditions. No single publication acts as standard-bearer for the comparative approach, but elements can be found in Adam Smith's long unpublished *Lectures on Jurisprudence* (1761 and 1766), Adam Ferguson's *Essay on the History of Civil Society* (1767), William Robertson's *View of the Progress of Society in Europe from the Subversion of the Roman Empire to the Accession of Charles V*

---

[24] For the political background see Riley 1978; Robertson 1995.

[25] On the intimate continuity between earlier natural law theories and the Scottish Enlightenment, see Haakonssen 1996. On the renewal of civic virtue in Scottish culture, see Sher 1985.

(1769), John Millar's *Observations Concerning the Distinction of Ranks in Society* (1771), and finally, in a book which embraces and transcends the trend, Adam Smith's *Inquiry into the Nature and Causes of the Wealth of Nations* (1776). Opposition to despotic rule and absolute monarchy may have been imbued with a greater sense of urgency in France, but Scotland was more receptive to an innovative perception of politics. Notwithstanding this, the differences should not be overplayed, given the regular exchanges of views across the English Channel.[26]

Adam Smith devotes an entire chapter to the law of nations in *Lectures on Jurisprudence* (1766), systematically examining the various underlying rules (Smith 1982, pp. 545–54), but it is in *The Theory of Moral Sentiments* (1759) that he lays the theoretical foundations for his attack on the traditional conception of relations between states.[27] In the opening passages of his *Theory of Moral Sentiments*, he posits his fundamental claim that sympathy is prevalent among men.

How selfish soever man may be supposed, there are evidently some principles in his nature, which interest him in the fortune of others, and render their happiness necessary to him, though he derives nothing from it except the pleasure of seeing it. Of this kind is pity or compassion, the emotion which we feel for the misery of others, when we either see it, or are made to conceive it in a very lively manner. That we often derive sorrow from the sorrow of others, is a matter of fact too obvious to require any instances to prove it. (Smith 1984, p. 9)

To substantiate his arguments, Smith draws on Mandeville, Hutcheson, and Hume; Hume's 1739 *Treatise of Human Nature* portrayed sympathy as the natural bridge between self-interest and the interests of society as a whole. Smith, however, goes one step further and explicitly describes his book as the pinnacle of moral philosophy. Commenting on Hobbes, Pufendorf, and Mandeville, he tellingly writes,

The idea, in short, which those authors were groping about, but which they were never able to unfold distinctly, was that indirect sympathy which we feel with the gratitude or resentment of those who received the benefit or suffered the damage resulting from such opposite characters: and it was this which they were indistinctly pointing at, when they said, that it was not the thought of that what we had gained or suffered which prompted either applause or indignation, but the

---

[26] Here I follow Donald Winch's reservations about the extension of purely Scottish perspectives to Adam Smith and David Hume. According to Winch (1983), these authors should be treated as being more responsive to European problems and audiences. For a critical view of the tendency to fragment the Enlightenment in eighteenth-century Europe into multiple Enlightenments, see Robertson 2005.

[27] The following presentation of Smith's moral theory is closely linked to the discussions on Smith's theory of rights found in Haakonssen 1983, especially ch. 3.

conception or imagination of what we might gain or suffer if we were to act in society with such associates. (Smith 1984, part VII, section 3, p. 317)

By crystallizing the notion of sympathy and distinguishing it from benevolence, Smith placed social order on a natural bedrock without resorting to politics like Rousseau or legislation as Bentham later did, thus epitomizing the need to *artificially* organize interests. Smith explains that sympathy forms in individuals and stems from the difference between their own feelings and the happiness or sadness they would feel in another's shoes. In a way, sympathy is an intimate yet broad market where supply matches demand and where our desire to exist meets our need for recognition. According to Adam Smith, men regularly view things from each other's perspective and, in doing so, feel each other's emotions. Just as citizens and nations prosper when trade and the division of labor grow, men are happier when sympathy is extended, since it means that burdens are shared. While Montesquieu praised commerce for pacifying states, Smith applauds the "extreme humanity" which softens hearts (Smith 1984, part VII, section 3, p. 317). In both cases, exchange is a form of mutual regulation which leaves everyone a winner and can never be equated with a zero-sum game.

Smith's view of sympathy echoes the Frenchman Pierre Nicole and the Dutchman Mandeville in that it zooms in on our desire or the need to coexist with others and also flags the unforeseen consequences of this desire.[28] However, Smith goes even further by asserting that, even in the absence of mutual benevolence, social ties prevail through utility:

Though the necessary assistance should not be afforded from such generous and disinterested motives, though among the different members of the society there should be no mutual love and affection, the society, though less happy and agreeable, will not necessarily be dissolved. *Society may subsist among different men, as among different merchants, from a sense of its utility*, without any mutual love or affection; and though no man in it should owe any obligation, or be bound in gratitude to any other, it may still be upheld by a mercenary exchange of good offices according to an agreed valuation. (Smith 1984, part II, section 2, pp. 85–86, emphasis added)[29]

In many ways, this extract from *The Theory of Moral Sentiments* represents a milestone in Smith's thinking. Contrary to popular belief, there is no real break between it and *An Inquiry into the Nature and Causes of the*

---

[28] For an interesting discussion of the role of Pierre Nicole on Adam Smith's theory of sympathy see Perrot 1990, pp. 345–50. For a recognition of Nicole's influence in seventeenth-century England see Wootton 1986.

[29] On the role of the idea of utility in Smith's philosophy see Campbell 1971, especially pp. 217–19.

Wealth of Nations (1776), no red line between an idealistic text and a realistic one. *Wealth of Nations* expanded upon what was most likely mere intuition in *Moral Sentiments*. In other words, the passage quoted above is fully consistent with the famous sentence from Book I (ch. 2) of *An Inquiry into the Nature and Causes of the Wealth of Nation*:

> It is not from the benevolence of the butcher, the brewer, or the baker, that we expect our dinner, but from their regard to their own interest. We address ourselves, not to their humanity but to their self-love, and never talk to them of our own necessities but their advantages. (Smith 1981, I, pp. 26–27)

It is thus in the furnace of *The Theory of Moral Sentiments* that Smith's "economic" vision of the world is forged. There he offers us a radically new way of depicting social order and, by extension, international order. Political economy is not a distinct area of research but rather the bedrock of society, the solid foundations upon which social harmony can be analyzed and achieved.[30]

The idea of an invisible hand is of course central to this rationale, and the corresponding pages in *The Theory of Moral Sentiments* (Part IV) have gone down in history.[31] Powered by the "wisdom of nature," the "invisible hand" gets around the whole problem of political obligation in the social contract without backtracking to an authoritarian conception of power. It also enables Smith to redefine the idea of the market as more than a tangible location where goods are traded. Instead, it embraces society as a whole. It is not just a way of allocating resources through unfettered price-setting. It is a mechanism organizing social coexistence rather than a tool to regulate the economy. Smith sees the market as a political and sociological concept, with the economic dimension a mere side effect. He does not justify nascent capitalism or boil our social existence down to economic activity. He believes that the market is the driving force of social order. It strikes a perfect balance between interest and justice. It nurtures shared interests and offers a silent and effective alternative to Rousseau's general will.

---

[30] On Smith's conception of political economy, see Winch 1996, especially pp. 20–25.

[31] "They [the rich men] are led by an invisible hand to make nearly the same distribution of the necessaries of life, which would have been made, had the earth been divided into equal portions among all its inhabitants, and thus without intending it, without knowing it, advance the interest of the society, and afford means to the multiplication of the species. When Providence divided the earth among few lordly masters, it neither forgot nor abandoned those who seemed to have been left out in the partition. These last two enjoy their share of all that it produces. In what constitutes the real happiness of human life, they are in no respect inferior to those who would seem so much above them. In ease of body and peace of mind, all the different ranks of life are nearly upon a level, and the beggar, who suns himself by the side of the highway, possesses that security which kings are fighting for" (Smith 1984, part IV, ch. 1, pp. 184–85).

Hence the idea of the market is a rich breeding ground in political terms. It does not just provide a theoretical answer to the social harmony conundrum, but also sheds fresh light on relations among states. In Part 6 of *The Theory of Moral Sentiments*, Smith dwells on this point in full awareness of the difficulties involved. Civil society is a collection of individuals bound by exchange, but can that be equally effective when applied to groups of individuals in the form of nations? Referring to Cato and his hatred of Carthage, Smith underscores the viciousness lurking in "the love of country" and appears to express a hope that alliance treaties will prevent conflict. We might wonder whether he is being drawn back to the doctrine of balance of power between nations, or perhaps implying that the invisible hand will not yield results until a world government is in place. Neither supposition hits the mark. In *Adam Smith's Politics*, one of the most inspired pieces on Smith's work, Donald Winch (1978) traces his "politics" back to a historical view of the emergence of human societies with commerce playing a key role. Like Montesquieu, Smith sees commerce as a linchpin of international order. The more we trade with our enemies, the better we can defend ourselves against them (Smith 1984, part VI, section 2, ch. 2, pp. 228ff.). More than anything else, free trade breeds closeness among nations and places their dealings in a diplomatic rather than a military context. Indeed, *An Inquiry into the Nature and Causes of the Wealth of Nation* sums this approach up nicely:

Hereafter, perhaps, ... the inhabitants of all different quarters of the world may arrive at the equality of courage and force which, by inspiring mutual fear, can alone overawe the injustice of independent nations into some sort of respect for the rights of one another. But nothing seems more likely to establish this equality of force than that mutual communication of knowledge and of all sorts of improvements which an extensive commerce from all countries to all countries naturally, or rather necessarily, carries along with it. (Smith 1981, II, pp. 626 27)

Be that as it may, peace based on commerce does not preclude what Beccaria called an "industrial war." Smith is all too aware of the limitations shown by the natural harmony of interests at international level. He argues that external markets can only ever complement and build on functioning domestic markets. Accordingly, he insists that local trade must come before remote trade (Smith 1981, book IV, ch. 9). He also understands that action taken at international level is often motivated by domestic concerns. Nevertheless, Smith views "industrial war" as an innovative beast. In actual fact, it is competition, and competition tends to reconcile all interests. As such, it puts all nations on an equal footing and nurtures peace all the more effectively in the absence of barriers. Hence, this new form of "war" is actually an instrument of peace. As Istvan Hont points out,

By contrasting national emulation to national animosity, Smith demonstrated that commercial reciprocity and intense competition were compatible. Cessation or reduction of trade could have easily eliminated jealousy of trade. Hume and Smith, however, never advocated economic isolationism. Rather, Smith replaced the negative and warlike model of commercial competition with a constructive one. Emulation was standardly used to describe activities as contests in sport, as at the Greek Olympiads, or cultural contention as in rhetorical competitions or in rivalry among city-states in religious and civic architecture. Emulation was the activity not of the virtuous but the ambitious. ... It redirected human passions toward honour and self-esteem as superior targets. Smith's story, like Hobbes's, was not about the passions and the interests but about interests and pride. (Hont 2005, pp. 119–20)

The *Wealth of Nations* is the best-known book to feature the term "nation" in its title. Smith also makes extensive use of the word throughout his opus in a bid to clear away any misunderstandings. The concept of civil society was already firmly established amongst his contemporaries, whereas the meaning of "nation" had yet to be enshrined. It was still very much linked to the word's etymological roots (*nascere*). Dictionaries published by Furetière in 1690 and Trévoux in 1752 offer the following definition of nation: "[It] describes a large group of people inhabiting the same area of land, which falls within set borders or comes under a common ruler." A similar line is adopted in the anonymous article on "Nation" published in Volume XI of Diderot's *Encyclopaedia* (1765): "Collective noun designating a sizable number of people inhabiting the same portion of land, which falls within set borders, and answerable to one and the same government." All these definitions are reminiscent of a highly prominent eighteenth-century model – that of the territorial state. The boundaries between the concepts of nation and state are still fuzzy. Indeed, the adjective "national" is not even used in the *Encyclopaedia*.

Basically, Smith uses the term "nation" to shift from a legal or political perception of civil society to one rooted in economics. He no longer sees the pivotal distinction as one between civil society and the state of nature, but rather between society and government or the state and the nation. That distinction is upheld throughout *The Wealth of Nations*. By understanding nations as markets, Smith makes a crucial distinction between territory and space. Up until then, mercantilist thinking had equated the economic arena with political borders, making territory the instrument of power and the yardstick for prosperity. Smith, however, argues that an economic area is forged, unlike territory, which is a fact of geography. A market is not circumscribed by borders or limitations, but rather generated from within through a whole system of human interaction and settlements. Political maps no longer mirror economic maps. Admittedly, this line of thinking can also be found in many eighteenth-century discussions on the dimension of states, and Hume had been one of the first philosophers to demonstrate the futility of rampant territorial acquisition. However, Smith's analysis was far more radical, in that it did not merely reshuffle the economic and political factors of power. It redefined politics in an economic light and, at the same time, freed the economy from any territorial straitjacket. His thinking on colonies is particularly instructive in this respect. Indeed, the chapter entitled "Of Colonies" (Book IV, ch. 7) is the longest in his publication. He believed that the "colonial illusion" epitomized the traditional views he opposed.

Smith saw little interest in having colonies that were a symbol of power rooted in land possession. He reluctantly acknowledged the military rationale for Roman colonies, but deemed the Conquistadors' pillaging to be shortsighted. He believed that the attraction of colonies lay elsewhere, in the fact that they held out the promise of new markets: "All [European] countries," he explains, "have evidently gained a more extensive market for their surplus produce, and must consequently have been encouraged to increase its quantity" (Smith 1981, II, p. 591). Trade, not plunder, was the real prize, and colonies, which "arose from no necessity" (Smith 1981, II, p. 558), were worth having because they broadened the scope of the market. Men as consumers, and not possessions such as gold and raw materials, would enable Europe to grow richer through its colonies. Consequently, he rejected moves to restrict trade with colonies, deeming monopolies to be destructive, as their sole purpose was to increase the wealth of a specific social class to the detriment of the nation as a whole.

The advantages a nation derives from increasing its market cannot therefore accrue to it alone. Markets are only truly effective when they "belong" to everyone. His rejection of the colonial illusion best illustrates this view. At times, his arguments foreshadow future events, a case in point being his attack on colonial policy, which Europe would continue to nurture through to the twentieth century.

To found a great empire for the sole purpose of raising up a people of customers, may at first sight appear a project fit only for a nation of shopkeepers. It is, however, a project altogether unfit for a nation of shopkeepers; but extremely fit for a nation whose government is influenced by shopkeepers. Such statesmen, and such statesmen only, are capable of fancying that they will find some advantage in employing the blood and treasure of their fellow citizens, to found and to maintain such an empire. (Smith 1981, II, p. 613)

In a way, the only empire Smith could tolerate was a global economic market which might imbue different peoples with a shared identity that cut across territorial divisions. "Were all nations to follow the liberal system of free exportation and free importation," Smith explains, "the different states into which a great continent was divided would so far resemble the different provinces of a great empire" (Smith 1981, I, p. 538).

By conceptualizing economy globally rather than nationally, Smith completed Montesquieu's philosophy and proclaimed the long and arduous journey towards the end of the idea of the nation state. In many ways, he was the first consistent advocate of internationalism. What made his thinking groundbreaking was the fact that he placed international policy in an economic setting, free from the constraints of the social contract. He did not strip social interaction down to mere economics, but rather *expanded* the horizons of international society to embrace the economy and proposed an alternative to the reasoning of natural law theorists. With Adam Smith, the idea of the market becomes the blueprint for analyzing international relations, mankind's new *patria communis* in which cooperation among states can flourish.

The idea that international trade drives forward cooperation among states gained a firm foothold in the eighteenth century. It can be found in major accounts of progress (a fairly widespread genre at the time), such as William Robertson's *View of the Progress of Society in Europe* (1769) and Condorcet's *Sketch for a Historical Picture of the Progress of the Human Mind* (1795). The German philosopher, Kant, provided one of the strongest cases in defence of this argument. In *Perpetual Peace. A Philosophical Sketch* (1795), he wrote that

The spirit of commerce sooner or later takes hold of every people, and it cannot exist side by side with war. And of all the powers (or means) at the disposal of the power of the state, financial power can probably be relied on most. Thus states find themselves compelled to promote the noble cause of peace, though not exactly from motives of morality. And wherever in the world there is a threat of war breaking out, they will try to prevent it by mediation, just as if they had entered into a permanent league for this purpose. (Kant 1991, p. 114)

In other words, Kant subscribed to the view that trade ultimately forged a world market which economically benefits all peoples and secures peaceful relations between states.

As we have seen, this thesis was posited by Montesquieu and analyzed in depth by Adam Smith as of the mid-eighteenth century. In a dual attack on Hobbes's pessimistic anthropology, Montesquieu and Smith identify growth in international trade as a means of ending wars and underwriting cooperation between states. The state of nature in which states are supposed to be found is not one of outright war between all, where life is "solitary, poor, nasty, brutish and short" (Hobbes 1996, p. 89), and there is no need for a "higher power" – a type of world government – to secure peace between nations. The market society is perfectly capable of fulfilling that role. It underpins a new approach to structuring international relations and paves the way for eliminating the contradictions between economic growth powered by the individualist revolution and efforts to ensure public welfare. It fashions a "mellower" human, one who is more honest, loyal, methodical, and disciplined, but also friendlier and more helpful, often willing to work through conflicts and opposing views.[32]

Nevertheless, this ideology vanished in Europe from the years 1830 onwards. The "doux commerce" thesis waned as the industrial revolution waxed. The "liberal" views championed by Montesquieu and Smith were conspicuous by their absence. In international trade, protectionism was the established rule and free trade the exception. Indeed, French legislation was highly protectionist until 1914, the only deviation from the norm being the 1860 Franco-British trade agreement, followed between 1861 and 1866 by further agreements with Belgium, Switzerland, the Netherlands, Spain, and Austria (Rosanvallon 1990, pp. 203–25). Similarly, the United States did not stray from its extremely restrictive customs policy throughout the nineteenth century. Germany shut itself off from the rest of the world once it had harmonized domestic customs through the Zollverein in 1834. The British alone bucked the prevailing trend, in 1846 when they abolished customs barriers to cereals trade and in 1850 when they repealed the infamous Navigation Act (1651) which banned the import of goods from colonies on non-British vessels. Be that as it may, Britain only advocated free trade for the simple reason that it was at the height of its industrial power and because free trade enabled it to deal with the situation of its working class, injecting stability through lower grain prices. The fact is that while most liberals continued to endorse free trade and set out its benefits, protectionism had in effect won the day.

The nineteenth century also saw most European countries indulge in unbridled colonialism, despite the fact that Adam Smith and every other classical economist had painstakingly refuted the colonial pipe dream on economic grounds. France, Britain, and Germany became embroiled in a fierce race to control Africa. Leading liberal thinkers such as Tocqueville and John Stuart Mill supported the conquest of non-European peoples (Pitts 2005, especially chs. 5, 6, and 7). The sheer strength of national

---

[32] For an early nineteenth-century version of this line of argument see Constant 1988, pp. 308–28.

political identities made it impossible to view the market as an instrument fostering cooperation among states.

One of the best examples of "economic nationalism" can be found in Friedrich List's 1841 publication, *Das nationale System der politischen Ökonomie* (The national system of political economy).[33] After the German free trade union was set up in 1834, List became an ardent supporter of protectionism, arguing that free trade would merely subjugate Germany to the overwhelming might of the British economy. He also wanted to form a Franco-German axis against Britain. Nevertheless, his theory should not be boiled down to a mere wish to safeguard German industrial interests. It stems from an inordinately complex critique of Smith's philosophy, the nuts and bolts of which he contests (Semmel 1993, pp. 57–84; Magnusson 1993, I, pp. 1–18). He attacks Smith's "cosmopolitical" economy, arguing that it prevents him from recognizing the pivotal role nations play in forging collective identities. In doing so, List echoes seventeenth-century mercantilist beliefs that drew no distinction between economic wealth and political clout. He resurrects the idea that international relations, expressed in terms of power, constitute a zero-sum game.

Simply put, like many of his contemporaries, List discarded Smith's core tenet, which was that economics was the expression of the political, and ultimately superseded it. Instead, he defined the economy as a science "which, emanating from the idea of nationality, teaches how a given nation, in the present state of the world and bearing in mind its own specific circumstances, can maintain and improve its economic conditions" (List 1857, p. 227 (my translation)). Protectionism is cautiously depicted as a means of safeguarding a "nation's industrial education." List does not dismiss free-trade theories outright and even hints on a number of occasions that it is a matter of ensuring favourable conditions. Nonetheless, he distances himself from Smith, whose theories he deemed to be outdated and rooted in an anachronistic worldview. The nation could no longer be seen merely from a social perspective. It was first and foremost a political entity, ring-fenced by geographical boundaries. The whole idea of a "world nation" was pure fantasy.

Hence the industrial society that emerged in the nineteenth century shaped a world diametrically opposed to the beliefs championed by eighteenth-century "liberals". As such, there was a clear break with

---

[33] List had written the *Système naturel d'économie politique* in 1837 as a prize dissertation to answer a question set by the French Académie des sciences morales et politiques. The largely rewritten German edition was published in 1841. List had intended to write a second volume to complete his *magnum opus*, but never completed it.

eighteenth-century philosophy. The market was no longer the corner-stone upon which social, political, and international relations were built. It amounted to nothing more than a theoretical concept or an economic mechanism to be adjusted. The idea of a global society of market-states gradually faded, the principle of unfettered competition ran foul of power-ful trusts and cartels, and rivalry between states became the norm as nationalist sentiment exacerbated.

More recently, however, the vision expounded by Montesquieu and Adam Smith has made a comeback. The twenty-first century is already witnessing the emergence of a global society of "market-states." And so, at a time when conventional political structures and models of national sovereignty are being called into question, there is much to be gained in taking these thinkers seriously. Their writings provide us with a comprehensive analysis on balancing economic globalization with sustained political pluralism. They urge us to reconsider the limitations of "economic nationalism" and help us to understand the prerequisites of an international order based on free and fair trade. As Istvan Hont put it,

History is the tool of the sceptics. It helps us to ask better questions. More precisely, it can help us avoid repeating some questions again and again, running in circles unproductively. ... The commercial future that many eighteenth-century observers imagined as plausible has become our historical present. We ought to recognize this and try to acquire at least as good a sense of our political predicament as they had of theirs, more than two hundred years ago. (Hont 2005, p. 156)

3   The two sides of multilateral cooperation

Charles Doran

What is multilateralism? Multilateralism is the strategic propensity to rely on the actions of multiple participants rather than on the actions of a single state. Decision making is shared, presumably. Because the outcome is shaped by the decision inputs of multiple actors, the agreement may be more broadly acceptable to the international community, though the terms of the agreement are likely to be less demanding (since the terms are of a lowest common denominator sort) than for agreements resulting from more narrowly based participation.

According to John Ruggie, multilateralism consists of (i) the principle of collective security that an attack on one member of a coalition is an attack on all members (indivisibility); (ii) the principle that members are "equal before the law" and will be treated equally (nondiscrimination); and (iii) the principle that members take the long view rather than the short-term view, or that the average is more important than the marginal decision, or that they look at all the bargains on balance, not just separate bargains with each individual member (diffuse reciprocity) (Ruggie 1992). Lisa Martin observes that avoidance of large transaction costs in bargaining is an important explanation of why multilateralism is employed even by large states (Martin 1999). James Caporaso asks whether multilateralism is a means or an end (Caporaso 1993). Part of its complexity, perhaps, is that multilateralism is both a means and an end. Arthur Stein points out that when structures change, interests may change, and these can undermine regimes including multilateral regimes (Stein 1990).

The thesis here is that multilateralism and unilateralism, sometimes treated as simple strategic opposites, involve complexity. This complexity lies deep within each strategy. For example, both for the small state and the large state, multilateralism is bifurcated. On the one hand, for the small state, multilateralism is desirable because it creates a foreign policy role for that state. On the other hand, for the small state, multilateralism is a burden because it drags the small state into responsibilities, as in peace-keeping, that many small states would prefer to abjure. Likewise, for the large state, multilateralism may be looked upon as desirable because it smoothes the way for policy agreement. But multilateralism also is a problem for the large state because of the difficulty of "getting everybody on board" in support of a particular policy.

But the argument in this chapter about complexity lies deeper. Multilateral cooperation is really a mix of multilateralism, unilateralism, and isolationism locked together in a dynamic relationship that changes over time. No state strategy is ever pure; the most that is possible is to try to shift state strategy in a particular direction such as toward multilateral cooperation.

Finally, complexity is evident in the tension between the strategy of multilateralism and unilateralism because each strategy contains a fallacy. The fallacy of small-state multilateralism is that it is not so much a technique of conjoint decision-making as it is a technique to bind the hands of the large state regarding the latter's foreign-policy conduct. The fallacy of the large state regarding unilateralism is its belief that, after it acts alone, it will still be able to obtain the affirmation and support of the international community (or from other powerful members of that community) when such support is urgently needed. These two fallacies tend to blind the practitioners of multilateralism and unilateralism to the opportunities and challenges of multilateral cooperation.

In sum, the argument here is that, in addition to several further complications discussed below, unless multilateralism is pursued in full awareness of strategic complexity, multilateral cooperation is likely to face unusual and perilous contradiction.

Cooperation and competition

Entire books have been written about cooperation as a self-contained concept. But that is a mistake. Cooperation and competition are linked inextricably. "Pure" cooperation alone cannot exist as a behavioral concept, that is, as an interactive concept, in human terms. In international relations, cooperation is often thought of as benign. Competition is thought of as aggressive, possibly violent, and always muscular. Competition involves influence, or force. Cooperation and competition are regarded as being at opposite ends of a spectrum of increasingly specialized options, as being binary opposites by definition.

But multilateralism reveals why cooperation and competition cannot be so separated. Cooperation can be used and often is used to compete. The operation of the balance of power is an excellent example of how states cooperate to compete. Historical illustration will explicate this example.

Suppose, as in the nineteenth century, the central international system is composed of five actors. Suppose, further, that one actor uses force to attempt to dominate that system. This act of aggression will cause the other four actors to cooperate so as to defeat the common external threat to the decentralized international system and to the security of each of the four actors. The greater the sense of threat the more likely is the cooperation among governments, governments that may be, in various ways, highly diverse and even disputatious. Indeed, it is the very act of competition with the aggressor that causes the other governments to cooperate among themselves. Moreover, according to realist thought at least, once the sense of common external threat disappears, cooperation with the other actors will also dissipate. Such cooperation, however, is interpreted differently from a liberal or a constructivist perspective.

What does history have to say about cooperating to compete?

When Napoleon was defeated for a second time, his attempt at hegemony had united Europe against him. The Congress of Vienna was an effort to build four pillars around France, never again to allow it to spill over militarily onto the system of states. Britain, by sea, and Russia, by land, were the two most powerful actors united in their determined opposition to revanche by France. But no less were Austria and Prussia willing to cooperate to this end. Not until the concert collapsed in 1822 was this particular, intense, interactive, and complexly overlapping form of cooperation among the great powers itself to dissipate in the face of a new emergent form of the balance of power.

Multilateral cooperation itself carries no connotation regarding war or peace, chaos or stability. Cooperation is a willing servant of any government that chooses to employ it regarding any goal that another government shares.

The content and purpose of multilateralism for the small and the large state

Multilateral cooperation can follow an open diplomatic forum of contact and negotiation. Or, multilateral cooperation can be highly institutionalized in such diverse forums as the World Trade Organization, the North American Free Trade Association, the North Atlantic Treaty Organization, or the United Nations Security Council. The type of issue, and whether the decision is regional or global, will determine the appropriate institutional framework of multilateral decision.

Multilateralism always has two sides. For the small state, multilateralism is a good, because it offers political participation in decision making, a foreign-policy role, or "a seat at the table." "All states are not created equal," observes former Canadian Prime Minister Joe Clark, "and one way to help level the playing field is to have rules of the game." (Quoted in Minden, Galant, and Irwin 1997, p. 121; Pekkanen 2005). But, for the small state, multilateralism is also a burden, because it involves duties and it mandates an input of resources to fulfill the foreign policy role that the state has appropriated. "Free-riderism" becomes impossible for the small state that participates.

For the large state, multilateralism is a boon because it legitimizes a foreign policy which it has had a large hand in shaping (Stein and Pauly 1993; Nye 2002). Multilateralism ensures that a number of other states, besides the large state itself, will accept the foreign policy role and policy that the large state adopts. But, for the large state, multilateralism is also a burden, because it requires persuading, and in some cases cajoling, smaller states to support the main message associated with the chosen foreign policy. This is not an easy task for the larger state, since smaller states may be either genuinely skeptical of the foreign policy or opportunistically opposed. Thus multilateralism, while a good thing in the abstract for both small and large states, in practice involves trade-offs, which neither may eagerly be willing to accept.

Isolationism

Isolationism is a foreign policy role that amounts to reduced participation in the international system. Isolationism is measured against the degree of involvement in world politics that would normally be associated with a state at a given level of power. Relative to the degree of participation of most other states at a given level of power, a state that practices isolationism is operating at a degree of foreign policy participation lower than would be expected for it.

Assumed here, as in power cycle analysis, is that, everything else being equal, the higher the level of its power, the more foreign-policy roles a state is able to perform and the greater the intensity of its participation in world affairs. Given the size of the German gross domestic product (GDP), Germany can fund more aid projects, and larger projects, than Sweden and thus occupy a more visible and influential role than Sweden. Yet relative to its power, Sweden is probably more of an international activist than Germany.

As the state progresses up the cycle of its power relative to that of other states, the potential for foreign-policy role increases. Normally there is a lag between increased power and the concomitant increase in foreign-policy role, for it takes time for other states to adjust. Isolationism, the opposite of extensive role participation, becomes less likely as the state moves up its power cycle over time. But what motivates isolationism in world politics?

1. *Tiny and vulnerable.* When a state is tiny and vulnerable, a policy of isolationism is not unexpected. Monaco and Liechtenstein may be

sovereign states, but their foreign policy role is negligible. Isolationism is a way of avoiding conflict and therefore reinforcing security. Even a state such as New Zealand, of considerably greater size, exploits this policy of isolationism, bolstered by the very real existence of geographic isolation.

2. *Singular focus on commerce.* In a system where security appears to be guaranteed, some states may subdivide their foreign policies. They may deal separately in commerce and emphasize it at the expense of other dimensions of foreign policy such as diplomatic leadership or the provision of military security. Switzerland or Singapore could attempt to offer a full agenda of foreign policy involvement and activity, but they do not. They focus on making money.

3. *Inward-looking because of a focus on economic or political development.* This motivation for isolationism is subtly different from the prior motivations. Moreover, it is often expressed more as a matter of degree than type. When a state concentrates on internal matters it has less political energy to focus on external policy. Economic development is often a dominant preoccupation. China, for example, limits its foreign policy participation in order to concentrate on internal economic development. Political development is no less confining; the European Union is less participatory in world politics, especially in Asian matters, than its size would predict. Likewise, the role it plays in military security is much less than its GDP would appear to justify.

4. *Unpopularity of governing regime.* When a government realizes that its mode of governance or the identity of its regime-type is unpopular internationally, it may withdraw inside its borders in order to avoid threats to its survival. Myanmar (Burma) is a country that attempts a low international profile in part because of the response it receives from other larger actors critical of its internal politics. During the Cold War, the communist government of Albania sought to reduce its international presence vis-à-vis both Moscow and Washington. Governments that are unpopular often have a lot to be unpopular about. Unpopularity is only a short step to political paranoia which in turn can further drive isolationism.

5. *Convulsed by civil war or revolution.* Temporary isolationism is often caused by the trauma and political distraction associated with civil war or revolution. A government internally torn by civil and political upheaval can scarcely be expected to play a larger international role. Anxiety about internal discord, highlighted in George Washington's farewell address, and ultimately experienced in the American Civil War, caused the United States to play a far smaller international role in the mid-nineteenth century than otherwise might have been the case. Likewise, the Russian Revolution caused Russia to withdraw from principal participation in World War I and thus in the diplomatic outcome of that war at Versailles.

6. *Neutral or "neutralized."* Almost by definition, a country that opts for the status of a neutral is attempting to isolate itself from fractious interaction with neighbors. Its single international legal responsibility, namely denial of its territory for use by belligerents, is often a responsibility that it cannot carry out. But through isolationism it sometimes tries to fulfill the responsibilities of a neutral. Likewise, a state that in effect becomes neutralized by the impact upon it of world politics often adopts isolationism or semi-isolationism as a strategy. During much of the Cold War, Austria assumed this posture both vis-à-vis the United States and vis-à-vis Western Europe itself.

7. *Strategic withdrawal.* Perhaps the most important form of isolationism is that expressed as strategic withdrawal. The most spectacular recent example in statecraft of strategic withdrawal was the posture of the allies prior to World War II. US wheat farmers wanted to recover from the depression, not influence governments abroad. French industrialists regarded good business with Germany as enough of a constraint on Hitler. British socialists thought that appeasement would work. Stalin believed that a bargain between dictators would not be broken. Everyone favored isolationism. And everyone (save Churchill) was wrong.

Strategic withdrawal is an important manifestation of isolationism. It is a characteristic of times and locations and issues as much as of power per se. The United States, by reason of proclivity as much as geophysical location, buffered by oceans, and surrounded by decent neighbors, is especially subject to strategic withdrawal. Any nation that believes that it is "an exception" to the norms of world politics is likely to be so afflicted. And yet, since 1945, the United States has shown few signs of this isolationist proclivity.

Periods of history in which virtually everyone is an isolationist are very rare. More common is the situation in which multilateralism and isolationism are opposed. Very much for historical reasons, both Germany and Japan today experience this tension in their foreign policies. Most countries reflect an amalgam of multilateralism, isolationism, and unilateralism, changing with period, issue, and administration, as well as with the circumstances abroad with which the government must contend. When governments are in extreme isolationist or unilateral postures, the management of world order is difficult. Multilateralism, as a bargaining strategy or a commitment to alliance, is the predominant mode of statecraft.

Situating multilateralism in strategic and historical space

"In the United States," according to Robert Keohane (1983, p. 153), "'internationalists' have been attracted to international agreements and international organizations as useful devices for implementing American

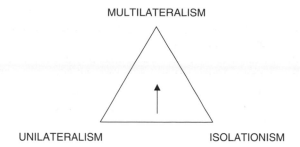

Figure 3.1. Multilateralism

policy; 'isolationists' and 'nationalists' have not." Other writers imply that foreign policies are pure – that they are either multilateralist or isolationist or unilateralist, but that their policy preferences do not include elements of all three strategies. But in actuality all foreign policy is a mix of the three propensities. In emphasis, they may be more of one propensity than another, but they contain elements of all three dispositions.

Multilateralism can be thought of as a concept at the apex of an equilateral triangle symbolizing overall policy space, with the strategy of unilateralism at one of the remaining points and the strategy of isolationism at the other (Figure 3.1). Each of these strategies is equidistant from the other. Each type of strategy dictates a kind of policy choice for the state with respect to each issue.

Regarding a given foreign policy issue, each government can then be situated in this foreign policy space at a given location. By situating each government in this policy space, one can determine how different or how similar each government is on a particular issue relative to the three general strategic dispositions, multilateralism, unilateralism, and isolationism. For ideological reasons, as well as reasons dictated by diplomatic circumstance (e.g., George W. Bush had to deal with the advent of the new terrorism – Laqueur 1999; Lesser, Hoffman, Arquilla, Ronfeldt, and Zanini 1999; Gunaratana 2002), Bill Clinton for instance was more multilateral in his foreign policy conduct than George W. Bush. Not only because Hillary Clinton is Secretary of State and the administration is also Democrat, the administration of President Barack Obama displays strong continuity with the prior Clinton administrations. But at the same time in energy, environmental, and security matters the Obama administration has pioneered its own sense of direction and indicates awareness of both the strengths and weaknesses of multilateralism.

Moreover, foreign policy is not static. As administrations change, so they change their foreign policy postures. Thus the policy–space triangle enables the analyst to trace the changing strategic propensities of subsequent administrations within a single country to determine each administration's strategic leanings. But what must be remembered is that these leanings will vary according to issue. The Bush administration was more unilateral regarding the environment and security considerations. But it was not more unilateral regarding multilateral economic initiative and human rights interventions. Each recent successive Mexican government has become less isolationist and more multilateral on most matters of foreign policy. On immigration issues, in contrast, Mexico has become more unilateral, especially regarding treatment of illegal aliens in the United States.

Although his main theme is the contrast between imperial Britain as the world's largest producer in the nineteenth century and "imperial America" as the world's largest consumer in the twentieth century, Charles Maier (2006) shows with vivid historical sketches what empire does politically to both colony and colonizer. John Vasquez (1993) observes that most wars do not occur in the absence of issues or grievances. He maps the steps to war in terms of the progression of those issues as they increasingly are perceived as grievances. Benjamin Miller (2007), on the other hand, argues that there must be "congruence" between state boundaries and "nations" for peace to prevail.

The analyst may believe that the choice of foreign-policy posture will dictate the strategy for dealing with an issue. But very often it is the issue that dictates the foreign policy posture, not the other way around. For example, regarding the response to the attack on the twin towers, the United States was prepared to act immediately and to act alone. This was understood by its allies. Yet in the end the United States was not obliged to act alone, for NATO – universally across its membership – regarded the attack on the United States as a clear act of aggression. NATO supported the decision to strike Al Qaeda and to intervene in Afghanistan.

In contrast, the decision to form both the Canada–US Free Trade Agreement and the North American Free Trade Agreement (NAFTA) was quite different. The United States was aware in each case that unilateralism would not work. Multilateralism is the anchor for all of this analysis. Every other strategic interaction with states involves a degree of multilateralism, including bilateral interaction. If the United States expressed its preference for an economic agreement with either of its smaller trading partners, the press in Canada and Mexico would play up the argument as though it were a diktat to states that were often characterized in the press as though they were in a dependency relationship to the United States. This would force the governments of Canada or Mexico to reject the US overture.

Instead, Canada had to take the lead in the Canada–US free trade agreement and be seen to take the lead by the press and public. With respect to NAFTA, Mexico did the unthinkable. For the very first time in history, a Third World country would declare that two of the richest countries in the world should follow *its* lead in forming a free trade area. Hence multilateralism worked for the United States, where unilateralism could not possibly have succeeded.

Of course, the form of unilateralism or multilateralism is less important, or should be less important, than the nature of the motivation for action. But this somewhat subtle point is frequently lost on observers. They think that the form of engagement is itself sufficient to determine whose interest is served by what form of strategic posture. Hence they argue that small states will almost always favor multilateralism, while big states will almost always favor unilateralism. In support of this argument, proponents may use the analogy of international trade as illustration.

International economic theory can quite easily show that international trade is more important, in relative terms, to small states than to big states. Why? Small economies cannot offer as much specialization, either in terms of production or in terms of consumption, as the large economies; therefore the small economies use the larger international marketplace, outside the economy of the state itself, to specialize through international trade, hence the relatively greater importance of international trade to the smaller economies as indicated in empirical terms by the ratio of the state's foreign trade to GDP. An inverse relationship exists between the size of the state and the importance of trade as a percentage of GDP. Small states exhibit a high percentage, as high as 40 percent or more. Large-economy states like the United States or Japan exhibit a much smaller percentage of exports to GDP, generally in the range of 10 to 20 percent. A small-economy state that is rapidly becoming a large-economy state, like China, will exhibit a decreasing ratio of foreign trade to GDP over time.

But what is true for international trade is almost certainly *not* true for multilateralism in international politics. An example may help show the argument. If both NATO and the UN Security Council approved of the decision to put down the threat to the Tutsi created by the Hutu in Rwanda, would the outcome have been any better for Rwanda and other African countries than if France alone had sent its paratroopers into Rwanda early in the violence? Involved here are complexities of agency, bias, and timing.

Critics have suggested that agency matters here, that is, collective involvement by a multilateral institution would have been fairer and preferable to unilateral intervention. Likewise some have regarded

France as too pro-Tutsi. But, in the end, did any of this matter? France, or any other interventionist agency, would have been obligated to confront Hutu extremists. For the slain Tutsi schoolchild, whether France, NATO, or the United Nations intervened mattered very little. What was necessary was for *somebody* to intervene before the killing started, and that did not happen.

There is no evidence whatsoever that Rwanda or the principle of human rights would have been advantaged by waiting for a larger multilateral effort. By delaying the response, and by debating military action endlessly in parliaments and in the United Nations, the opportunity to save hundreds of thousands of Africans from murder by rivals and by crazed militias was lost. As it turns out, neither unilateral action nor multilateralism occurred in time to save Rwanda. Surely the hesitancy caused by the felt need to pursue a multilateral course (to his credit the Secretary General of the United Nations, Kofi Annan, tried desperately to persuade governments to intervene to stop the slaughter, but without success) undoubtedly failed to serve this small state well.

Dual fallacies of multilateralism and unilateralism

From the small state perspective, the fallacy of multilateralism is that the small state will be able to use multilateralism to "tie the hands" of the large state. The claim here is that multilateral cooperation really means that the purpose of multilateral strategy is not to find mutually acceptable policies, but rather to "handcuff" the larger state or group of states by merely opposing whatever policies that state or group of states advocates (Fearon 1995).

Sometimes the view is that the small state has greater wisdom than the larger state about a foreign-policy issue, especially an issue involving the use of force. Multilateralism is seen as a true reflection of the knowledge and preferences of the larger community of (smaller) states, and on this moral basis ought to be able to define the policy direction that the multilateral initiative adopts. Thus the small state seeks influence by counterposing its own moral virtue to the material capability of the larger state. The fallacy here is that the larger state will agree to this unusual bargain. The small state ignores the assumption of the large state that, although it may see an issue differently from the small state, it believes that it, too, possesses moral virtue.

This was largely the strategy of those governments that wanted the United States, Britain, Spain, and the other supporters of intervention to go back to the UN Security Council before seeking a regime change in Iraq, in order to obtain a resolution that would reimpose inspections. The strategy of France, Russia, and Canada was to tie up the United States in procedural disputation inside the Security Council, where the threat of a Security Council veto would hang over the discussions. The focus was not on whether Iraq had observed the prior UN resolutions regarding inspections or had primarily given up the attempt to acquire chemical and biological weapons. Nor was the debate about the morality of intervention, since France had frequently intervened in Africa, Russia continued to pursue what it regarded as its interests in Georgia and Azerbaijan, and Canada had just encouraged the members of the Organization of American States (OAS) to intervene in the affairs of Peru, all without formal UN mandate. The purpose of the multilateral initiative was to obtain a resolution that would delay, and if possible prevent, Anglo-US military intervention in Iraq; it was not to ensure that through regime change Saddam Hussein would be prevented (preempted) from obtaining weapons of mass destruction.

From the small-state perspective, the fallacy of multilateralism occurs when it is used by one group of states to frustrate and oppose the initiative of another group of states, rather than for some positive, new joint enterprise that would appeal to all parties to an agreement, including the large states involved. When the sole effort becomes that of the restraint of a large state and its allies, rather than conjoint diplomatic initiative for some more encompassing common goal, the fallacy of multilateralism becomes apparent. In such instances, multilateralism becomes virtually indistinguishable from an attempted use of the balance of power.

From the large-state perspective, the fallacy of unilateralism is that the state can act alone (because it has the military or economic power to do so) and still obtain the respect and support of the community of states for its actions (Krauthammer 2002; Kane 2006; Chua 2007). The large state forgets that its own capability and the legitimacy it seeks from the larger community of states are not identical. It mistakenly believes that "success" for a venture in terms of initial action is the same as success in terms of eventual political implementation of necessary policies or reforms. It neglects to take into account that resistance to an action from the smaller states occurs either because they do not interpret a threat as so imposing, or because they are deeply skeptical about whether there will be sufficient follow-through to make the initiative truly worthwhile.

The decision of two of the larger states in the western hemisphere, the United States and Canada, to encourage intervention in Haiti for the purpose of promoting democracy and bolstering the Aristide forces in the government is illustrative of the unilateralist fallacy. Other governments in the hemisphere were opposed to the intervention, not because of a lack of esteem for democracy, but because they thought that intervention would transgress the OAS norms against such intervention once more, and once again reinforce abridgments of small-state sovereignty by large states. But, despite commendable efforts by Canada in particular to try to clean up the lack of professionalism in the Haitian police force and the court system, these other states were skeptical of the "staying power" of the initiative in terms of willingness to invest resources and time such that the government would be fundamentally reformed. They were worried that military intervention was just a short-term fix that would do damage to the principle of state sovereignty in the hemisphere without producing any long-term benefits to Haitian society.

Hence the unilateralist fallacy of the larger state is that its wisdom is greater than that of smaller states, or other states in the system, and that military force is a reflection of this wisdom rather than an instrument shaped by practical exigency. Moreover, the unilateralist fallacy is to exaggerate short-term decision criteria, and to minimize the long-term consequences of an action, especially if these consequences are negative or lacking in credibility regarding whether the action should ever have taken place.

The "anchoring" of multilateralism

Either a single state can move away from the issue status quo and from the structural status quo of the many states, or the many states can move away from the issue and structural status quo of the single state. Just as the new position adopted by the many states may be called multilateralism, so the new position adopted by the individual state may be called unilateralism. But in reality the true answer to whether unilateralism or multilateralism is the more valid strategy is determined by who has moved away from the issue status quo, the single state or the many (and whether this movement is regarded as normatively acceptable by the community of states) (Hoffmann 1998, pp. 102–03).

Whether multilateralism is anchored in the issue status quo or in change is thus a very important strategic matter. The unilateralist state can be accused of "revisionism" if the multilateral majority wants to remain with the status quo. An example is that of Charles de Gaulle in 1966, when he attempted to alter the institutional nature of NATO, ultimately withdrawing France from the Organization but not from the Alliance. His actions were regarded by the other members as revisionist because he wanted to change NATO into something it currently was not.

Or the unilateralist state may be accused of "reactionary-ism" if the rest of the states in the system want to move forward and the unilateralist state stubbornly does not. An example here is the establishment of an international criminal court, preferred by many states in the system, but rejected by the United States as too subject to politicization. Another example where the United States is regarded as the "reactionary state" concerns the Kyoto Protocol on global warming, where perhaps a majority of states favor involuntary reductions of emissions but where the United States appears recalcitrant because it is skeptical, not about the fact of global warming but about the reliability and validity of the scientific explanation for the bulk of the variance in the independent variable – that is, that which causes the increase in global temperature. It is even more skeptical about the reliability of the mechanism to guarantee compliance and about the likely inclusion of states such as China and India which are soon to become among the largest polluters in the system but remain free riders with respect to the Kyoto process. How multilateralism is anchored in the issue dynamic of history thus determines much about how unilateralism and multilateralism will be characterized and about how they will be applied as descriptors of state behavior.

Of course, extreme "unilateralist" states are sometimes territorial aggressors, challenging world order at the regional or global levels (Schweller 1998; Newman 2007). In reality, most states, large or small, do not want to adopt a unilateralist position of any sort. In reality, most states cannot adopt such a position or strategy because they cannot withstand the pressure from the international community to conform.

Government decisions about foreign policy conduct are much different during critical intervals of structural change when long-held expectations about future role and security are suddenly proven wrong. Unilateral aggressive behavior is more likely, but so is alliance behavior. Empirical evidence confirms that a government tries to mitigate fears about security at a critical point by joining an alliance and forming bigger alliances (Chiu 2003), and that deterrence challenges increase while rate of deterrence success declines (James and Hebron 1997; Tessman and Chan 2004).

Only a few large states, or states backed by some monopolist advantage such as regarding oil exportation, are likely to persist with policy unilateralism over time. However, to the extent that the unilateralist position becomes that of the majority of states, in the form of a new multilateral posture and outlook, that adoption of unilateralist position by the multilateral majority is often due to the size, status, or capacity for persuasion of the large state. Not many examples in history illustrate such movement from individual state outlook to the outlook for the system of states as a whole. US preference for the establishment of a new international trade order in the post-1945 period, reflected in the establishment of the General Agreement on Tariffs and Trade (GATT), is, however, one such example.

Normally, initiative is multiple in conception and implementation. For example, regarding the formation of NATO, two smaller states, Britain and Canada, were largely responsible for the idea of the alliance. The United States was a very important future member, but it was a somewhat laggard participant. So it is with many multilateral enterprises. The large state is not necessarily the initiator of the idea (see the discussion below on NAFTA), although often it is the critical participant, and the chief "sherpa," in the long process of making the multilateral enterprise a reality.

Anchoring multilateralism not only in the "hierarchy" of issues, but also in the shift and movement of the issue agenda over time, is thus key to determining whether a state will be categorized as "revisionist" or "reactionary," and thus whether it is truly a unilateralist state in the proper meaning of the term. That the "many" and the "few" or the "one" are often at odds in world politics is probably unavoidable. The key is how to interpret this issue opposition in terms of how issues change over time. This is truly a twenty-first century kind of analysis, made particularly relevant by the increasing number of democracies in the system, where "participation" is becoming the talisman for legitimacy and order.

"Inside" and "outside" strategies of multilateral actors

Multilateral actors can opt for either of two basic strategies to influence larger states, an inside and an outside strategy. The inside strategy is that of former Prime Minister Tony Blair of the United Kingdom and of former President George W. Bush of the United States. It is a strategy of working from the inside to influence choices and events, even if the overall goal of military intervention and regime change for Iraq was not Blair's first choice. By supporting the president of the United States, Britain hopes to prevent US isolation. But Blair also hopes to prevent US attempted hegemony (in that the United States would act alone and thus would feel no pressure to consider the will of other governments that are less enamored with the policy of regime change and its consequences than is the United States). Blair has enjoyed some considerable success with this strategy.

The outside strategy is that of former President Jacques Chirac of France, who, like Bush, is a political conservative. France offers its full participation only belatedly and perhaps qualifiedly. It attempts until the last moment to shift the policy orientation of the large state through criticism, procedural obfuscation within the UN Security Council, coalition formation, and attempts at inspiring counter-coalitions. The French objective is to influence decision-making from outside the circle of the principal proponents of Iraqi regime change (Britain and the United States). The tactic is to use delay and international legal recourse to alter the direction of decision. This tactic does not mean that in the end France, Russia, or Canada will remain opposed to collective foreign-policy action regarding, for example, Iraqi stabilization and reconstruction. But France was not likely to support stabilization and reconstruction efforts unless certain of its demands were met, usually expressed in terms of UN resolutions, through which France expected to transfer greater control over Iraqi policy to itself.

While likewise rejecting US intervention in Iraq, President Nicolas Sarkozy also chose to forego Chirac's outside strategy. He replaced the outside strategy with a peculiarly inside strategy with respect both to NATO and to bilateral relations with the United States. Insofar, the Bush administration responded far more positively to the French initiative even though the substance of French foreign policy vis-à-vis a number of traditional Franco-US concerns changed very little.

Thus inside and outside strategies may have the same purpose, even though they possess different content, are pursued by different means, and may be justified by different moral imperatives. A reviewer has noted that these inside–outside strategies possess characteristics similar to balancing versus bandwagoning (Walt 1987; Pressman 2008). It is true that inside strategies and bandwagoning appear similar to outside strategies and balancing. Inside strategies involve cooperation regarding a common agenda; outside strategies involve opposition and competition. But outside strategies also involve cooperation among alliance members resisting a common external threat. In bandwagoning, the alliance leader tends to define the agenda which the other members cooperate to promote. Cooperation in the operation of the balance of power is internal to the alliance and restricted to the alliance members. Cooperation in bandwagoning among other actors is limited to support for the objectives as defined by the alliance leader.

The difference between these inside–outside strategies and bandwagoning is that bandwagoning involves coalescing behind the coalition leader regardless of the terms because the small state is weak, isolated, and unable to affect the strategy of the larger leading state or states. The small state is also vulnerable to inducements. In the case of a true inside strategy, the multiple members of the international community support the strategies of the leading state provided that an accommodation occurs. Likewise the outside strategy is different from balancing because the smaller states seek to alter the strategy of the leading state while in the end supporting that strategy. Moreover, no issue of a balance of power to promote territorial security is involved.

Notwithstanding the differences in content and implementation between the inside and outside strategies, the goal of the strategies may still be identical. A final example will perhaps illustrate how inside and outside strategies are intertwined.

Regarding Fidel Castro's Cuba, the United States has long sought a shift toward a more democratic government and toward more market-oriented policies. The strategy employed has been the US embargo of Cuba in terms of trade and the mobility of citizens. This strategy might be regarded as equivalent to the above "external" strategy. In contrast, Canada and Mexico have also sought the same ends of greater democracy and greater market reform. But they have chosen a different strategy, the equivalent of an "internal" strategy of engagement with Cuba and the attempt to use communication and interaction to modify its governing policies. The goal of each strategy is the same; the means are different. So it is with the inside and outside strategies of the attempt at multilateral influence by small states with respect to the behavior of large states within coalitions of collective action.

Origins of multilateral success: the NAFTA example

Success in multilateralism involves two stages. First, there is the successful multilateral negotiation. Then there is the demonstration that what has been negotiated is a success in terms of output or production or purpose. That these two stages are not the same, but that both are needed, may be apparent; but what is apparent is often not heeded by statespersons. After all, it is much easier to negotiate an agreement that does nothing than to negotiate an agreement that does something. The more a multilateral agreement attempts to achieve, the more difficult is the task of negotiating participation to that agreement. Ambitious terms complicate negotiation success. Moreover, the easiest thing in diplomacy is to negotiate a document to which every state's signature is attached, but which elicits not a single state's actual implementation. That is the history of many a UN resolution.

For many reasons, NAFTA stands out as the quintessential success of multilateral negotiation. First, although power was highly unequal among the three partners to NAFTA, the most powerful state did not take the lead in proposing the agreement (Doran 2001). That would have been the death knell for the negotiation. Instead, it was the weakest of the three partners, Mexico, that proposed the formal ideal of NAFTA. This over-came suggestions of "imperialism" and "manipulation" that often accompanies, sometimes with justification, such asymmetric negotiations. Because the government of President Carlos Salinas initiated the idea for NAFTA, and invited the United States to consider that idea, the Mexican press and elites were much more likely to accept the notion of a preferential North American trade area than if the United States had been the government that tried to introduce the idea. Insofar, the United States and its coalition partners overcame the unilateralist fallacy of acting precipitously and alone. Hence, by managing the process of integrated action properly, legitimacy was retained for the NAFTA idea.

Second, NAFTA was a success because the NAFTA negotiation turned the conventional idea of First World–Third World relations on its head. For the first time in the history of modern international political economy, a Third World country negotiated head-to-head on trade matters without asking for dispensations and prior concessions from the larger, more mature economies. Admittedly, Mexico had some very fine technocrats as advisors to the Mexican president, and as negotiators, who in turn were backed by neo-classical trade theory which said that all states are very likely to benefit from trade liberalization regardless of their economic base (Noguez 2002; Cooper 1995). But translating theory into policy is scarcely easy, especially when there are centuries of fear and self-inhibiting propaganda to overcome.

Third, the NAFTA negotiations were successful because a simple rule was observed. He who commits most to the negotiation stands in the end to receive the largest benefits. He who places the most at stake reaps the largest eventual returns. This rule saw Mexico taking higher risks and obtaining the greatest relative gains. The United States, on the other hand, was required by the circumstances to assume the least risks; it thereby also received the smallest relative gains. But the very notion of disproportionate incentives drove Mexico to adopt the timing and the format of negotiations that led to a successful agreement.

Fourth, the second stage of NAFTA multilateralism was extremely rewarding. The negotiation was about "something" rather than nothing – that is, empty symbolism. That something continued to produce benefits for years to come. But such benefits required long-term planning, very intense negotiation that at various times nearly broke down, and highly creative design such as was ultimately incorporated into the trade dispute resolution mechanisms. Thus NAFTA was a multilateral success at both stage 1 and stage 2.

Fifth, NAFTA was a success because it was a transparent negotiation that was open to others in future trade arrangements, not a beggar-thy-neighbor arrangement that sought one-sided advantage. This does not mean that all of its provisions were conspicuous examples of trade liberalization. The provisions regarding textiles and automobiles employing domestic content legislation were not very forward looking. But the balance of the agreement did create and enhance trade, both globally and regionally. NAFTA was a multilateral success because other governments, not members to the agreement, could also benefit from it.

Sixth, NAFTA was a successful agreement because it contained or generated involuntary side-payments and benefits that led to greater interdependence among the members. For example, NAFTA broke economic ground in Mexico so that the country had the confidence to move toward genuine party competition and democracy. NAFTA strengthened the financial sector so that when crisis came, that crisis could be dealt with largely inside the North American context. NAFTA implicitly assisted in dealing with other problems such as illegal migration by increasing the Mexican economic growth rate, thereby offering jobs to hard-pressed peasants and others who chose to migrate to Mexico City or northern Mexico instead of attempting to cross the US border illegally. A multilateral agreement that increases interdependence among its signatories is a positive achievement.

The reader should not conclude that NAFTA was a successful multilateral negotiation because there were no losers. Inside each country certain firms, industries, and individuals were losers. Not everybody was able to increase productivity through specialization. Californian tomato growers and Mexican maize farmers both lost out to competitors across the border in the name of more efficient production elsewhere. Some of these losers were compensated from the greater economic gains made elsewhere in the economy and then transferred through taxes and incentive payments. Some individuals and firms moved to other industries where their productivity would be higher. But the overall economy in Mexico, Canada, and the United States benefited from this example of multilateral economic and political success.

Exemplified by the tomato industry, a further consequence occurred. The advantages of sun and low labor costs in Mexico, and of a comparatively long growing season and good soil in California, were offset in Canada by technological innovation. Hydroponic tomatoes, assisted by greenhouse nurturing and artificial light, turned out to be highly competitive to tomatoes grown naturally in Mexico and California. A new approach technologically to tomato production returned tomato production to the most unlikely of the three economies for such production, that of Canada. NAFTA competition stimulated technological innovation, already ongoing, in each of the countries.

At the heart of the multilateral success of NAFTA is that both at stage 1 and at stage 2 of the negotiated arrangement all of the governments member to the agreement saw benefits that would flow to them, not necessarily equally, but proportionate to the risks and to the political costs that they were expected to assume. NAFTA has much to teach the student of multilateralism regarding how and why multilateralism can be a success.

In conclusion

The argument. According to the thesis of this article, not only is multilateral cooperation regarding every issue a mix of multilateralism, unilateralism, and isolationism that varies for every state, and over time, but multilateral cooperation must also take into account other complexities. One of these complexities is that the large state should not pursue a policy that is largely bereft of multilateralism and then expect the international community to come to its assistance so as to make that much-disputed policy a success. A policy that is not considered legitimate at the outset is unlikely to be regarded as legitimate and worthy of material support, no matter how much that support may be needed, at a subsequent point in the implementation of the strategy.

Similarly, the complexity of multilateralism is such that the smaller state in pursuit of its own objective and seeking to "handcuff" the larger state, rather than to pursue a truly conjoint foreign policy effort, is likely to see multilateral cooperation fail. If the purpose of a multilateral strategy is only to stop a larger state from pursuing a specific policy, that form of so-called multilateral cooperation contains a troubling flaw. Multilateral cooperation must possess positive elements that are broadly and mutually attractive.

As the new unipolar system emerges, it displays elements of multilateralism, unilateralism, and isolationism. Through the disappearance of the second pole of the bipolar relationship in the aftermath of the collapse of the Soviet Union and the end of the Cold War, unipolarity emerged. But unipolarity is not the equivalent of hegemony, an impossible reach for the United States, or any other state, concerning politics within the central international system. Nor is unipolarity the equivalent of multipolarity, which would impose a kind of equality among the principal states of the system that does not at present exist. Yet regardless of the degree of polarity in the international system, multilateral cooperation may or may not exist within that system depending upon actor, issue area, and time point.

Multilateralism is evident in such US projects as the Central American market initiative (CAFTA), the six-power talks on North Korea, and the G8 summit (Tepperman 2004; Pauly 2005). Although governments other than the United State were involved as well, unilateralism was reflected in US policy towards Kosovo, Afghanistan, and Iraq. Tinges of isolationism color the foreign policies of Germany, Canada, and Australia, as they downsize their militaries, reduce the relative size of their aid budgets, and begin to neglect large areas of the world in all but rhetorical policy. Sometimes such foreign policy tendency is expressed as "free-riderism," for that is its ultimate result. Claims to hegemony at the top of the system of course abet the proponents of free-riderism elsewhere in the system.

Countries like Germany stress regionalism within the European context rather than globalism on a worldwide scale. Iran is part of this ambient extension, for example, but North Korea may not be. Unable to exercise a global reach, some of these rich states tend to withdraw into the region within which they reside, often veiling such policies for domestic political consumption with expressions of global moral preference.

Thus behind the disparity between multilateralism and unilateralism lies the specter of isolationism. The contrast between a US foreign-policy budget that is overstretched and German or Canadian budgets that have been sharply downsized is reflected in the disparity in the capacity actually to sustain multilateralism with troops, material, or emergency aid. While absolute disparities in power will always exist, the percentage of GDP devoted to these individual endeavors (a partial index of relative power) is a rough measure of global involvement for a number of individual states at the top of the central system.

Hence multilateralism is not merely a matter of whether the United States is inclined to act in multilateral fashion (Newman, Thakur, and Tirman 2006). The answer here is indisputable; certainly the Obama administration is willing to act conjointly with other governments. Zbigniew Brzezinski argues that Americans favor multilateralism as a strategy over the unilateralism that is implied in hegemony. Opinion poll data backup Brzezinski's claim. In an elite opinion poll, 75 percent of the respondents supported multilateralism, while just 12 percent favored iso-lationism, and only 10 percent favored unilateralism (Brzezinski 2004, p. 199; Chicago Council on Foreign Relations 2006). The real question for President Obama is whether other governments feel confident enough politically and economically to take on multilateral responsibilities.

Inside the G20 all kinds of gaps have emerged. The European role in the IMF exceeds its contributions. US international responsibilities exceed its financial capabilities. The Chinese aspirations for foreign policy role exceed China's contributions and capabilities. Despite its absolute decline in size, Russia is dissatisfied with its diminished role. In terms of disruption to world order, however, these gaps are not felt so immediately because of the global security deployment of the United States, a deploy-ment that is thus sometimes rather strained, and is often likely to be misunderstood. But the reality remains that the only truly global interna-tional security presence today, on the part of any single country, is that of the United States.

Fen Osler Hampson

International cooperation can take many forms, some of which are highly institutionalized forms of cooperation, others of which are not. One of the most discussed – and controversial – form of institutionalized cooperation is "multilateralism." At its heart, the concept of "multilateralism" rests on the relatively simple notion that when three or more states choose to cooperate it is with the expectation that their cooperative arrangement will yield roughly equal reciprocal benefits. For example, when three or more states agree to an alliance partnership it is with the expectation that the security guarantees they offer to each will be reciprocated – that is, an attack by a hostile force against one of the members of the alliance will rally the others to its defense.

Ambrose Bierce's definition of a Hydra – as a kind of animal that the ancients catalogued under many heads – captures some of the definitional quandaries associated with the concept. "Multilateral" literally means "many sided." It is typically used as an adjective, not a noun or a verb. "Multilateralism," however, is a noun – but a noun to describe what? A set of belief systems about how the world should be organized? A set of norms or principles for action that are informed by the expectation of reciprocity? A description of different kinds of world order? A description about international institutions and how they should operate? A description of international negotiation processes? A surrogate for "international regimes?" An exhortation about how foreign policy should be conducted – that is, the "liberal" response to "unilateralism" (or "realism")? Or a term of endearment (or derision) depending upon one's ideological point of view? The answer is "all of the above and then some."

This chapter argues that there is much debate today about the real meaning (and purpose) of "multilateralism" in international relations. There are several different conceptions of "multilateralism" that are reflected in the scholarly and policy literature. Although some of these conceptions overlap, they also differ in a number of important ways. The absence of consensus about the meaning and purpose of multilateralism also extends into policy circles. "Multilateralism" is often presented as an alternative to "unilateralism." In debates about intervention, "multilateralism" is often presented as the only legitimate recourse when the use of force is involved. Interventions led by "coalitions of the willing" or the "co-opted" are dismissed by multilateralist partisans as illegitimate (or illegal) forms of state practice and action unless they receive the formal blessing of the United Nations Security Council (Evans and Sahnoun 2001; Weiss and Hubert 2001). Many lay the blame for the current "crisis" or "failure" of international institutions and "multilateralism" at Washington's door, arguing that Washington's "sheriff's posse" approach to global problems, especially under the Bush administration, flies in the face of evolving international norms and precepts.[1]

The roots of the purported "crisis of multilateralism" lie not simply in US foreign policy behavior and actions as argued by some, but in deeper, underlying assumptions about the real meaning of "multilateralism" in world affairs. Enthusiasm for "bottom-up" visions of multilateralism is greater in left and center-left circles in North America and Europe than in other parts of the world, encouraging as much attention to South–North differences as to longstanding transatlantic ones. In recent years, however, the idea that reciprocity among states is the bedrock of multilateralism has come under challenge from left-of-center critics and, for different reasons, from states in the South which have long felt that international institutions are dominated by the interests of Western countries in "multilateral" decision making. Concepts of equity, empowerment, fair representation, and even democracy now infuse the concept of multilateralism. So too has the somewhat radical notion that multilateralism is a form of international cooperation that is not confined to state actors but, in the eyes of some, involves a wide variety of non-state actors as well. These conflicting notions of multilateralism – compounded by general dissatisfaction with the performance of international institutions – will undoubtedly make efforts to strengthen and reform international institutions even more difficult than they already are. As one commentator astutely observes,

International politics is at a crossroads: on the one hand, the path towards an elite multilateralism, which shifts decisions on global policy increasingly into exclusive clubs and political circles while excluding democratic control and participation; on the other, the path to a multilateralism of solidarity, which emphasizes and strengthens the responsibility of democratically legitimate public institutions and complements this through a comprehensive involvement of social society organizations and the well regulated interaction with the private sector. (Martens 2007)

---

[1] For different views on current US foreign policy challenges and behavior, see Byers and Nolte 2003; Holzgrefe and Keohane 2003; Glennon 2003; Brzezinski 2004; Lennon and Eiss 2004; Nye 2002; and Slaughter 2004.

Formal ("top-down") multilateralism

"Formal" multilateralism centers on the collective norms, rules, and principles that govern interstate behavior. It is most closely associated with the liberal tradition in international relations, although some elements converge with rational choice theory, constructivism, and institutionalism. Much of this scholarship has focused on explaining why states choose to accept multilateral institutions and arrangements over other forms of cooperation.

Scholars have struggled to bring some analytical rigor and consistency to the concept of multilateralism. John Ruggie (1993a, p. 8) suggests that the term refers to different kinds of principled institutional arrangements among three or more states that serve to coordinate their policies and behavior.[2] According to Ruggie, multilateralism covers three institutional domains: international orders, international regimes, and international organizations (Ruggie 1993, p. 12). Multilateral "constitutive" rules generally tend to govern the behavior of state actors in these different domains. There are three issue areas where multilateral arrangements typically arise. The first is the area of property rights, where there are strong incentives to invoke indivisible, general principles of ownership that are reciprocal and diffuse. The second are coordination problems where states are "more or less indifferent in principle about the actual outcome, provided that they accept the same outcome," as in the case of international telecommunications regimes regulating the use of different radio frequencies and bandwidths. The third are collaboration problems marked by genuine conflicts of interest (or mixed motives) where multilateral arrangements are generally more difficult to develop (Ruggie 1993, pp. 15–17).

In a similar vein, Brian Job (1997) argues that multilateralism is a form of state practice that accords with certain principles and that involves the development of shared norms, collective identities, and institutions, which can be formal or informal. These principles can govern cooperative relationships between and among states in conflict management, although for genuine multilateralism to exist such cooperation must be deep-rooted and extend over a lengthy period of time. Like Ruggie, Job argues that multilateralism has taken a variety of different institutional forms in international relations, specifically in the area of global conflict

---

[2] Ruggie defines the "principles" of multilateralism as follows: (1) general principles which specify conduct without regard to the particularistic interests of the parties; (2) principles that are indivisible among the parties with respect to the range of the behavior in question; and (3) relations that are marked by diffuse reciprocity, i.e., they yield roughly equal benefits to their members in the aggregate over time.

management. Balance of power arrangements, collective defense, collective security, concerts, and pluralistic and integrated security communities are all different manifestations of multilateralism. However, he concedes that the "depth" and "breadth" of "qualitative multilateralism" vary substantially in these different institutional settings.

Much of the formal scholarship on multilateralism is concerned about explaining why multilateral institutions and governance arrangements among state parties take a particular form. Ruggie, for instance, argues that the chief reason why major, global institutions have taken the form that they have is because of the hegemonic impact of US preferences and power in the immediate aftermath of World War II and the fact that the United States was keen to project on to the world its own experience with the New Deal regulatory state (Ruggie 1993a, pp. 24–31). President Franklin Delano Roosevelt also believed that the only way to prevent the United States from returning to isolationism was to bind the country in a series of multilateral institutional frameworks and commitments. According to Ruggie, these arrangements will persist so long as the state parties to those arrangements continue to share similar expectations about diffuse reciprocity and rewards; these arrangements continue to be based on generalized principles that are elastic and open to modification; and the domestic polities of those state parties to these arrangements remain open and politically stable.

Although interstate cooperation in the twentieth and twenty-first centuries is marked by a proliferation in the number of organizations and international regimes that adhere to multilateral norms and principles, there are obviously other ways to secure international cooperation. In some regions of the globe, states have quite consciously avoided formal multilateralism. A case in point is the Asia–Pacific region. As Christopher Hemmer and Peter Katzenstein (2002) explain, the lack of formal, *de jure*, regional, multilateral institutions in the Asia–Pacific region has both a normative and a domestic, political explanation. In their international relations in the postwar period, many countries in the region have eschewed multilateral arrangements in favor of direct, bilateral economic and security ties with the United States. The Chinese and the Japanese, in particular, have had a strong politico-cultural disposition to avoid becoming involved in formal institutions. Prevailing political norms at the national level have also been antithetical to liberal internationalism because of colonial legacies that favored "rule by law" instead of the "rule of law" and custodianship in state–society relations.

But there are others tensions that thwart the development of stronger institutions in the region. The voluntary multilateralism and institutional weaknesses of the Asia–Pacific Economic Cooperation (APEC), for example, are due to "the on-going creative struggle between ambitious multilateralists and national sovereignty realists." In addition to great power rivalries between China, Japan, and the United States, the broader regional framework for cooperation has been held hostage to the countries of the Association of Southeast Asian Nations (ASEAN), which preferred their own "incipient sub-regional architecture," centered on the "Asian way" of informal agreements and consensual decision making. Nevertheless, APEC has been somewhat successful in promoting a "cognitive diffusion of values and information" while advancing policies that promoted greater levels of economic integration and more effective national responses to successive global economic crises and shocks (Feinberg 2008, pp. 239, 246).

Clubs versus universality

A number of questions come to mind about the requirements of formal multilateralism as discussed by Ruggie and others. For any collective good, the benefits of membership grow as more join the collective arrangement, but so, too, do the potential costs of free riding with enlarged membership. Cooperation is usually difficult when numbers are large, because it is difficult to impose penalties or sanctions against free riders; it is difficult to identify shared interests; and there are "recognition and control" problems with declining transparency regarding the actions of other players. Thus the traditional response to the collective action difficulties that are experienced in most multilateral settings, including most UN bodies, is what Miles Kahler (1992) refers to as "minilateralism" – that is, cooperation through smaller group interactions usually involving the most powerful actors in the international system (or what Duncan Snidal (1985b) calls the privileged "K" group – i.e., a club which has the authority and power to impose its preferences on weaker or smaller players). The relationship of the permanent members of Security Council to the rest of the members of the United Nations is an obvious example of "minilateralism" in practice in the maintenance of international peace and security. So, too, is the way voting shares are allocated among different state members in the Bretton Woods institutions (the International Monetary Fund and the International Bank for Reconstruction and Development), where the most powerful and wealthy states in the international system have a disproportionate voice and influence over the way these institutions are managed.

Inevitably, minilateral arrangements are necessary to make international institutions work, and sometime exclusive clubs are seen to work better than nonexclusive ones. As Steve Weber notes (1992, p. 633),

NATO was successful in providing security to its members during the Cold War, on the multilateral principle that "security was indivisible, the external borders of alliance territory were equally inviolable, and diffuse reciprocity was the norm," in spite of the fact that "it did not distribute decision-making power and responsibility equally among the allies." In contrast, a recurring criticism of the UN Conference on Disarmament (CD) is that its universal membership – and consensus-based approach to any decisions it takes – has rendered that body all but ineffective in promoting new arms control and disarmament schemes, which is why those countries which were intent on securing a new convention to ban anti-personnel landmines took their negotiations out of the CD through a bypass negotiating mechanism otherwise known as the "Ottawa Process" (Hampson and Reid 2003). One of the arguments that is advanced against expanding the permanent membership of the UN Security Council is that the Council would become even less effective than it is now, especially if new permanent members were also to get the veto (Weiss 2003; USInfo 2005).

The awakening of the global South

Another criticism of "formal multilateralism" is that small or weak states are disempowered and fail to receive commensurate benefits from their participation in multilateral arrangements. It is readily apparent that many developing countries feel profoundly disadvantaged by global multilateral financial and trading arrangements. They believe that the normative principles and political architecture of the Bretton Woods system are biased towards the interests and values of the North and the most powerful states in the international system. Many developing countries also believe that the North has traditionally been the normative and legal trendsetter in international institutions, with the South being on the "receiving end" of those norms and rules (Newman, Thakur, and Tirman 2006; Thakur 2001).

In some multilateral forums, however, developing countries have begun to spearhead normative change. For example, Argentina and Brazil have played a key role in bringing the "development agenda" into talks on international patents and copyright claims in the World Intellectual Property Rights Organization (Williams 2004). In other institutional settings, however, more profound kinds of structural reform may be required to bring about the kind of normative and political change desired by developing countries. In the words of Kevin Watkins and Ngaire Woods (2004; also Woods 2001), "Rich countries are ardent advocates of democracy all around the world. But when it comes to the International

Monetary Fund and the World Bank, government of the many by the few is the preferred option." Accordingly, developing countries must be given a greater voice in the decisions of these bodies that affect the lives of their citizens: "In international economic governance, as in national governance, greater democracy can improve the quality of policy" (Watkins and Woods 2004).

A similar assessment is offered in a 2007 Brookings Institution policy brief, which contends that global governance institutions are undergoing an existential crisis, suggesting that they are "fragmented, unrepresentative and ineffective ... increasingly fragile and unable to address the global challenges of the twenty-first century" (Bradford and Linn 2007; see also Lesage 2007). Although it contains a rather bleak assessment of the potential for meaningful reforms to take place in the United Nations, the World Bank, and the International Monetary Fund, this brief concludes that the growing momentum to expand the G8 indicates the potential for this kind of leaders' forum to remain a legitimate, functioning, and relevant institution. For several years this school of thought has garnered increased attention and support, notably from the former Canadian prime minister, Paul Martin, and others who perceived the 1999 financial crisis as an impetus to shift the G7–G8 summit process in a more globalized direction, toward an enlarged body of some twenty countries whose membership would include the major countries of the developing world (Crane 2008).

In November 2008 such a G20 meeting was convened by US President George W. Bush to grapple with the worsening global financial and credit crisis. The summit was not much of a meeting of minds. Rather, it underscored the continuities and disparities of how global governance is perceived. In the Strategic Economic Dialogue between the United States and China prior to the summit, US Treasury Secretary Henry Paulson was chastised by Chinese officials for US overconsumption and overreliance on credit – which China perceives as the root cause of the international financial crisis (Dyer 2008). Other European countries share this criticism, encapsulated by Christian Sautter, former finance minister of France, who complained, "Whether the reason was ideology, short-sightedness or lobby group pressure, the US authorities did not put their financial house in order. We all are paying the price today" (Starr 2008). American moral and economic leadership has been severely undermined through this crisis, and the world – especially the developing countries – will likely no longer be as receptive as it once was to US criticism and direction on fiscal matters.

The attitudes of the developing countries towards global governance have also been shaped by their perception that they are paying the price for the follies and irresponsibleness of the wealthy countries. India's prime minister, Manmohan Singh, complained at the November 2008 G20 meeting that "emerging market countries were not the cause of this crisis, but they are amongst its worst affected victims." India has been especially vocal in expressing the idea that the evolution of global governance institutions must be focused on mitigating and ameliorating economic inequalities in the developing world. There is also a rather pragmatic incentive for this shift in focus: the managing director of the International Monetary Fund, Dominique Strauss-Kahn, pointed out that the developing economies are projected to lead world economic growth, and so there is an incentive – even an imperative – for the wealthier countries to empower and protect these nascent developing economies (Artlow 2008).

Even so, developing countries' criticisms of "inequalities of multilateralism" should be tempered by the recognition that the multilateral system does allow some countries – especially activist states – to punch above their weight. Sometimes small countries have lobbied for their interests in ways that are helpful. Consider, for example, Vanuatu's vigorous advocacy of new measures to combat climate change that have dramatized the plight of small, low-lying, island states.

But multilateral institutions can also empower small countries in ways that are damaging. For example, Cuba, Libya, and Malaysia have done much to thwart the advancement of human rights with obstructionist tactics and bullying behavior in bodies such as the UN Human Rights Commission and its successor body, the Human Rights Council.[3] Developing countries also collectively wield considerable influence over the budgets of some UN agencies, such as UNESCO, and have used that power to thwart reform (Wells 1987; Dutt 2002).

Informal ("bottom-up") multilateralism

Formal, liberal theories of multilateralism focus almost exclusively on state-to-state or intergovernmental forms of international cooperation and the principles and rules under which various kinds of cooperative arrangements emerge within international institutions and occasionally outside them. In recent years, however, there has been growing disquiet even among liberal, international relations scholars about the legitimacy of formal international institutions and the principles, norms, and rules

---

[3] This has prompted widespread debate and discussion about the new bid to reform the UN human rights machinery. See the recommendations of the UN's High-level Panel on Reform.

that inform the membership, the participation of non-state actors, and the behavior of those institutions. Many believe that international institutions are afflicted by a growing "democratic deficit" (e.g. Reinisch 2001; Porter 2001; Simai 1994; Cox 1997). This deficit emerges in the systematic exclusion of key branches of civil society – especially the poor and otherwise marginalized – from participation in the powerful institutions of international governance (Reinicke 1999–2000). It also emerges in the failure of those institutions to provide for the necessities of human life, not to speak of the necessities of global survival (see, e.g., Report of the Commission on Human Security 2003).

Whereas traditionalist multilateralists argue that international institutions were never intended to be democratic and have always functioned as intergovernmental bodies, "bottom-up" multilateralists argue that civil society is playing an increasingly important – if not critical role – in many areas of international public policy. In some areas, they are in the vanguard by raising public awareness, setting the agenda, and helping negotiate new international treaties. In others, civil society actors and nongovernmental organizations are helping to implement and monitor compliance with new international agreements. These new multilateralists are ambivalent about the utility of formal international organizations, such as the United Nations, in promoting key human values, because they believe that entrenched state interests are opposed to the values and interests of the public and civil society.[4] Accordingly, they want to create new international institutions and instruments of cooperation to harness and better engage the talents and interests of an increasingly proactive, global, civil society.

Driving much of this change in global affairs, according to "bottom-up" multilateralists, is the globalization phenomenon.[5] On the one hand, the communications revolution is allowing various "messages" to be carried on a global scale (Warkentin and Mings 2000). This revolution is also transforming individual and communal self-identities and images while empowering local communities in ways that were unthinkable in earlier times (Keck and Sikkink 1998). On the other hand, powerful social, economic and technological pressures are opening up the boundaries of national life. The internationalization of production has also created new challenges to national regulatory structures. There are, in James Rosenau's words,

---

[4] For a dissenting view that the United Nations has adapted to the challenges posed by globalization, see Ruggie 2003.

[5] On the challenges of globalization see, e.g., Held et al. 1999; Keohane and Nye 2000; and Mittleman, 2000.

strong micro and macro reactions against the internationalization of production ... Some individuals feel their livelihood is threatened by freer trade and a wider distribution of production facilities ... [and] it is doubtful ... that the localizing tendencies inherent in economic nationalism are likely to offset the globalizing tendencies associated with free-trade orientations. (Rosenau 1997, p. 71)

Ideas about what should replace current systems of multilateral governance differ. Rosenau, for example, believes in the emergence of what he and others refer to as a "Third System" of governance that is marked by the emergence of new, "imagined communities" and/or social movements that "tend to improvise from issue to issue, sometimes circumventing national governments and sometimes working with them, but at all time eschewing efforts to develop and intrude formal structures into their deliberations and activities" (Rosenau 1997, p. 68). Taking a somewhat different approach, Inge Kaul (Kaul et al. 2003) argues that new multilateral structures, which can be created out of the old, can help with the provision of "global public goods," especially if the public is more fully engaged in global public policy making within existing international institutional frameworks. In a global context, the growth and expansion of international civil society has increasingly blurred the line between public and private activities, because many "diverse actors define the public and contribute to the provision of public goods." According to Kaul, "publicness" is a social construct, and, in an increasingly globalized world, a wide range of non-state actors are involved in both populating the domain and providing global public goods. Kaul and her co-authors make a convincing case for inclusive, coordinated public stewardship and management of such problems as climate change, security, and poverty. They point to the need to legitimize the role of non-state actors in international institutions, to open up governance of the International Monetary Fund, to enhance parity and strengthen the negotiating capacity of developing countries in various forums including the World Trade Organization, and to promote global equity along with efficiency in international economics.

The challenge of integrating different stakeholders in new, multilateral instruments of cooperation is also taken up in Jean François Rischard's (2002) discussion of new "problem-solving" approaches to address major global threats to planetary survival. Rischard's metaphor – "no pilot in the cockpit" – conveys the powerful image of a global population traveling uncontrolled at high speed toward imminent disaster. Rischard argues that although we have international institutions supposedly competent to fly this plane, they are demonstrably not up to the task. And, in fact, international treaties and conventions commonly work too slowly to deal with the most burning global issues. Intergovernmental conferences lack proper follow-up mechanisms. The current G8 and G20 systems have serious limitations of exclusivity, unrepresentativeness, and leadership far too removed from the people whose interests they purport to serve. In sum, argues Rischard, the current global multilateral machinery cannot manage the international global issues that confront us all.

Given that there is little chance of establishing a world government in the next twenty years, Rischard recommends that we look to alternative forms and procedures of multilateral, global governance. His key proposal focuses on the successes and promise of a growing phenomenon in global government – the spreading web of global issues networks (GINs) that are forging vigorous and innovative new partnerships among public, private, and civil society actors. GINs are not intended to legislate or regulate, but to pressure national governments – and simultaneously enhance their capacity – to enact conforming legislation and take practical action on global problems such as the management of the biosphere, population growth, and global warming. By rating government performance, and by "naming and shaming" those authorities that are failing to conform to new global standards, they can help persuade them into line by exploiting political rewards and punishments already in place. Rischard emphasizes that new technologies also provide new forms of communication and information exchange. Global electronic town hall meetings can be run through the Internet. Independent panels of experts can also be assembled to bring concrete scientific knowledge to bear on policy solutions to global problems. Nor is this airy theory. As Rischard argues, even in fields as controversial as large-scale dams and forestry conservation, issue-based networks are already having some positive effect.

There is an unquestioned and usually unspoken assumption in these discussions of "bottom-up" multilateralism: if international institutions are made more inclusive by opening them up to new political participation, they will not only enjoy more political legitimacy, but they will also become more effective in treating global problems. This is not an assumption that should be taken on faith, especially if we remind ourselves of Kenneth Arrow's (1951) impossibility theorem. The desirable properties of a social choice function no doubt include universality and citizen sovereignty, non-dictatorship, and the positive accommodation of social and individual values. But Arrow shows with rigorous analysis how hard it is – even impossible – to organize social choice in a way that satisfies all these criteria simultaneously. There are not only practical difficulties associated with concepts of social empowerment, the expansion of global civil society, and the democratization of international institutions. There are theoretical limitations as well.[6]

Instrumental (utilitarian) multilateralism

Another kind of multilalteralism is what might be called "instrumental" or "ultilitarian" multilateralism. According to this conception, multilateralism is a valuable, cost-cutting management tool in global affairs, especially for great powers that have global responsibilities but finite resources to discharge them. If the costs of a given course of action for a great power are deemed to be too high – or the costs are such that the public is unwilling to support a particular course of action – then the appropriate (and indeed rational) response is to look for allies who can share costs, as we have seen in recent (and somewhat unsuccessful) US efforts to secure greater troop contributions from NATO allies for combat mission roles in Afghanistan and elsewhere around the globe.

Such debates about the instrumental (as opposed to intrinsic) value of multilateral institutions are not new. During the Cold War there was a recurring debate within NATO about the need for "burden-sharing." Throughout the 1980s, patience ran thin in some quarters of the United States that the Europeans were not living up to their commitments under the Long-Term Defense Plan (1978) to increase defense spending. Many Americans wondered openly why they should continue to support the Alliance and shoulder the burden of Europe's defense if Europeans themselves did not make a more concerted effort to look after their own interests. And there were recurring threats in the US Congress to reduce the US troop presence in Europe unless the allies boosted their levels of defense spending (Hampson and Flanagan 1986).[7]

In post-Cold War discussions about international security, multilateralism has sometimes been presented as a kind of burden-sharing "solution" to the problems of "imperial overstretch," especially in addressing the problems of "failed states" and the succession of humanitarian crises that have plagued some regions of the globe, such as the African subcontinent. Barry Blechman (1996) for example, argues that multilateralism is an appropriate response to a US public that has grown increasingly wary of paying the costs of peacekeeping (and the attendant costs of peace building and state building that follow military

---

[6] There are also important issues of accountability concerning NGOs and the groups they represent; see Willetts 2000; Wapner 2002; Spar and Dail 2002; and Spiro 2002.

[7] Many of the same concerns within NATO resurfaced during the Balkans wars; see Clément 2003.

intervention). Burden sharing is easier if governments share similar goals and are prepared to use collective means of intervention. Intervention also has political costs (along with human and financial costs). Multilateral approaches likewise permit these political costs to be shared. The United Nations, in particular, provides much-needed legitimacy at the domestic level when the costs of intervention are deemed to be high. When interventions run awry (or the costs escalate out of control), states can also shift the locus of responsibility for failure onto multilateral institutions. Multilateral institutions are not simply useful for "buck-passing"; they are also potentially useful instruments of "blame avoidance" when things go wrong.

Some of the sternest critics of US foreign policy in recent years have adopted "instrumentalist" arguments in their defense of mulilateralism. David Malone and Yuen Foong Khong (2003, p. ix), for example, argue that "US foreign policy must be informed by a deeper appreciation of the way the United States is perceived abroad" but also because "unilateralism undercuts US national interests." They and their co-authors also underscore the fact that "the US foreign policy agenda is being transformed by a wide range of challenges that cannot be addressed successfully by any single state, no matter how powerful" (Clément 2003; also Patrick and Foreman 2002) (i.e., the United States must look to other ways to share its "imperial" burdens).

What is interesting is that similar arguments about "burden sharing" are coming from some unexpected quarters. Some traditional, self-styled American "realist" scholars now argue that the United States must recognize that many countries in the world are undercutting and/or opposing US interests with their superior bargaining and negotiating tactics. To address these challenges, the United States must do a better job of recognizing and defining its national interests and building a system of strategic, regional alliances and multilateral security arrangements that will allow the United States to reduce its overseas military presence and "resume its traditional role as an 'offshore balance'" (Walt 2005, p. 118). Public opinion polls also consistently show that Americans have lost their appetite for using force to advance US interests abroad and are increasingly enthusiastic about "multilateralism," because they believe that international institutions can facilitate burden-sharing (Dresner 2008; Lyons 2007).

There are a number of practical (and conceptual) problems with "instrumental multilateralism." Marriages of convenience, by definition, will not withstand the test of time unless they are informed by deeper and more lasting commitments based on shared values as well as clearly articulated norms, rules, and principles of cooperative behavior and joint action as argued by students of "formal multilateralism." Champions of "burden sharing" must also recognize that those who are being courted to share costs will usually insist on some kind of reciprocity – that is, calls for burden sharing usually lead to demands for decision sharing. And demands for reciprocity (as well as resources) will also come from those allies of the United States that are being courted and groomed to help the United States disengage from some of its overseas military commitments.

Amour propre *multilateralism*

Much of the contemporary political rhetoric about the meaning, purpose, and utility of "multilateralism" has a highly charged, partisan flavor. On both sides of the Atlantic there is more than just a tinge of national (or Euro-centric) hubris in the way the term is used and applied. What is striking about these debates is the degree to which different national (or collective) understandings about "multilateralism" are infused by national (and collective) identities and historical experience (Kagan 2003). Europeans and Americans all have their special view of what "multilateralism" means in normative, institutional, and even practical terms. And there is little evidence that either side of the Atlantic is prepared to concede much ground to differing views. Hence we use the term *amour propre* multilateralism to describe these different – and somewhat uncompromising – attitudes.

The European concept of "multilateralism" is born out of Europe's experience with building the European Union – but it is also a conception that is wedded to a deeply held set of beliefs about the primacy of the rule of law and human rights in international affairs. As Jeremy Rifkin (2004) argues, Europeans have developed their own cosmopolitan solution to the problems of peaceful cooperation among a group of countries that have traditionally had highly antagonistic relations and which remain culturally and economically diverse. Whereas Americans have responded to the challenges of globalization by reasserting their own "exceptionalism," Europeans have adopted a collective approach that is premised on the exercise of "soft power" and consensus-based decision making within a highly institutionalized and rule-bound setting. It is also perhaps no accident, given their history, that Europeans have championed their own, distinctive model of international cooperation. As Ralph Dahrendorf and Timothy Garton Ash (2003) observe, Europeans see themselves as the champions of a new, Kantian-like confederation of democratic states:

We are Kantian. Like Kant, we seek ultimately a cosmopolitan society of citizens, universally administering law, ever imperfect and rife with conflict but, above all, open. A renewed Europe can contribute considerably toward this, as America has done for more than two hundred years and always in new ways.

With the relative decline of the West and the rise of new centers of power and influence in Asia, such as China, India, and perhaps even Russia, some argue that Europe should actively eschew a return to the balance-of-power diplomacy of the nineteenth century, which could see a division of the world between Western (democratic) powers and "an axis of autocracies" centered on China and/or Russia. Rather, Europe should become a champion of a new multilateral/multi-polar world order that is based on "a stronger international society, well-functioning international institutions and a rule-based international order." This is because among "the major power and potential powers, only the European Union starts from the assumption that multilateralism is desirable. Faith in the rule of international law, and in the potential of international institutions, runs deep in the DNA of Europe's political elite" (Grant 2007).

Other scholars and social activists would like to see the European Union improve its effectiveness as a global actor by adopting the concept of human security as an enduring and dynamic organizing frame for security action, a frame which European foreign-policy texts and practices currently lack (Kaldor, Martin, and Selchow 2007). Under such a new frame of reference, respect for human rights, the rule of law, well-functioning systems of justice, and "effective multilateralism" – this last defined as a "commitment to work with international institutions, and through the procedures of international institutions" as well as a "commitment to creating common rules and norms, solving problems through rules and cooperation, and enforcing the rule" – would become the new cornerstones of Europe's common foreign and security policy (p. 285).

American "exceptionalism," coupled with a deep-rooted historical ambivalence towards international institutions, has meant that the United States is generally the reluctant bride in formal, multilateral undertakings (McCrisken 2004; Washbum 2001; Patrick and Forman 2002). However, it would be a mistake to characterize the United States, even under the second presidency of George W. Bush, as unrepentantly "unilateralist" – the doctrine of unilateralism states "that nations should conduct their foreign affairs individualistically without the advice or involvement of other nations" (FreeDictionary.com). The second Bush administration made some effort to reach out to other nations following a series of blunders during the first administration. Fareed Zakaria (2004), for example, saw multilateralist leanings in the Bush administration's grudging acceptance of World Trade Organization authority, even when that body's rulings have run directly against US interests, as in the case of farm subsidies like cotton. And he and others note that Bush has negotiated new, free multilateral and bilateral free-trade agreements with the countries of the Central America region, the Dominican Republic, and Australia (Denton and Solomon 2004).

Multilateralist impulses were also evident in the administration's foreign aid record – for example, the Millennium Challenge Account (MCA), which boosted development aid by 50 percent, and the President's Emergency Plan for AIDS relief. In its policies toward North Korea, the administration also adopted a shared, multilateral approach through the Six-Party Talks, directed at a nuclear-free Korean peninsula, and the Proliferation Security Initiative, which included more than sixty countries in a variety of interdiction and counter-proliferation efforts. The United States also gave its support to EU efforts to curb the growing nuclear danger from Iran and is unambiguously working through the International Atomic Energy Agency, a rather traditional multilateralist venue, to deal with this problem. Even more remarkable is US insistence on referring Iran to the UN Security Council in spite of the United States' traumatic experience in attempting (and failing) to get Council approval for its military intervention in Iraq.[8]

Brendan Taylor (2008), an Australian scholar, suggests that in its overall approach towards the Asia–Pacific region, the Bush administration was "a more active and stimulatory advocate of multilateral approaches than is common acknowledged," but that its "enthusiasm for multilateral approaches ... encountered a high degree of regional reticence," especially with respect to US membership in the east Asia summit process.

Of course, for some, the real test of a country's multilateralist commitments (and credentials) is whether it is prepared to relinquish some of its sovereign authority to the United Nations, or any other intergovernmental body, especially when resorting to the use of force. Accordingly, in the eyes of some (Heinbecker 2004), the US intervention in Iraq, which failed to secure the support of several key permanent members of the Security Council, has altogether discredited any claims the United States might have of "multilateralist" leanings or respectability. These critics also saw the US refusal to engage itself in the new, multilateral institutions of human security, such as the International Criminal Court, the Anti-personnel Landmines Convention, and so on as further evidence of its unilateralist, "je-ne-regrette-rien" approach to foreign policy (*The Economist* 2004).

---

[8] At Heiligendamm (G8 Summit 2007), some observers attributed the marked improvement in transatlantic relations to the "return" of the United States to multilateralism as well as greater unity of Europeans. Kaiser 2007.

Another way of looking at this debate is to regard the United States as offering a different vision of multilateral cooperation, one that is *not* based on striking a formal consensus, where each state has the right of veto (as in the European model), but rather where cooperation emerges out of an informal process of consultation and where final, decision-making authority continues to reside with national authorities (which is historically how the United States has approached most cooperative ventures). For the Bush administration it would seem that professed intentions – or lip service to multilateralism – are important too. As Vice-President Richard Cheney once asserted, the United States "wants to work multilaterally. But being multilateralist does not mean 'submitting to the objections of a few.' And being multi-lateralist does not preclude a policy of staying 'on the offense'" (quoted in Shales 2004).

An Obama foreign policy will almost certainly be pragmatically inter-nationalist and multilateralist – resembling that of President Clinton and President Bush at the end of his second term. Some sense of Democratic thinking can be gleaned from the report coauthored by James Steinberg, Anne-Marie Slaughter, Ivo Daalder, Kurt Campbell and others, (Steinberg et al. 2008), which emphasizes that the United States should work through international institutions and alliances and support a con-ception of "common security" that gives priority to the problems of failed and failing states and using force for humanitarian as well as counter-terrorist objectives.

Conclusion

This chapter's efforts to "deconstruct" the different meanings and uses of multilateralism in international relations point to a number of key con-clusions. First, we should recognize that there is continued debate in scholarly and policy circles about the real meaning of "multilateralism." For some, multilateralism is defined by the existence of indiscriminate rules and principles of behavior in international relations which are informed by the expectation of reciprocity – that is, that all parties will benefit in roughly equal measure from the institutional arrangements in question. To others, however, the concept is tied to the workings and performance of formal, international institutions as well as other criteria about the requirements for effective international cooperation (such as principles of equity, empowerment, and fair representation). And to others still, the concept refers to a wide variety of different historical and regional approaches to international cooperation in which formal institu-tions may or may not be present.

A second conclusion is that there is growing disenchantment in many quarters regarding the legitimacy of formal, multilateral institutions – a disenchantment that is not limited to Washington's (or Brussels') frustrations with the United Nations. The "legitimacy" and "accountability" deficits in multilateral institutions play out at two levels. At one level, many would like to see a better representation from the South in the major, decision-making organs of the United Nations and the Bretton Woods system of institutions. These calls have mounted in response to the 2008–09 international financial and credit crisis. At another level, many would like to see international institutions become more accountable to the public by engaging citizens to a much greater degree in their decision-making processes than they do now. Some would also like to see the creation of new institutions of global governance that will lead to radically new kinds of partnership between civil society, business, and government actors, as well as a commitment by the members of these institutions to advancing and promoting new concepts of human security.

Finally, when it comes to matters of state practice and assessing how major actors in the international system view multilateralism as a tool and instrument of foreign policy, we should acknowledge that there is a rather narcissistic quality to these debates at the national political level. In recent years, Europeans and Americans have taken to criticizing each other's respective "multilateralist" intentions and credentials. It is time that both took a deep breath and recognized that there is more than one way to secure international cooperation.

5   Negotiated cooperation and its alternatives

Saadia Touval

This chapter explores what happens to multilateralism when the idea is implemented. Implementation requires negotiation, because participants in a multilateral process need to agree about their joint project. Yet, despite this intimate linkage, it appears that studies of multilateralism have not given much attention to its negotiation component. Interest has been directed mainly at structures – institutions, regimes, norms, and rules – and much less at the processes of negotiation that are an integral part of multilateralism.

I use the term "multilateralism" to refer to a diplomatic strategy employed by states in order to coordinate policy among three or more actors, more succinctly termed in the introduction "a philosophy of multilateral cooperation." It stands in contrast with "unilateralism" – a strategy of aiming to advance a state's goals alone, without coordinating with other states – and also with "bilateralism" – a strategy of coordinating with single partners, through separate arrangements with each of them. This definition is broader than Ruggie's, which defines multilateralism an "an institutional form that coordinates relations among three or more states on the basis of generalized principles of conduct" (Ruggie 1993b, p. 11). The term, as used here, encompasses the meaning given by Ruggie, but goes beyond it by including multilateral initiatives that take place outside institutions.

As used here, the term "multilateral" comprises universal frameworks like the United Nations or the World Trade Organization, as well as regional ones such as the European Union or the Organization of American States. It also involves alliances consisting of more than three members, such as NATO. Smaller groupings of states are also included, such as the five permanent members of the Security Council, the various G-groups (G7, G8, G20, G77) and ad hoc groups through which states conduct their diplomacy: "contact groups" (e.g., on southern Africa or the former Yugoslavia), the Middle East "Quartet", as well as the six-nation negotiating forum on North Korea's nuclear program. The diversity of the frameworks is significant, and produces important consequences. But here we shall consider mainly some common characteristics of multilateralism. This chapter addresses mainly the process by which multilateralism is practiced. That process is negotiation.

The exploration will begin with an examination of the main arguments presented by advocates of multilateralism. The benefits attributed to multilateralism in international relations fall into two principal categories: one is functional – the presumed effectiveness and efficiency of multilateral strategies – and the other is moral–political. Next is a description of negotiation processes through which multilateralism is implemented. I shall point to typical problems encountered in such negotiations and types of outcome that multilateral negotiations often produce. As I shall show, some of the presumed benefits of multilateralism tend to undergo erosion when they are implemented through negotiation. Multilateral strategies are not particularly efficient or effective. On the other hand, certain moral–political benefits ascribed to multilateralism tend to be advanced through multilateral negotiation.

Why multilateral cooperation?

States protect and pursue their goals by all three approaches: unilaterally, bilaterally, and multilaterally. Which approach to choose is often debated in many countries. Debates revolve both about principles and about the suitability of an approach to the problem at hand. Opposing positions in the debates between unilateralism and multilateral cooperation can be summarized in two maxims: "Unilateral when we can, multilateral when we must," as opposed to "Multilateral when we can, unilateral when we must." (The phrase is taken from Patrick 2002, p. 13.) The maxims imply that both sides in the debate acknowledge that, in practice, states' policies are a mixture of the two. Still, these maxims express opposing principles of capability and necessity, or interior assertion and exterior imposition, that, according to their proponents, ought to guide state policies. The debate is about preferences.

Two key arguments are made on behalf of cooperation: the functional argument and the moral–political argument. The functional argument has two components – efficiency and effectiveness, related to "cooperation for us." The first (probably of greater interest to theorists than practitioners) refers to transaction costs. Some scholars believe that institutions and regimes (which by their very nature are multilateral) help to reduce the costs of coordinating policies. According to Keohane (1984, p. 90), international regimes make it "cheaper for governments to get together to negotiate agreements" and "allow governments to take advantage of potential economies of scale." This view, however, is not universally accepted. Caporaso

(1993, pp. 61–62) has claimed that "the costs of transacting almost certainly increase with an increase in actors," although the two are arguing diachronically versus synchronically. The differences depend in part on the definition and methods of estimation of transaction costs. Nevertheless, it seems that the view that multilateralism reduces transaction costs is held by many proponents of multilateralism because they emphasize the institutionalized aspect of multilateral regimes, which saves the costs of ad hoc reinvention of the wheels of cooperation each time (Ikenberry 2001, p. 13; Lipson 2004).

Underlying the justification of multilateralism by its presumed effectiveness is the phenomenon of interdependence: in view of the high degree of interdependence among states, their policies need to be coordinated. In the absence of coordination, states' policies may contradict each other, and their outcome will be suboptimal. Therefore effective policy responses to many international issues require coordination among states affected by the issue. Interdependence is generally recognized as a fact, and the desirability of coordination is not disputed.

A number of political–moral justifications for multilateralism have been proposed. The emphasis placed on particular arguments varies, depending on the advocate's perspective – a policy maker in a small or weak state or in a major power, or an academic analyst. Who advocates multilateralism and in what context should not concern us here, because our purpose is to assess what happens to multilateralism when it is being put into practice through negotiation. But it is interesting to note that the political–moral justifications offered for multilateralism tend to share the view that multilateralism contributes to international stability and reduces the risk of war, harking back to the notion of reciprocity. Many policies pursued by states affect other states – not only foreign and security policies, but also economic, social, environmental, and other matters. Therefore policies ought to be coordinated with others who may feel affected. This is a social obligation that states owe to other members of international society, advisable for prudential and practical reasons: states that feel adversely affected by another state's policies are likely to take steps to counter those policies or to diminish their effects. It is, therefore, wise to coordinate with those who may be affected by addressing issues through multilateral forums and multilateral action. Related to this is the widespread assumption that policies are legitimized by the consent of others; the broader the consensus, the more legitimate the policy.

Another frequently voiced argument for multilateralism is that it helps constrain actions of those who may disregard the interests of others who are affected by such actions. A general rule derived from this is that it is in the interest of every state to bind itself by accepting the constraints of multilateralism, because by doing so it helps other states to do so as well and to accept limits on their freedom of action. This argument pays back reciprocity on the initial cooperator, enmeshing it in a mutually beneficial Future Shadow.

Yet most of the attention is directed at great powers: multilateralism helps to constrain powerful states. It is a balance of power mechanism. It is not military power against which states balance, but rather egoistic and inconsiderate policies of those who have the capacity to act alone on a wide array of political, economic, social, environmental, and other issues. It is the great powers that are most able to act unilaterally, and are often inclined to utilize their capability, free of the constraints of involving others. Great-power actions are likely to have a greater impact on others than unilateral actions by small and weak states. Were Albania to manipulate the value of its currency, it would have a lesser impact on the international economy than manipulation of the value of the Japanese or Chinese currencies. Multilateralism provides the weaker states with a voice, with an opportunity to influence the policies of others that affect their interests. It provides the weak with a method for counterbalancing that is non-offensive. It is formulated as a constructive policy aimed at facilitating cooperation and improving everyone's welfare, rather than as the "balancing against" of traditional balance-of-power politics.

A different justification for multilateralism makes the opposite argument, namely that it is a strategy that can work to advance the interests of the powerful hegemon. This can be labeled as a "Realist" argument, though probably unintentionally so. It starts from the premise that a hegemonic state would not be inclined to accept the constraints of multilateralism. Yet this theoretical premise appears to be contradicted by the historical example of the US predilection for multilateralism after World War II. According to this explanation, the United States promoted the establishment of multilateral institutions after the war in order to "lock in" norms, rules, and practices that would serve US interests if and when it loses its primacy (Ruggie 1993b; Ikenberry 2001; Martin 2004).

How negotiate?

Turning the purposes of multilateralism into reality requires international multilateral negotiation. By multilateral negotiation is meant a discussion between three or more states aimed at arriving at a joint decision (Zartman 1994b). Decision making by intergovernmental negotiation is a constant activity within international institutions. Even when decisions are made by voting, proponents of decisions need to persuade other members to vote for the proposal – and that usually requires negotiation. There is no escape from negotiation.

This section will describe the typical features of multilateral negotiation (Touval 1989; Zartman 1994a; Hampson 1995). The description will pay special attention to the structure and the process, to decision rules, and to the outcomes of multilateral negotiation. The portrayal of these typical features will subsequently help us in assessing how well the purposes of multilateralism survive the processes of getting them implemented. In doing so, it is important to point out that multilateral negotiations often involve bilateral negotiation as well as unilateral moves. Bilateral negotiations are often an essential building block toward multilateral agreements. And, unilateral moves come into play both in attempts to exercise leadership, and as bargaining tactics (Underdal 1994).

Structure and process of multilateral negotiation

By definition a multilateral negotiation consists of three or more parties. Obviously, the more parties participate, the more issues come up for discussion. When, as in some UN- or WTO-sponsored negotiations, almost all members of the international community participate, matters tend to become complicated. Most participants have interests that need to be accommodated. The larger the number of participants, the greater the likelihood of conflicting interests. Small wonder, then, that reshaping the participants' positions and rendering them compatible is a difficult and time-consuming process. Although there are examples of speedy multilateral negotiations, the typical negotiation is a protracted affair. Among the numerous examples one can list the UN Law of the Seas Treaty, which took fifteen years to negotiate; the Uruguay Round of trade negotiations, which took eight years; the negotiations among NATO allies about the US proposal for a "flexible response" strategy in the event of war with the Soviet Union lasted five years, from 1962 to 1967; the negotiations to establish a new regime to replace CoCom (Coordinating Committee on Multilateral Export Controls) for regulating export of technologies that can be used in the manufacture of weapons of mass destruction (WMD) were launched in 1993 and expected to take a few months, but actually lasted more than two years; the urgent efforts of the UN Security Council to reduce tensions in the aftermath of the 1967 Arab–Israeli war took four months to produce the ambiguous text of Resolution 242.

Multilateral negotiations are characterized by coalitions. States band together in the expectation that a bloc of like-minded states has a greater chance of having their position accepted, than by pursuing their goals individually. But establishing a coalition may require a difficult negotiation.

Once established, a coalition tends to hold to its position inflexibly because of the high costs that the formation of the coalition entailed. Expanding the membership of a coalition, by winning over individual states or groups of states, would entail a difficult renegotiation of the coalition's initial joint platform. Since coalitions are reluctant to renegotiate their initial agreements, their existence tends to introduce a certain rigidity into the negotiation process, making the attainment of a consensus encompassing all participants more difficult.

The negotiation process is strongly affected by these structural features. The sheer quantity of information and communication, increasing with the number of participants, is difficult to manage. Each participant is likely to experience difficulty orchestrating the different signals to be sent to different audiences, and interpreting the statements and signals made by other participants. A further difficulty stems from trading concessions in a multilateral forum. In bilateral negotiation, the norm of reciprocity facilitates the exchange of concessions. But the reciprocal exchange of concessions often loses its meaning in multilateral negotiation because a concession offered to one participant may have a differential impact on others, and may even be considered by some as detrimental to their interests. This may serve as a basis for a claim for compensation. Thus devising a package containing concessions and compensations that satisfies all participants is a complicated and time-consuming process.

Decision rules

The multilateral negotiation process ends when a draft is proposed to the assembly for acceptance. While the acceptance takes the form of a vote by some decision rule, it is in the interest of those in favor to negotiate a draft that will achieve the necessary votes. Thus negotiation anticipates acceptance rather than simply producing it as if there were no ratifying vote in usual negotiations, where unanimity is the characteristic rule. Three types of decision rule are typically practiced in multilateral negotiations. They are all premised on the principle that states have the sovereign right to accept or reject a decision. One is unanimity, according to which agreements require the positive affirmation of acceptance by all participants in the negotiation. Unless all participating states agree, the negotiation ends without any conclusion. In other words, each participating state has the right to veto a decision.

A more flexible rule is consensus. The term has come to mean that proposals are considered to have been agreed upon if none of the participants formally objects. This rule, too, allows each participating state to exercise the right of veto. But practice has shown that states are reluctant to veto outcomes that enjoy wide support. This can be explained by the differentiation of interests and motives among the participants. Parties in multilateral negotiation do not necessarily hold strong views about the subjects under discussion. Some may participate for reasons of status, or mere membership in the case of international organizations, rather than a substantive interest in the issue on the agenda. They wish neither to affirm support, nor to lodge an objection. But they are ready to go along with a conclusion endorsed by an overwhelming majority of participants. Once the person chairing the negotiation ascertains that none of the participants intends formally to oppose a proposal, the chair announces that agreement has been reached by consensus.

A third alternative is to allow for decisions by majority vote. This requires a preliminary acceptance of states to forego the exercise of their sovereign right to veto decisions and, instead, to abide by decisions endorsed by the majority of participants. Yet negotiation is an integral part of decision making even when decisions are made by voting. Negotiations are required to form a coalition of states. Members of a coalition need to agree on a common platform, and they need to persuade a sufficient number of states to vote on a proposal to assure its adoption.

Outcomes

All three decision rules tend to produce ambiguous agreements. Ambiguity in the wording of decisions is usually necessary in order to accommodate a wide variety of interests and opinions. Accommodating parties with different interests and priorities usually requires wording that is not objectionable to anyone, and allows the parties some latitude in interpreting the meaning of the agreements they have consented to in accordance with their interests. If the wording fails to reassure all participants, the practice of allowing parties to place their reservations and interpretations on the record helps in winning the passage of many multilateral agreements. Under this practice parties sometimes announce that their assent does not apply to certain clauses, or that their interpretation of certain provisions differs from that of other participants. The end result is ambiguity and equivocation.

The disadvantages of ambiguity are obvious. It produces an illusion of accord when little agreement actually exists. Such pretense can sometimes be justified by the argument that an ambiguous agreement is preferable to none, that it is "a step in the right direction," and by the expectation that the outcome may later be improved in a future negotiation. It therefore provides a cooperative base for further cooperation.

How evaluate?

Does multilateral cooperation through negotiation produce outcomes that are effective and efficient and advance the political–moral vision of multilateralism? The typical process and outcome of multilateral negotiation described above suggests a mixed result. Functionally, in terms of efficiency, negotiation falls short of the promises advanced in the justifications for multilateralism. The functional deficiencies are indicated by several elements. Multilateral negotiations usually exact high transaction costs. Effective participation in a complex negotiation involving many parties and many issues in dynamic interaction requires large staffs with an array of qualifications. The length of the process, sometimes extending over several years, adds to the cost. Thus, from a purely functional perspective of efficiency, multilateralism is a costly strategy, although compared with bilateral arrangements it may be cost-saving. Bilateral agreements would subsequently need to be coordinated to be multilaterally harmonious. The US-sponsored bilateral and plurilateral free trade agreements, competing with the laggard progress on a multilateral trade agreement such as the Doha Round, are an apposite example.

As for effectiveness, and the political and moral promises of multilateral cooperation, multilateral negotiations may produce mixed results. The characteristic ambiguity of the agreements produced means that only part of the functional purposes of negotiations are achieved, and that agreements often do not effectively address the issues that prompted the negotiation. A unilateral or a bilateral strategy of narrower cooperation might do better, exacting lower transaction costs and producing outcomes that are less ambiguous and better focused on solving substantive issues. To be sure, many issues cannot be solved unilaterally or bilaterally, and with respect to such cases the arguments of inefficiency and ineffectiveness are irrelevant; the only way to cooperate is multilaterally, even if the results fall short of what is needed.

As for the moral and political purposes of multilateralism, the verdict is mixed. These purposes are all related to the overall goal of reducing international tensions and improving the prospects for peace. Policies emanating from multilateral negotiations are usually perceived to be legitimate, in contrast to unilateral and bilateral policies whose legitimacy is sometimes challenged. Such challenges are common with respect to security matters, such as deployment of troops and use of force. Challenges to the legitimacy of unilateral and bilateral policies also occur regarding other issues that impact on other states, such as utilization of resources (e.g. rivers, maritime fishing). Policies on such issues are perceived to be more legitimate if emanating from a multilateral forum.

Policies that carry a stamp of legitimacy tend to arouse less opposition, and are less likely to generate international tensions.

The ambiguity of multilateral agreements can have mixed and contradictory consequences. On the one hand, they muffle conflicts and reduce tensions. On the other hand, ambiguity may give rise to disputes over the interpretation of documents. These can turn into bitter accusations of violation of promises, cheating, and bad faith, and increase interstate tensions. Furthermore, although the compromises and ambiguities that characterize multilateral cooperation agreements detract from their effectiveness in addressing or resolving issues, their legitimacy reduces the motivation of potential opponents to act against such agreements.

Multilateralism and the process of pursuing it through negotiation can also spread and expand tensions and conflicts. Multilateralism can serve as a transmission belt: conflicts limited to two states (or a small number of states) may spread and impact other members, as participants in multilateral negotiations are pressed to take a stand and support one side or another in a dispute, as is developed in Zartman's chapter below. This has happened numerous times at the United Nations during the Cold War, and continues to occur when the Security Council is called upon to act on contentious issues. This is so not only because of the norm of indivisibility that characterizes multilateral cooperation (Ruggie 1993b), but mainly because of linkages among issues that characterize multilateral negotiation (Hampson 1995).

The claim that multilateral cooperation serves to constrain the more powerful states seems to be only partially valid. Cooperation here is a two-way street. As has been pointed out in Doran's chapter, great powers sometimes resort to multilateralism, establishing institutions that lock in rules and norms that are advantageous to them. But multilateralism can also provide an opportunity for small and weak states to balance against the powerful. They can block agreement by refusing to give their assent where unanimity is required, or object to proposed terms of an agreement and thus prevent a decision by consensus from being achieved. Small and weak states can band together to form coalitions, thus augmenting their bargaining power vis à vis powerful great powers, and thus can influence the shape of an emerging agreement. But the ability of small and weak states to constrain the powerful and to influence the course of negotiations is limited. The resources at the disposal of powerful states can usually provide them with greater bargaining power. They can use "sticks and carrots" to break up opposing coalitions and win over states to join them in a coalition. Even when multilateral negotiations constrain somewhat the ability of great powers to impose their will, they still enable the powerful to achieve their objectives to a greater extent and more frequently than weak and small states. While it is true that the means used by great powers in negotiations provoke less antagonism than threats or use of force, it would be a misapprehension to view multilateral negotiation as producing harmony (Zartman and Rubin 2000; Steinberg 2002; Drahos 2003).

Obviously, powerful states that consider multilateral negotiations as inefficient or constraining have an additional option. They can "exit" – withdraw from a negotiation, or change their strategy to one of pursuing goals unilaterally or bilaterally. It is less difficult for the powerful to exit, and act outside the multilateral framework, than for the smaller and weaker members to do so. France's withdrawal from the integrated command of NATO in 1966 is an example. Having long objected to the Anglo-American domination of the alliance's decision making, and having seen its request for an equal voice rebuffed, de Gaulle withdrew from some of NATO's military structures. Another example was the diminished US readiness to pursue multilateral strategies in 2002–03, and its increased tendency to prefer unilateral action. This has been attributed to the growing gap in military power disparity between the United States and other great powers, as well as to a changed domestic political climate. While these changes are indisputable, an additional factor probably contributed to these trends. Since the end of the Cold War the United States has experienced greater difficulty in persuading its allies to accept its preferences. The allies seem to have been more willing to defer to the United States during the Cold War, when their dependence on the United States was greater, than after the Soviet Union collapsed. Furthermore, the European Union has become not only a more significant economic power, but also more of a political entity which formulates common policies on many international issues. Once it formulates a common policy, it is difficult for it to change its internal agreement in order to accommodate US views; indeed, it is a general characteristic of plurilateral as well as multilateral agreements that they are harder to achieve and harder to alter. Thus it appears that the United States' greater propensity to act unilaterally stemmed not only from its immense capabilities and domestic ideological changes, but also from the frustrations its policy makers experienced from their diminished ability to persuade allies to defer to US preferences.

As these illustrations demonstrate, multilateralism is not devoid of contentious politics.

Remedies and trade-offs

Awareness of the functional deficiencies of multilateral negotiation has led to the emergence of various techniques and devices to minimize this disadvantage. One is to strive to limit the scope of negotiations and narrow the agenda as much as possible. This is combined sometimes with an incremental approach to addressing issues – dividing the subject matter into segments and dealing with them sequentially. These negotiating techniques may help to simplify issues, thus helping to reduce the time and effort required for keeping track of the multiple issues and the linkages among them. Narrowing the focus of negotiations may also make it easier to devise more effective measures for addressing substantive issues and to avoid ambiguities that blunt the capabilities for effective action (Simmons and de Jonge Oudraat 2001; Hampson 1995).

Since the difficulty in negotiating efficient and effective agreements tends to grow with the number of participating states, another technique for improving outcomes is to narrow down and limit the negotiating forum (Simmons and de Jonge Oudraat 2001; Kahler 1993; Hampson 1995). There are a number of ways to accomplish this. One is the creation of an ad hoc forum for negotiating a specific issue, and the avoidance of negotiation within a wide-membership organization. By this approach one could include in the negotiation only those governments that are relevant to an issue. Relevance might refer to having a stake – that is, being affected by the issue. It might also suggest the desirability of including governments capable of contributing to common action, or of interfering with such action. Among the examples of this approach is the Contact Group, consisting of the United States, the United Kingdom, France, Germany, and Russia, created for dealing with the Yugoslav wars of the 1990s; the Middle East Quartet, consisting of the United States, Russia, the European Union and the United Nations, created for dealing with the Israeli–Palestinian conflict; and CoCom and its successor regime, the Wassenar Arrangement on Export Control for Conventional Arms and Dual-Use Technologies. A more restrictive ad hoc forum is the "coalition of the willing," comprising governments capable and willing to contribute to resolving the problems arising from the issue. This was used in regard to Kosovo, and approved after the fact by the UN Security Council, and to Iraq, and subject to divisive disagreement ever since. Thus ad hoc forums can also carry disadvantages. The process of selecting and forming a negotiating forum may be contentious and provoke resentment and opposition among some of those who are excluded. As a result, the legitimacy of the forum and the policies adopted by it may be called into question.

To avoid these risks, governments resort to existing wide-membership organizations, but engage in "forum shopping" to select the most congenial among them. Issues may be addressed by geographically defined organizations such as the Organization for Security and Cooperation in Europe (OSCE) or the OAS. If such organizations seem too large and unwieldy, smaller, more cohesive, regionally oriented organizations may be chosen. For example, the interested European states chose the European Union as the principal European forum for dealing with the problems of the former Yugoslavia, in preference over the OSCE, which was relegated to a secondary role (Touval 2002); the United States and its partners preferred NATO over the United Nations for punishing Serbia over its policy in Kosovo. Although advantageous in terms of efficiency and effectiveness, this approach, too, carries the risk of controversy and of provoking opposition among those who wish to influence the handling of the issue, but are excluded from the process. The technique further opens the possibility that the legitimacy of the policy agreed upon by the forum may be challenged.

Still another approach for reducing the inefficiencies of multilateral negotiations is by formally placing issues on the agenda of a universal membership organization, but holding actual negotiations within a small and select group of states. The most obvious example is the five permanent members of the UN Security Council. When they agree, the majority of the ten non-permanent members of the Council almost always go along. Other examples can be drawn from trade negotiations in the WTO (and its predecessor GATT). The practice there, sometimes called "minilateralism," is to negotiate issues within small "working groups" consisting of the principal stakeholders. On some issues negotiations are conducted in the even narrower forum of the United States, the European Union, and, occasionally, Japan. Once the small group reaches agreement, the rest of the membership is co-opted (Kahler in Ruggie 1993b; Steinberg 2002).

Through such techniques some of the deficiencies of the multilateral negotiation process can be alleviated: negotiations can be simplified, they can be better focused, the time they take can be shorter, and agreements reached may be less ambiguous. As for the moral–political purposes of multilateralism, some can be advanced, others cannot. Since the agreements reached require the formal approval of a broad multilateral framework, those states excluded from the actual negotiation maintain an ability to exert some influence and protect their interests. The aura of legitimacy can be acquired. However, the friction and tensions that such techniques generate may be as high as the antagonisms provoked by unilateral action.

Conclusions

As this chapter has shown, cooperation requires negotiation. The purposes of multilateral cooperation were described in this chapter as falling into two broad categories. The first justifies multilateralism on the grounds of efficiency and effectiveness, the second for its moral and political values: constraining the strong and requiring that state policies which affect other states be pursued by consensus. The chapter then examined certain typical features of multilateral negotiation, pointing out some of its deficiencies, which in turn give rise to the question of how well the purposes of multilateralism survive the process of putting this strategic principle into practice. An evaluation indicates that the purposes of efficiency and policy effectiveness are not well served. As for the moral and political purposes of multilateralism, the results appear mixed. The legitimacy of policies is usually enhanced, and the weaker members of the multilateral set gain influence by balancing against the strong. But powerful states still retain significant bargaining power and use it to shape or influence the terms of any agreement reached. They often also have the ability to abandon the cooperative approach and pursue their goals through bilateral or unilateral strategies. Furthermore, multilateralism does not eliminate conflict and antagonism among participants in multilateral processes.

More profoundly, a review of tactics aimed at improving the efficiency and effectiveness of multilateral negotiations suggests that an improvement of the efficiency or effectiveness of multilateral negotiation through such tactics often has the unintended consequence of undermining the moral–political purposes of multilateralism. The improvements in efficiency and effectiveness that can be achieved through a variety of tactics tend to generate friction and discord, increasing international tensions. On the other hand, opting for less efficient and effective negotiation processes allows states to form a consensus and thus reduce the political friction that the negotiation process might otherwise cause.

As happens with many ideals, attempts to realize them reveal their shortcomings. This is perhaps the reason that governments do not adhere strictly to either of the two principles of unilateralism or multilateralism, but follow a policy of "mix and match." Even when their rhetoric gives the impression of ideological commitment, the practice of governments seems to be mixed, sometimes pursuing goals unilaterally and sometimes multilaterally. For example, the German Federal Republic, whose foreign policy is often characterized as distinctly multilateralist, chose in 1990 to pursue its goal of reunification unilaterally, without associating its NATO allies and European partners, and concluded agreements with the Soviet Union and the German Democratic Republic to that effect on its own. Another example is offered by some of the policies of the Bush administration, whose rhetoric was unilateralist, but whose practice nevertheless was to form the Middle East Quartet for the purpose of cooperating with the European Union, Russia, and the United Nations in the pursuit of an Israeli–Palestinian settlement, or the six-power talks with Russia, China, and South Korea for the purpose of negotiating cooperation with North Korea, or the Group of Five working with the other four members of the UN Security Council and Germany on conditions of cooperation with Iran.

Perhaps theorists and analysts should not preoccupy themselves with justifying why multilateralism (or unilateralism) ought to guide foreign policy. The more relevant question is: *when* to pursue a multilateral strategy and *when* to be unilateral.

Part 2

Multiple strategies of cooperation

6   Synthesizing rationalist and constructivist perspectives on negotiated cooperation

P. Terrence Hopmann

The literature of international politics often focuses either on the *structure* of the relations between states and other actors within the international system or on the role of *agents* (or actors) within those systems, usually states, but sometimes substate collective actors or even individuals. A third and important form of analysis evaluates the interactions among actors that are both shaped by and shape the structure of relations between them. These patterns of interaction are generally treated in terms of two primary dimensions: hierarchy (that is, relative power positions among them, whether symmetrical or asymmetrical) and a conflict–cooperation continuum.

The two dimensions are largely independent of each other. For example, power relationships between the United States and Canada as compared with those between the United States and Iran are quite similar – both are highly asymmetrical. But the nature of the interactions is nonetheless quite different, as the former is characterized by a high degree of cooperation whereas the latter exhibits substantial conflict. While the first dimension tends to focus mostly on material relations among the actors, the latter operates much more in the ideational domain, that is, on the extent to which the actors share common interests and identities versus holding divergent interests and values. Thus, to return to the example above, the asymmetrical relationship between the United States and Canada is largely cooperative, due to the presence of common interests and, even more importantly, common identities as Western (and especially North American) democratic nations, whereas the United States and Iran have relatively few common interests and share even less in terms of common values and beliefs about the world; each one views their counterpart as an alien "other" set very far apart from itself on almost any ideational dimension. Thus understanding and analyzing the critical dimension ranging from intense conflict to close cooperation requires analyzing more than the power dimension generally emphasized by Realists; they also require an evaluation of ideas and values and the extent to which they converge or diverge between states or other international actors.

Realist theorists of international politics have tended to focus almost exclusively on the first of these dimensions, relative power, leaving it almost impossible for them to explain cooperative relationships among former enemies, such as the cooperation that has evolved between France and Germany since 1945 at the core of the process of European integration. Liberal theorists focus more on the presence of common interests, noting, for example, how common economic interests enabled the West European states to build a cooperative political order initially based on common material interests such as trade, environment, and monetary policy, expanding eventually into significant, if still incomplete, cooperation over "high politics" issues such as common security policy. Changes such as these represent not only a shift in the degree of cooperation, but a fundamental change in the nature of the relationship, to one in which cooperation has become fully embedded within the "deep structures" of the relationship itself. In order to explain the emergence of cooperation of this sort, constructivist theorists, with their emphasis on "ideas all (or almost all) the way down," have added an essential element to our understanding of international cooperation that cannot be fully appreciated in realist and even in liberal interpretations alone. The change in identity that transformed Germans and French as the "other" for one another into what Karl Deutsch (Deutsch et al. 1957) many years ago referred to as "we feeling" constitutes a fundamental change in international relations at a deeper psychological and social level that cannot be explained in terms of material interests alone.

Theorists who study international negotiation have a great deal to contribute to this debate because their subject matter focuses on how these patterns of interaction may be transformed along the conflict–cooperation continuum (Wendt 1999; Adler and Barnett 1998). Negotiation involves the interactions between two or more parties who generally search for cooperative solutions to a problem entailing a significant degree of conflicting preferences among them (Iklé 1964). In one sense, all negotiation is about seeking cooperation in mixed-motive situations where two or more interdependent parties share common and conflicting interests and thus strive to identify agreements that reflect or upgrade those common interests without necessarily overcoming all conflicts of interest. In these situations, however, cooperation involves more than finding agreements: it entails joint efforts to identify "efficient" agreements that maximize joint benefits, "fair" agreements that share benefits, and "durable" agreements that facilitate future cooperation (Hopmann 1996, pp. 28–30). Furthermore, negotiations may even make cooperation a constitutive element in mutual relationships that no longer depends on short-term, joint material interests as a basis for cooperation, as in some regimes and international communities where shared identities constitute newly created common preferences. Finally, negotiations may be helpful even in situations of pure cooperation, where unilateral behavior by all parties theoretically would converge on a single shared point of convergence; in reality, however, imperfect information may impede convergence around a single point, so negotiations serve the purpose of sharing information and thus facilitate coordination among parties with joint, but otherwise unrecognized common interests (Stein 1990, pp. 27–30). As Robert Keohane (1983, pp. 153–55; also Haas 1966, p. 96) has noted in his classic neo-liberal work on "regimes," bargaining and negotiation within international regimes "reduce[s] transaction costs" and "upgrade[s] common interests." But where such common interests do not appear to exist or are perceived only dimly by the parties to a dispute, the effort to transform the conflict and to create a deeper level of cooperation requires an approach to negotiations, and to international relations *writ large*, that goes beyond the contributions evident in realist and liberal theories alone.

In this brief chapter I propose to start by returning to the fundamental foundations of negotiation theory, based largely on some principles illustrated most succinctly by game theory, which presumes that the parties operate at least to a certain degree on the basis of making rational choices to maximize their perceived benefits and minimize their expected losses. However, I also propose to build bridges between this traditional understanding of bargaining and negotiation as a means to achieve international cooperation and more recent constructivist theories by showing how our understanding of negotiated cooperation is also consistent with at least some of the core theoretical precepts of contemporary constructivist theories of international politics. While recognizing the important ontological and epistemological differences between rationalist and constructivist paradigms, I do also believe that negotiation analysis may provide a useful device for illustrating how these two approaches may be bridged and thus provide a more complete understanding of the origins of conflict and cooperation in international relations in general.

As theories of negotiated cooperation have matured over roughly a half century of systematic research, certain foundational principles have continued to serve as basic axioms, even while the process is increasingly seen as complex and multidimensional. In particular, recent theoretical developments in international relations theory, especially the appearance of constructivist approaches, require us at least to demonstrate how some of these fundamental principles may also be subsumed in constructivist arguments. That is, we need to explain not only how interests are upgraded as in liberal theory, but we also need to examine how identities are formed and transformed through a process of negotiation that literally produces a continuous process of reframing the issues under negotiation and opens up new possibilities, not just because preferences change but because identities may change as well. Most importantly, cooperation is enhanced when "they" become "we," when the "other" is no longer viewed as an enemy but as a necessary partner in the solution of common problems that can only be resolved by joint, cooperative efforts. Social psychological concepts frequently employed in negotiation analysis, such as empathy, and techniques to enhance mutual perspective-taking such as role reversal exercises, provide important insights into how these fundamental changes may be facilitated in the process of negotiating cooperation.

Game theory as a metaphor for negotiations

I shall now turn to a brief restatement of what I assume to be the "basics," the fundamental foundations of all theories of negotiated cooperation, using formal game theory as a metaphor that will help us to understand the basic tensions that underlie the dynamics of all negotiation processes. Negotiation is fundamentally about cooperation in mixed-motive situations, where both common and conflicting interests and identities are present simultaneously. The game theorist does not claim to tell us where those interests and values came from, but only claims to explain how independently derived preferences (utilities) may create combinations of cooperative and conflictual outcomes between two or more interdependent parties. The parties are interdependent in the sense that all have direct influence over outcomes that affect them directly and significantly. That is, negotiation situations pertain when no single party has absolute control over outcomes, but rather where the consequences of their decisions interact with the decisions made by others to produce a joint outcome that may be mutually beneficial (i.e., it expands value for all parties), mutually harmful (i.e., it reduces value for all), or produce gains for one and losses for the other (i.e., exchange of fixed value among the parties) (Hopmann 1996, p. 28).

In some such interdependent situations, negotiations would not be necessary. If both parties have a dominant strategy that they will select no matter what the other chooses, then the outcome of the game may be determined analytically without any presumption that it will require negotiation to achieve a stable outcome – the outcome is predetermined by the intersection of those dominant strategies (with the partial exception of a few unique, but theoretically important games like the Prisoner's

Dilemma, where the dominant strategies produce a sub-optimal outcome, leaving another, "Pareto superior" outcome that would make both players better off). If only one player has a dominant strategy, and if the other player has perfect information about the preferences of the first, again no negotiation is necessary and the game may be "solved" analytically. However, in the many situations where neither player has a dominant strategy, it is usually necessary to negotiate some combination of "mixed strategies" that will produce mutually beneficial outcomes or at least avoid mutually harmful ones (Hopmann 1996, pp. 37–45). Furthermore, negotiation may be a useful tool for overcoming uncertainty, so that the two parties are at least "playing the same game" as they seek cooperative solutions (Stein 1990, pp. 55–86).

Largely for this reason, one of the first analysts to develop a systematic theory of international negotiations, Fred Charles Iklé (1964, pp. 3–4), defined negotiation as a process in which proposals are put forward for reaching an agreement "for the realization of common interests when conflicting interests are present." The mixed motive game – such as the classic "battle of the sexes" depicted in Figure 6.1 – provides a metaphor (not a formal model as used here) for understanding the tensions between cooperation and conflict in negotiation situations. The polygon determines the range of possible negotiated agreements, with its borders being determined by exogenous constraints that mark off the environmentally imposed limits of possibilities. The value of any given outcome within the polygon is intersubjectively determined by the agents responsible for the choices made by each actor: party A's value is expressed on the vertical dimension and B's on the horizontal axis. Movement in any direction within the negotiation space from a given status quo point may be defined as cooperative (0°–90°), conflictual (90°–180° and 270°–360°), or mutually harmful (180°–270°). However, any movement towards the northeast (the upper-right quadrant between 0° and 90°) except at 45° suffers from the problem of "relative gains" – both parties gain, but one gains "more" than the other. In some, but not necessarily all situations, this difference may matter; where power differentials are important in controlling outcomes, relative gains may matter a great deal, but in other situations they may matter less or even not at all (Rapoport 1966, ch. 8; Snidal 1993, pp. 170–208).

In these situations, cooperation may be defined as achieving a mutually beneficial outcome that all parties consider satisfactory within the context of their *own* values. It is often averred that such considerations of utility are biased in favor of some specific definition of "rationality," but this in fact is not the case. Preferences are determined by each party within its own value system, and from a formal point of view it does not matter to the

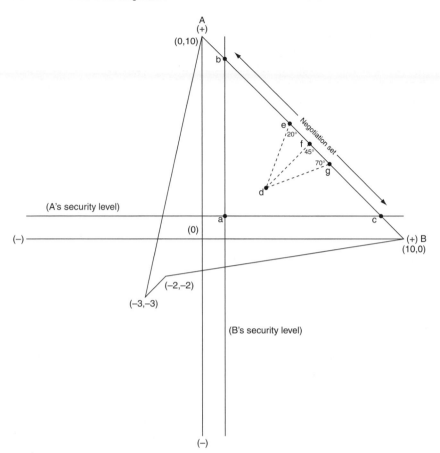

Figure 6.1. Absolute versus relative gains in a "mixed motive" game

game theorist where these values came from (although this is obviously an important, even necessary issue for negotiation analysts, but answering it requires us to go beyond pure game theory). In this context cooperative outcomes may be defined as any agreement that falls along (or at least approaches) the northeast ("Pareto optimal") frontier. If this frontier consists of a single point then theoretically negotiation is not necessary, as the unilateral optimal choice of each party would produce the mutually cooperative outcome; due to incomplete information this single mutually cooperative outcome may not be recognized, so in this case negotiation serves as a "learning" or "coordination" process. This northeast frontier is seldom a single point, however, and more often takes the form shown in

Figure 6.1 of a continuum, whereas agreement at a specific point along this "optimal frontier" introduces an element of conflict into what might otherwise be purely a game of coordination.

If the Pareto frontier is linear (going from northwest to southeast), then any movement along this line benefits one party at the expense of the other, making stable, cooperative outcomes difficult to reach *if* relative gains matter. The importance of relative versus absolute gains is largely a subjective matter, influenced by the socially constructed values of the actors rather than by an objective measure of gains and losses. However, fear of exploitation may cause even cooperatively oriented actors to behave defensively if they fear that the other party may exploit their cooperativeness.[1] Thus achievement of cooperative outcomes depends in large part upon a cooperative process, and it is here that the negotiation process enters as the key intervening variable between initial preferences and final outcomes.

Two kinds of dilemma focus our attention on ways in which game theory may help us to identify cooperative outcomes in conflictual situations; these are often referred to as "dilemmas of common interests" and "dilemmas of common aversions" (Stein 1990, pp. 32–38). The first situation, typified by the classic Prisoners' Dilemma game (PDG), illustrates a case where two definitions of rational choice produce two different outcomes. The classic game theory solution, based on the "minimax" theorem, produces a mutually conflictual outcome due to the fear of each party that its cooperation could readily be exploited by the other for its unilateral gain. However, this equilibrium or "saddle point" is suboptimal, in the sense that there is another combination of choices that can make both parties better off. The dilemma posed by these situations of "common interest" is how to move towards a cooperative solution without running a risk that the other may cheat and leave its partner worse off. Negotiation, then, in a series of repeated Prisoner's Dilemma games, is an opportunity for the parties to communicate with one another about the joint benefits that can be obtained from both making the cooperative choice, and to develop either mutual trust, or some mechanism or system of guarantees to assure each party that the other will not defect from the cooperative solution.

Robert Axelrod (1984), in a series of computer experiments, has found that the best way to reach this equilibrium is through a strategy known as "tit for tat," in which each player does to the other in a subsequent play

---

[1] For the debate between the neo-realist emphasis on relative gains versus the neo-liberal emphasis on absolute gains, see Baldwin (1993), especially the discussion of the behavior of relative gains protecting "defensive positionalists" in Grieco (1988, pp. 116–42).

of the game what its partner did to it in the previous iteration. Axelrod finds that in a surprisingly short time players can learn that cooperation on their part will be reciprocated to produce joint benefits, whereas conflict will also be reciprocated, making both worse off. Thus in an iterated series of games, especially an infinite series (or at least one in which the end of the game is not known to the players in advance, which is what we presume international relations to be), both parties should quickly learn that cooperation is mutually beneficial and that any defection by one will be punished by a reciprocal defection by the other. Axelrod notes that this simple rule quickly becomes internalized, and the behavior of the parties becomes governed by a mutually shared normative set of rules about how to play the game cooperatively. The main problem with this "tit for tat" reciprocity is that it does not offer any mechanism for escape from a continuous spiral of conflict, when both parties continue to reciprocate defection strategies in a seemingly infinite series of interactions, a problem that Stanger addresses in the next chapter. The problem of breaking out of such vicious cycles has been a major concern of negotiation theorists from virtually all theoretical perspectives, and it is evident that such a breakout cannot be achieved within a purely mechanistic model of reciprocity; what is needed is thus some mechanism to "start over" and to create a virtuous rather than a vicious cycle.

The second situation is generally referred to as a "dilemma of common aversions," often represented by the game of the Chicken Dilemma (CDG), pursued in greater detail in chapter 8 by Goldstein. Here, the main common interest is not in achieving a mutual benefit, but in avoiding a mutually hurting outcome. The "chicken" game, however, also reveals an underlying dilemma, because it suggests two equally valid outcomes or equilibria, in which one player swerves to avoid a crash while the other continues straight ahead and is proclaimed a hero; the "cooperative" partner is branded as a "chicken." The mutually beneficial outcome in this case occurs when both swerve at the same time to avoid a crash and both suffer a minor blow to their prestige with their "in-group," but this is not a stable outcome. Each player wants to move to a "winning" situation, but the consequence of both moving there is that they suffer the joint losses that both seek to avoid. Any outcome in which one wins while the other loses may be optimal in some technical sense, but it creates exactly the asymmetry in "relative gains" that leads to unequal outcomes, in which one party wins while its partner feels humiliated. Such inequality clearly does not make for normatively "fair" outcomes, and in practical terms it also produces pressures for defection over the long haul that are likely to make highly asymmetrical outcomes unstable, prone to cheating and defections.

Again, negotiation is usually required to reach agreement on the choice for both to swerve, since each must be assured that the other will not defect at the last second and seek to win by continuing straight ahead on the collision path as soon as it sees the other begin to swerve. And, of course, if both continue on course until they see the other swerve, then neither will swerve and they will end up in a collision that produces the worst outcome for both, where both are dead. In the CDG, "staying the course" may prove to be fatal if one's opponent also commits itself to the same strategy. The only acceptable solution to avert the common danger is a negotiation that assures both players that they can swerve without risking defection by the other, which will lead to victory for the latter and humiliation for the former. As in the PDG, at the outset of a series of interactions either some degree of mutual trust must be created or a mechanism must be established to guarantee compliance or to punish defection. In this case, however, the threat of reciprocal defection may not work as well as in the Prisoner's Dilemma, since that will lead to mutual annihilation, the outcome both seek to avert.

Therefore, especially for dilemmas of common aversions, institutionalized systems of rules and enforcement mechanisms are more likely to assure mutual compliance in the common interest, but as these patterns of cooperative interaction become institutionalized over time the fear of defection may recede and eventually even disappear completely. It was largely for this reason that Germany and France began the process of economic integration in 1952 by placing the two major commodities needed for the conduct of warfare – coal and steel – in a single economic community, the European Coal and Steel Community, essentially making defection through pursuit of unilateral armaments physically impossible. After a period of time this kind of material constraint was no longer needed, as the "idea" that a war between Germany and France was possible began to fade from the collective consciousness, to be replaced eventually by a sense of belonging to a common community that Deutsch et al. (1957, p. 5) and Waever (1998, pp. 81–93) famously referred to as a "no war" community, one in which the idea of war disappeared altogether, to be replaced by a "pluralistic security community" characterized by "dependable expectations of peaceful change." Thus "negotiated cooperation" is eventually converted to an internalized cooperation that no longer depends on negotiated agreements, although specific negotiations may still occur from time to time to reinforce the modalities of the underlying cooperation. Rather than the kind of "tit for tat" reciprocity described in Axelrod's model of cooperation, reciprocity becomes "diffuse"; parties reciprocate cooperation, not so much because they expect an immediate reward but because they have a relationship built upon trust in which they can expect the other to reciprocate whenever necessary at any indefinite time in the future. In this sense, expectations of reciprocity and peaceful change have become a constitutive part of the relationship; they are expected as an inherent part of the relationship and not necessarily because of some expectation of immediate reward.

Therefore achieving cooperative outcomes generally requires a cooperative process to negotiation to maximize the possibility for realizing optimal, fair, and stable outcomes. The negotiation process may be viewed as falling along a continuum from tough, oppositional bargaining to cooperative, joint problem solving. Jean Monnet (cited in Fisher and Ury 1982) depicted the two ends of this continuum by the simple metaphor of the arrangement of table and chairs; in positional bargaining the parties sit on opposite sides of the table and essentially "arm wrestle" with one another; in joint problem solving they sit on the same side of the table, place the "problem" on the other side of the table, and then work together to solve the problem to the satisfaction of both. Thus the first approach consists in strategic bargaining in which each actor seeks to "win" relative to the other; they view one another as opponents in a strategic contest in which one wins and the other loses – that is, as a largely zero-sum game in which asymmetric outcomes are expected reflecting relative gains that favor one at the other's expense. By contrast, the second approach consists of a cooperative problem-solving exercise in which the parties work together to define, confront, and resolve a common problem in ways that will be beneficial to both (all) parties (Hopmann 2001).

How the process evolves along this continuum, and where an agreement is reached, depend on a number of factors.

1. *Mutual trust (confidence) between the parties.* Will cooperative behaviors be reciprocated or exploited? In highly cooperative relationships, mutual responsiveness may become a constitutive element of the relationship; it becomes embedded and diffuse rather than a response to specific cooperative acts by the other. But naïve cooperation in the absence of established trust or an enforcement mechanism of some sort may induce exploitative rather than cooperative responses, especially when the parties face dilemmas of common interests and/or common aversions. And the temptation to take advantage of a naïve partner may drive out cooperation and return the process to a largely conflictual one.

2. *Their joint framing of the issue.* Are they inclined to move together in a northeasterly direction or to exploit the other by moving towards the northwest (party A) or towards the southeast (party B)? That is, do they frame the issue as one where absolute gains or relative gains matter more?

How close are they prepared to work together to move from the status quo along a 45° angle to produce approximately equal mutual benefits in comparison to the starting point? Once they reach the northeast frontier this would normally identify an agreement that is both optimal and mutually acceptable. However, how each party approaches the northeast frontier throughout the negotiation process will be conditioned by each party's knowledge that they may be locked into an agreement once they reach the frontier, in order to avoid the opprobrium that would be associated with appearing to retract previous cooperative moves. Bargaining about where their agreement should fall along that frontier reintroduces a purely zero-sum situation. The awareness that once they reach the northeast frontier pressure will develop from both internal and international quarters not to engage in zero-sum bargaining and moving back and forth along that frontier means that each party has an incentive from the outset of the bargaining process to move the angle of approach to one that favors their unilateral interests. However, efforts by both to do this may also undermine their ability to coordinate their negotiation strategies in a cooperative fashion to achieve a mutually satisfactory as well as an efficient and equitable agreement on the frontier. It is this tension that creates the fundamental "negotiator's dilemma," defined by Sebenius (2002, p. 241) as one in which "competitive moves to claim value individually often drive out cooperative moves to create it jointly. Outcomes of this dynamic include poor agreements, deadlocks, and conflict spirals."

3. *How they manage the endgame.* As they approach the northeast frontier, do the parties succumb to the temptation to behave conflictually as each tries to move the point at which they reach the frontier in the direction that they prefer? Fortunately, this may be offset by the pattern of cooperative interaction throughout the preceding negotiation that was required to reach the Pareto frontier, especially if it has contributed to trust, empathy, and a belief that the other can be counted on to continue to behave cooperatively.

4. *Whether a third party is available.* Do third parties assist in managing a "fair" cooperative process in which exploitation will be discouraged and cooperation will be rewarded? That is, are mutually acceptable third-party mediators available to assist the parties in reaching a "fair" and "optimal" agreement by the most efficient means possible? Left to their own devices, one or more parties to a negotiation may succumb to the pressures mentioned above and bring a cooperative process to an end. However, a third party may serve as a kind of referee in these circumstances to ward off unilateral, self-interested behavior and to reinforce a cycle of mutually cooperative reciprocity once it has been initiated.

Therefore negotiated cooperation may best be facilitated by a process in which two parties coordinate their behavior to achieve outcomes that they regard as fair – that is, in which neither perceives that it is being exploited by the other – efficient, in the sense that it represents the optimal joint benefits that could possibly be achieved within existing constraints, and stable, in the sense that neither party has a strong incentive to defect from the resulting agreement. Game theory models may serve as metaphors that help us understand the conditions under which such cooperative outcomes may be achieved in negotiations, while also presenting clearly and simply the underlying dilemmas that often make such cooperation so difficult to achieve in "real world" situations of conflict.

Beyond game theory: constructivist cooperation

Beyond these simple, basic principles most negotiation theory essentially consists in the elaboration of how these principles operate in a wide range of highly complex contexts that normally frame conflicts. However, the constructivist "turn" in international politics also reminds us that this is not a simple, linear process in which given preferences are mediated through a negotiation process to produce outcomes; the process also conditions, frames, and structures the original preferences, which then may be modified as a consequence of the negotiation process itself and through other interactions among the parties outside formal negotiations that nonetheless frame the political context (Hopmann 1996, pp. 195–220). Preferences are no longer viewed as being wholly exogenous to the game-theoretical model, as the preferences and processes become mutually constitutive and preferences are constructed and modified through the negotiation process itself. In this sense, the negotiation process may lead to the reframing of preferences which then begin to merge, until eventually the negotiation process itself creates a new identity for the participants as part of the interdependent system constituted by the fundamental problem that created the need for the negotiation in the first place.

Interestingly, this basic concept was captured quite well in one of the pioneering works on international negotiation employing game theory, Anatol Rapoport's 1960 classic *Fight, Games, Debates*. In this seminal work, Rapoport outlined the basic game-theoretic models that underlie all work on bargaining and negotiation, especially the classic "battle of the sexes" game discussed above. However, Rapoport concludes his discussion of game theory by noting that it may help us think about conflict situations, but it often produces indeterminate solutions or makes assumptions about the nature of human conflict that are inadequate to explain many situations of conflict. This, he contends, means that we must "look around for other frameworks into which conflict situations can be cast" (Rapoport 1966, p. 242). Therefore Rapoport concludes by looking in the realm of psychology and realizing that conflicts may be a product of the way in which we frame situations, often characterized by what he calls a "blindness of involvement." To overcome such one-sided blindness, he suggests (pp. 259–72) that negotiations must focus on a process of discourse, debate, and mutual learning that may lead to the development of "empathetic understanding." When such understanding is achieved, issues may be reframed, new identities may be created, and (in the language of game theory) preferences may be transformed in ways that open up new possibilities for reaching agreement. In effect, the "payoff polygon" may be expanded and the Pareto frontier may move further outward, opening up new possibilities for mutually advantageous agreements.

In many ways, Rapoport's analysis in 1960 foreshadowed many of developments in international relations theory that emerged decades later, especially the move towards a constructivist approach in the discipline. Unlike that of many social constructivists, Rapoport's analysis focused primarily at the individual level, and thus reflected an approach derived from individual psychology rather than from sociology. However, it shared with the constructivists some forty years later the assertion that conflicts are often as much about ideas as they are about material interests, and therefore that the best way to negotiate a resolution of international conflicts is to modify the structure of shared ideas that provide the primary sources of conflict in order to make the conflict more amenable to resolution.

Thus the essence of this approach is that issues need to be reframed, something which may emerge from the process that Rapoport called "debate." As he used the term, "debate" is not very different from Habermas's (1998) notions of "discourse," in which parties may explore their beliefs and attempt to find common ground through the development of empathetic understanding (Crawford 2002). It is thus through debate, argumentation, and persuasion that our ideas about the world change, and eventually these changes may become great enough to constitute a fundamental rethinking of our concrete interests, but even more importantly of our subjective identities. As Risse (2000, p. 10) has noted, Habermas believed that "argumentative consensus seeking requires the ability to empathize" and to "share a 'common lifeworld,'" that includes a "shared culture, a common system of norms and rules perceived as legitimate, and the social identity of actors being capable of communicating and acting." It is in this way that enemies may be transformed into participants in the same "community," as, for example, France and Germany during the second half of the twentieth century transformed their relationship from that of mortal enemies into joint participants in a new European Union. Thus the "idée européenne" reframed the animosity that had been the foundation for three major wars between 1870 and 1945 into a new shared *weltenschang* of belonging to the same pluralistic security community. When these new ideas literally extend "all the way down" in the relationship so that it becomes completely transformed, internalized, and even institutionalized, new patterns of cooperative negotiation become possible that are no longer characterized by widespread fears of exploitation or defection. Once this stage is reached, a consistently cooperative process of negotiation may emerge even when parties still encounter occasional conflicts of material interests. This is the case, for example, between the United States and Canada, where issues such as environment and trade often arise, but where negotiations on these issues generally take place on the basis of the underlying assumption that they will occur in a cooperative relationship and that both parties intend to reach a cooperative agreement in spite of their different interests. In this case, the common identity of North American democratic states trumps the frequent conflicts of interest and other irritations that enter into the relationship from time to time, to ensure that the community is preserved and strengthened.

This reframing of the issue is also generally accompanied by a qualitatively different negotiation process that occurs within highly cooperative and institutionalized international regimes, organizations, and communities. Positional bargaining, and the related method of concession–convergence negotiation generally characteristic of the bazaar setting, is usually replaced by a process more widely characterized as joint problem-solving. Concession–convergence bargaining generally occurs along a fixed issue dimension, in which two parties start off at somewhat different positions on that dimension and seek to converge towards agreement through a series of mutual concessions. However, the "toughness dilemma" often encourages using various tactics such as commitments, threats, and promises to try to induce the other party to make greater concessions, thereby resulting in an agreement that is unbalanced in favor of the tougher bargainer (Zartman and Berman 1982, p. 170). Mutual employment of these tactics, however, may induce a stalemate in which neither concedes, leaving the parties far apart. And even when such tactics do lead to agreement, it is often perceived as "unfair" and "imbalanced." The solutions reached through concession–convergence bargaining are thus more likely to reflect the power differentials among the parties. Since at least one of the parties will generally regard such an agreement as "unfair," the temptation to drag their feet in implementing an agreement or even to defect altogether is likely to make such unbalanced agreements highly unstable and of limited durability.

In conflictual situations, however, "defensive positionalists" may fear exploitation that could lead to greater relative gains by their opponent, and they are thus likely to approach these negotiations by digging in their heels rather than by searching for an optimal and mutually beneficial solution to their differences. Thus deep-seated conflicts of opposing material interests and opposed identities (where the conflict is perceived as one between good and evil) are likely to produce negotiation tactics that reinforce rather than ameliorate those conflicts. In these cases, the probability of reaching any kind of mutually agreeable outcome is likely to be low.

By contrast, negotiating parties that have learned from previous experience that mutual toughness tends to make both parties worse off over the long term may reframe their relationship as one of cooperation, which may initially be based on specific reciprocity, but which evolves over time into what Deutsch and his colleagues referred to as "diffuse reciprocity." One cooperates, not necessarily expecting immediate rewards, but rather because the "other" has become "us," so that cooperation is perceived to be in "our" own interest when conceived in terms of the new and redefined identity of who "we" are (Adler and Barnett 1998, p. 32).

In the final analysis, constructivist theories synthesized with social psychological theories of "social learning" suggest that negotiation may be viewed as a process through which conflictual relations may be transformed into more cooperative relationships, as mutual "reflected appraisals" of the parties begin to identify each other as potential partners rather than as rivals (Wendt 1999, pp. 326–55). In this sense, negotiations may be viewed as more than an effort to reach cooperative solutions to common problems, but also as a form of discourse, debate, and argumentation that may be used to promote long-term embedded habits of cooperation that entail not only the realization of a common interest in the midst of conflicting ones, but also a process that contributes to the development of shared identities in which cooperation becomes institutionalized and even a constitutive part of relations among formally sovereign states. Coming to construct, understand, and reproduce international relations in Kantian rather than Hobbesian terms can only emerge through a process of interaction, in which negotiation plays a fundamental role. In short, we may understand international cooperation to be a fully negotiated understanding of how to engage in international relations *writ large*, as well as a more specific process of reaching cooperative solutions to common problems within formal diplomatic settings. Since these emergent understandings of shared goals lead to a transformation of the preferences of parties previously in conflict with one another, agreements based on a new set of preferences thus also meet standard criteria of rational convergence around common interests and values.

Thus if we relax the assumption often made by rational choice and game theoretic approaches to conflict and cooperation in international relations generally (and in negotiation analysis specifically) that preferences are exogenous and fixed, it is no longer necessary to view rational models and constructivist interpretations as fundamentally opposed to one another. As Risse (2000, p. 34) has observed, "the logic of arguing [i.e., negotiating] challenges the assumption that actors hold fixed interests and identities during the process of interaction." At the same time, this approach to interaction along the conflict–cooperation continuum "brings agency back in and allows us to overcome the structuralist bias in some social constructivist statements."

Particularly since one of the purposes of negotiation is to change attitudes, beliefs, and preferences in such a way as to enlarge prospects for agreement, preferences evidently need to be treated as endogenous to the negotiation process and can be modified in the course of negotiations. Insofar as constructivist approaches aid in understanding the social and psychological processes that bring about such changes of preference, they contribute a necessary element to traditional rationalist theories of conflict and cooperation, without requiring us to throw out altogether the fundamental logic of rationalist explanations.

7   The shadow of the past over conflict and cooperation

Allison Stanger

Why do individuals and states choose cooperation over conflict? Common sense tells us that the context in which such a choice is made is critical, but defining the salient contours of context is a challenging task. Robert Axelrod's influential work on the evolution of cooperation, cited in over 4,000 articles, identifies a long shadow of the future (simply, when the players expect to continue interacting frequently) as a critical precondition for sustainable cooperation in a world of self-interested actors with no central authority. In the pages that follow, the terms "societal cooperation," "systemic cooperation," and "a cooperative regime" are used interchangeably to refer to such emergent multilateral cooperation.[1] While affirming Axelrod's central insight, this chapter ultimately demonstrates the extreme fragility of the long shadow of the future. It is in reality a prisoner of the past – of historical context – to a greater extent than has been heretofore acknowledged.

The chapter introduces agent-based modeling, a variant of computer simulation, as a tool for advancing our understanding of the origins and development of cooperative regimes. By agent-based modeling, I mean "a computational methodology that allows the analyst to create, analyze, and experiment with, artificial worlds populated by agents that interact in non-trivial ways and that constitute their own environment" (Cederman 2001a, p. 16). As Robert Axelrod has argued, agent-based modeling facilitates a new way of conducting scientific research:

Simulation is a third way of doing science. Like deduction, it starts with a set of explicit assumptions. But unlike deduction, it does not prove theorems. Instead, a simulation generates data that can be analyzed inductively. Unlike typical induction, however, the simulated data comes from a rigorously specified set of rules rather than direct measurement of the real world. While induction can be used to find patterns in data, and deduction can be used to find consequences of assumptions, simulation modeling can be used as an aid to intuition ... Simulation is a way of doing thought experiments. (Axelrod 1997, p. 5)

---

[1] On international regimes, see Keohane 1984, 1989, 2002; Keohane and Nye 1977.

Axelrod characterizes the goal of agent-based modeling as the enrichment of "our understanding of fundamental processes that may appear in a variety of applications" (Axelrod 1997, p. 6). For our purposes, it is a largely untapped resource for systematic counterfactual reasoning that might be deployed to explore the origins of both conflict and cooperation.[2]

Agent-based modeling is above all a tool for better understanding the significance of context. Computer simulation enables us to specify parameters that define a given geostrategic context and then observe how those assumptions influence conflict and cooperation processes over time. In its quest to implement Axelrod's third way of doing science, this chapter will probe the plausibility and robustness of three candidate mechanisms for shedding light on the mechanics of multilateral cooperation.

Mechanism 1: A long shadow of the future increases the likelihood of emergent systemic cooperation (a central insight of Axelrod's 1984 book).

Mechanism 2: A long shadow of past discord decreases the likelihood of emergent systemic cooperation.

Mechanism 3: The capacity to learn from the "other" increases the likelihood of emergent systemic cooperation.

It does so by constructing a virtual world in which we can attempt to "grow" the anticipated outcome through each postulated mechanism. Success in "growing" the desired result will lend further support to the plausibility of the mechanism. In turn, failure will mean that either the model's implementation is flawed or the mechanism is spurious – or both. The paper's central argument is that our understanding of strategic interaction must be wedded to a rich understanding of the context in which that engagement takes place if we are to know when and under what circumstances cooperation is most likely to carry the day.

The discussion that follows is divided into five principal sections. The first reviews Robert Axelrod's early contributions to cooperation theory and his subsequent agent-based modeling of the iterated Prisoner's Dilemma, laying out the building blocks that comprise TopolCon (for Topology of Conflict), the proxy model I construct to replicate Axelrod's central findings. The second section reviews TopolCon's basic framework and demonstrates the emergence of a cooperative regime in the TopolCon virtual world. The third section then conducts an experiment in which Axelrod's traditional practictioners of tit for tat (TFT) are replaced with Suspicious

---

[2] On the case for agent-based modeling, see Axelrod 1997b; Axtell 2000; Cederman 1997, 2001a, 2001b, 2005; Clough 2001; Dean et al. 1998; Epstein and Axtell 1996; Lustick 2000; Lustick, Miodownik, and Eidelson 2004; Schelling 1978; Tesfatsion 2002. For a popularized account of agent-based modeling, see Rauch 2002.

TFTers (Suspicious TFTers defect rather than cooperate on the first move but are otherwise identical to Traditional TFTers), demonstrating that this simple tweak to the model's ontology undermines entirely the prospects for cooperation based on reciprocity. The fourth section conducts a second experiment with TopolCon, introducing the possibility of difference-conscious learning (whereby agents will only "see" and learn from the successes of those who resemble them; prejudice prevents them from learning anything from those unlike them). The results demonstrate that difference-conscious learning, contrary to our expectations, in some circumstances produces better long-term results for society as a whole than when difference-blind learning prevails. The fifth section concludes.

Adaptation and Axelrod's shadow of the future

Robert Axelrod's brilliant 1984 book, *The Evolution of Cooperation*, redefined standard approaches to the study of conflict and cooperation, becoming a classic and winning its author the MacArthur prize. Based on an innovative use of the iterated Prisoner's Dilemma,[3] Axelrod deployed computer simulation to demonstrate that cooperation can be a stable outcome in a world of self-interested actors with no central authority if two conditions are fulfilled: (i) all players know that the game will be repeated for the foreseeable future; and (ii) the stream of potential future payoffs is of sufficient value to all participants (the discount parameter w is sufficiently large). Thus "mutual cooperation can be stable if the future is sufficiently important relative to the past." Cooperation is possible and stable, relatively speaking, when the shadow of the future is sufficiently long (Axelrod 1984).

Axelrod reached his conclusion by deploying a novel form of experiment. He solicited strategies or programs to participate in a round robin computer tournament in two rounds, where any proposed strategy would be systematically teamed with each of its rivals, with a copy of itself, and with a random strategy. Outcomes for the system as a whole and the players that comprise it were systematically tracked. After the results of the first round of the tournament had been announced, participants were

---

[3] In the Prisoner's Dilemma, there are two players, each of whom has two choices: either to cooperate or defect. Each must make this choice without knowing what the other is going to do. Regardless of what the opponent does, defection always yields a higher payoff than cooperation, but if both players defect (as they are each likely to do, given the alternatives as described), each experiences the worst possible outcome. Yet if both can cooperate, the best possible outcome for both is secured. Among other things, the game captures quite nicely the inherent difficulties in promoting collective action for the common good. If all cooperate, each individual will be better off, but the gains from defecting when others are cooperating (free riding) are so large that collaborating for the common good is an elusive goal.

given the opportunity to revise their strategies and the entire tournament was run again. Axelrod found that the simplest of strategies, tit for tat – a "golden rule" maxim where the player cooperates on the first move and then responds in kind to subsequent moves by his or her opponent – outperformed its rivals across a range of settings.

TFT's robust success is due to being nice, provocable, forgiving, and clear. Its niceness means that it is never the first to defect … Its retaliation discourages the other side from persisting whenever defection is tried. Its forgiveness helps restore mutual cooperation. And its clarity makes its behavioral pattern easy to recognize; and once recognized, it is easy to perceive that the best way of dealing with TFT is to cooperate with it. (Axelrod 1984, p. 176)

The results from the second tournament were particularly striking: "The single best predictor of how well a rule performed was whether or not it was nice, which is to say, whether or not it would ever be the first to defect" (Axelrod 1984, p. 133).

Axelrod also demonstrated that the world need not be comprised of enthusiasts of reciprocity for cooperation to take hold and endure. Rather, small clusters of individuals prepared to reciprocate cooperation can successfully convert a majority who are not initially inclined to cooperate. Stable cooperation at the global level can be catalyzed by a handful of self-aware actors and, once established, such a population can protect itself from invasion by uncooperative strategies (Axelrod 1984, pp. 169–91).

As Axelrod himself acknowledges in *The Evolution of Cooperation*, the stellar performance of the TFT strategy in his two-stage tournament does not mean that it is always the best strategy to deploy. The success of the strategy, as Axelrod repeatedly emphasizes, is contingent on a sufficiently long shadow of the future – that is, on a sufficiently large value of w, the discount parameter in Axelrod's book. What might increase the value of w? There are two basic ways of increasing w and thereby lengthening the future's shadow: by making the interactions more frequent and by making them more durable. TFT shines as a strategy when the game is constantly played *and* one's opponents remain the same. Mutual cooperation can be stable and TFT the means to that stability "if the future is sufficiently important relative to the past" (Axelrod 1984, pp. 126–32, quote on p. 126). Thus "the foundation of cooperation is not really trust but the durability of the relationship" (Axelrod 1984, p. 182).

In more recent work Axelrod has utilized agent-based modeling to explore further the significance and implications of his findings when learning is endogenized and made a dynamic part of the simulation itself. In his 1984 work, learning and adaptation were exogenous to the computer tournament; the first stage was played, participants were given the opportunity to reassess, and new strategies were submitted for the second stage of the tournament. In a 2001 article in *Rationality and Society* that began as a 1999 Santa Fe Institute working paper, Axelrod and his Michigan colleagues Michael Cohen and Rick Riolo ran a more sophisticated version of the computer tournament, where the players, or agents, can scan the results of the game to date and update their strategies without any external intervention. (Cohen, Riolo, and Axelrod 1999). What is striking about this subsequent modeling experiment is that the concept of a discount parameter, a central feature of Axelrod's 1984 book, drops out of the modeling exercise entirely. It is explicitly set to 1, thereby maximizing the prospects for cooperation. In a sense, that is, Axelrod and his collaborators make interactions so frequent that for all practical purposes, $w = 1$. This enables them to explore the significance of durability – what Cohen, Riolo, and Axelrod in the paper refer to as "context preservation" – for the degree of emergent cooperation in the system.

Cohen, Riolo, and Axelrod find that generalized or systemic cooperation is most likely when interactive processes lead to context preservation or using the parallel language from the 1984 volume, when interactive processes are durable – basically when players play the same game repeatedly over an extended period of time with the same players. The authors label this emergent cooperative behavior a "cooperative regime," arguing that "social structure, by channeling which agents interact with others, can sustain cooperative regimes against forces that frequently dissolve them." Cooperative regimes "create a 'shadow of the adaptive future,' allowing even a small set of cooperative strategies to grow into a cooperative regime, a coherent, self-sustaining entity that is something more than the sum of pairwise interactions among its members" (Cohen, Riolo, and Axelrod 2001, quotes from abstract).

TopolCon and the Emergence of Systemic Cooperation

In what began as an effort to replicate Cohen, Riolo, and Axelrod's results, I extended an existing model, Lars-Erik Cederman and Lazslo Gulyas's EvolIPD to include some of the same functionality. The extended model I produced is hereafter referred to as TopolCon, an acronym for the Topology of Conflict. The aim was to dock the Cohen, Riolo, and Axelrod model, written using the Swarm simulation package (an objective-C based system), with one written using the RePast simulation package (a Java-based system).[4] Successfully producing the same

---

[4] On Swarm, see www.swarm.org/. For information on RePast, see www.repast.sourceforge.net/.

results from a model written in different languages deploying different simulation packages only strengthens the inferences drawn from the Cohen, Riolo, and Axelrod framework (Axtell et al. 1996).

TopolCon consists of a population of agents playing the iterated Prisoner's Dilemma with each other. In each time step (round of iterative play), agents play four games of Prisoner's Dilemma with their opponents (more on how opponents are chosen below) and may deploy one of four binary strategies: ALLC or the "always nice" strategy (cooperate on the first move and subsequently, regardless of the opponent's response), ALLD or the "always mean" strategy (defect on the first move and there-after, regardless of the opponent's response), TFT (cooperate on the first move and respond in kind thereafter), and ATFT (defect on the first move and do the opposite of whatever the opponent does thereafter).

At the end of each time step, agents survey the results of play (each agent has an average payoff for the round), and then adjust their strat-egies. They do so by simply adopting the strategy of their most successful opponent. Round by round, agents interact in this artificially con-structed world in one of three ways. When interaction process 2DK prevails, the agent chooses his north–east–west–south neighbors (his Von Neumann neighbors) as opponents and keeps these opponents throughout the entire run. 2DK provides for both spatial proximity and context preservation. For interaction process FRN, each agent initially chooses four opponents at random (no spatial proximity is required), but then keeps these opponents for the duration of the run. FRN provides for context preservation without spatial proximity. Finally, interaction process RWR represents the proverbial soup. For each time step, four opponents are randomly selected for each agent, four rounds of Prisoner's Dilemma are played, results are evaluated and strategies adjusted, and then each agent chooses four new opponents for the next round of the iterated Prisoner's Dilemma.[5] Since new

---

[5] The payoff matrix for our prisoner's dilemma (payoff for player 1, payoff for player 2):

	Cooperate	Defect
Cooperate	(3, 3)	(0, 5)
Defect	(5, 0)	(1, 1)

R (reward for mutual cooperation) = 3; S (sucker's payoff) = 0; T (temptation payoff) = 5; P (punishment for mutual defection) = 1. T > R > P > S AND R greater than the average of T and S defines the classic prisoner's dilemma payoff matrix in its myriad forms.

opponents are chosen for every time step, RWR represents an interaction process without *any* context preservation.

To replicate the Cohen, Riolo, and Axelrod results, I ran TopolCon with the same parametric assumptions and initial conditions. Agents are randomly assigned one of the four strategies with equal probability and are randomly placed on a 16 x 16 grid. Thus at the beginning of time, any given agent is equally likely to be a born deployer of TFT, ATFT, ALLC, or ALLD. Each is also equally inclined to be cooperative or uncooperative on the first move. With these parallel assumptions, we then let virtual history unfold. To allow for maximum comparability in our experimentation, I continue to use the Cohen, Riolo, and Axelrod parametric assumptions in the following section as a springboard for extending their findings, while at the same time probing some ambiguities in their results. Since under most scenarios the system converges to equilibrium quite rapidly, the figures below summarize and report on the first twenty time steps only (except in instances where it proved necessary to explore the action further down the road).

In facilitating connections between bilateral (micro) and societal (macro) cooperation, the TopolCon universe is distinctive. At the micro-level, in each round of the endlessly iterated Prisoner's Dilemma game, individual agents choose to cooperate or defect. At the macro-level, the strategies of all players are aggregated to express the level of societal cooperation at a given time step. The degree of societal cooperation at any discrete time step is reflected in the step average payoff measure (the sum total of all payoffs divided by the total number of players, who together constitute the virtual society), which can be deployed as a crude barometer of systemic cooperation and tracked over time. What TopolCon does nicely is to highlight the potential discrepancy between individual and societal utility. One must take care to note that individuals can flourish while society despairs and suffer while society as a whole flourishes, and that very fact is an engine of considerable systemic instability.

With respect to the strategies themselves, when the most frequently deployed strategies are ALLD or ATFT, daily life in TopolCon virtual society is nasty, brutish, and short, with step average payoff converging to the lowest possible level (1.0). In this context, when the differences between individual payoffs and step average payoff vanish, the system equilibrates, and both the individual and society at large pay the price. In contrast, the ALLC and TFT strategies are most likely to facilitate sustainable societal cooperation, and societal cooperation emerges and is stable when the TFT strategy predominates. In such a world, the golden rule prevails, and step average payoff converges to the TFT individual payoff of 3.0. Where a stable TFT equilibrium has emerged, the potential utilitarian gap between individual and societal good melts away, with each individual's benefit mirroring the societal norm. Both the individual and society at large benefit from this state of affairs.

The images given here – snapshots of a TopolCon run in progress – illustrate the potentially contagious character of the TFT strategy, the qualities that Robert Axelrod first identified. In this particular run, TopolCon is set to 256 players, with each agent playing its Von Neumann neighbors. On the grid, the ALLC strategy is coded dark grey, the ALLD coded white, the ATFT light grey and the TFT strategy black. The emergence of a cooperative regime is represented by the spread of blue across the grid over time. In the final snapshot (time step 11), only a few white deployers of ALLD swim in a sea of TFT black. By time step 14, the entire grid has gone black, and a stable equilibrium of systemic cooperation has been secured, although the initial configuration of the grid at the outset (see snapshot 1) made this outcome seem highly unlikely.

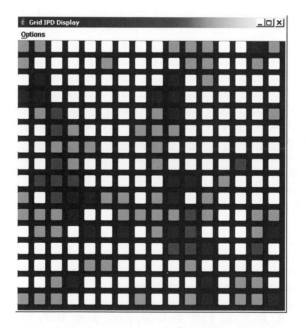

Grid snapshot 1. Traditional TFT, 2DK, 256 players, random seed 1, tick count 1

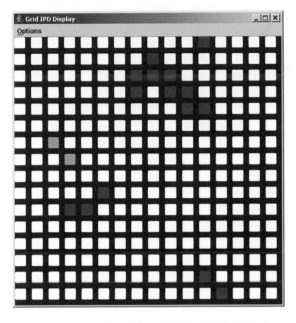

Grid snapshot 2. Traditional TFT, 2DK, 256 players, random seed 1, tick count 3

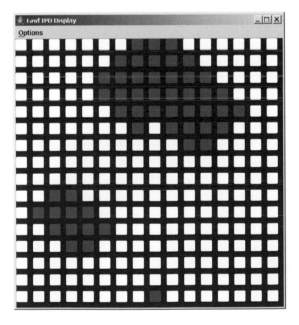

Grid snapshot 3. Traditional TFT, 2DK, 256 players, random seed 1, tick count 5

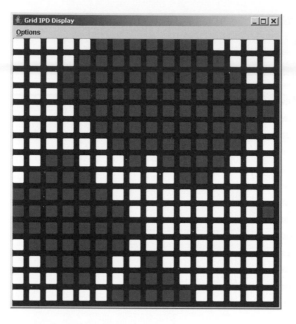

Grid snapshot 4. Traditional TFT, 2DK, 256 players, random seed 1, tick count 7

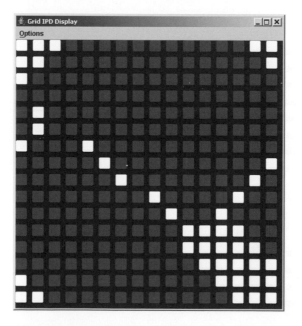

Grid snapshot 5. Traditional TFT, 2DK, 256 players, random seed 1, tick count 9

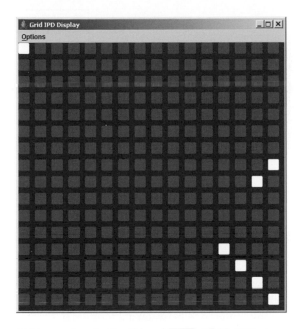

Grid snapshot 6. Traditional TFT, 2DK, 256 players, random seed 1, tick count 11

The shadow of the future's fragility

Axelrod's 1984 book and his subsequent experiments with the iterated Prisoner's Dilemma using agent-based modeling persuasively demonstrate that factors (especially context preservation and a high discount rate) that lengthen the shadow of the future increase the likelihood of systemic cooperation (reflected in the triumph of the TFT strategy) that is stable over time. Once established, the TFT equilibrium can resist invasion by other strategies. The TFT strategy in all of Axelrod's work presupposes cooperation on the first move, regardless of context. Deployers of TFT are nice by nature, assuming the best of their opponents until proven otherwise. Once crossed, they immediately retaliate, but they by definition lead with cooperation. They trust until proven otherwise. Let us call these deployers of trusting TFT "Traditional TFTers."

Yet one might conceive of individuals who embrace the golden mean as an important moral principle, but who come to the table with different historical baggage, their point of departure being suspicion rather than trust. Indeed, it is not so uncommon for humans who have experienced

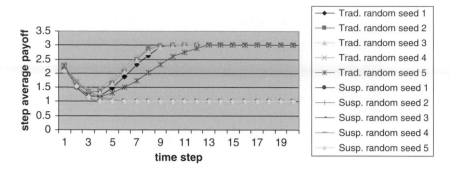

Figure 7.1. Traditional v. suspicious TFT, 2 DK, 256 players

deception to expect more of the same. Over time they come to be suspicious until proven otherwise. We can model this tendency by having such players open with defection in the first round of a game with new opponents but then deploy an eye for an eye and a tooth for a tooth – classic TFT behavior – thereafter. Let us call these players Suspicious TFTers. To be crystal clear, the only difference between a Traditional TFTer (a player deploying Axelrod's version of TFT) and a Suspicious TFTer is what he or she does on the first move. Traditional TFTers cooperate on the first move. Suspicious TFTers defect on the first move. Their responses to opponent strategies are identical thereafter.

We have all the tools we need to test how this aspect of the general model's initial conditions affects outcomes. We can run TopolCon with all other parameters save the first move of the TFT strategy remaining exactly the same. Since the model starts up by randomly placing the TFT, ATFT, ALLD, and ALLC strategies on the grid in equal proportions, this means that the suggested tweak changes the strategy of only 25 percent of the total number of players, with every other feature of the model remaining exactly the same. Since the basic patterns emerge quite quickly and we are interested in relative patterns over time rather than discrete data points, we run the model for each combination over five random seeds for twenty time steps. For now, just as did Cohen, Axelrod, and Riolo, we assume a world with 256 players.

Figures 7.1 and 7.3 vividly demonstrate the explosive nature of this simple tweak to TopolCon's initial conditions. Figure 7.1 shows what replacing Traditional TFTers with Suspicious TFTers does to Axelrod's most cooperation-inclined scenario, the 2DK interaction topology, which provides for context preservation that is spatially derived (each agent plays its four von Neumann neighbors). A minority of Traditional TFTers is

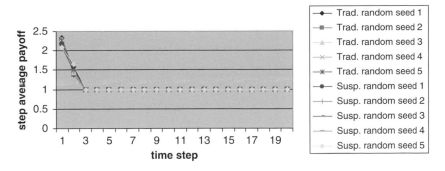

Figure 7.2. Traditional v. suspicious TFT, RWR, 256 players

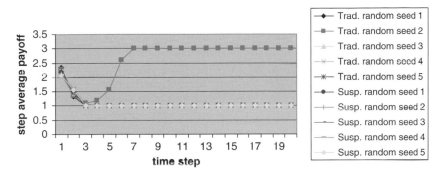

Figure 7.3. Traditional v. suspicious TFT, FRN, 256 players

a precondition for the emergence of reciprocity-based cooperation. With Suspicious TFTers present at the creation, cooperation can never get off the ground. This effect is only all the more pronounced with the FRN interaction topology, where the spatial component of context preservation is not present. Under 2DK and FRN, a long shadow of the future is a precondition for systemic cooperation and reciprocity, but the shadow of the past, insofar as it influences the attitudes that individuals bring to the game at hand, can shorten, if not eradicate, the future's shadow.

Only the results for the RWR topology, where agents randomly choose opponents at each time step, eradicating all aspects of context preservation, are not influenced profoundly by this simple reconceptualization of the model's initial conditions. The RWR or random soup interaction framework represents an ideal typical Hobbesian state of nature, one completely devoid of networks and enduring relationships and thereby all potential instruments for context preservation. In such a world, as

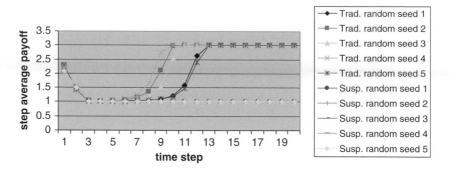

Figure 7.4. Traditional v. suspicious TFT, FRN, 10,000 players

Figure 7.2 demonstrates, it does not matter whether players come to the table initially trustful or distrustful; the structure of the system in which all social interaction must take place determines the bleak societal outcomes.

Similarly, with FRN, a bit of good luck (as exemplified by the Traditional TFT run under random seed 2) can produce contagious systemic cooperation, but the simple fact that each agent plays the game against four randomly selected opponents who need have no further connections with each other (as by definition players in the 2DK interaction do) diminishes the prospects for cooperation. But note the surprising systemic outcome, conveyed in Figure 7.4, which results when we run the iteration with 10,000 players rather than 256. In this larger world, cooperation rather than discord is the emergent societal outcome under the Traditional TFT scenario. Interestingly, the prospects for pockets of contagious cooperation rise with the number of individuals playing the game, and these small centers of goodwill at the micro level can multiply and shape macro outcomes – assuming there is a sufficient reservoir of goodwill (as represented by the presence of Traditional TFTers) present at the creation.

To summarize, with the standard 25 percent of the population leading with Traditional TFT, we find two overarching patterns. First, increasing the number of players can increase the prospects for emergent systemic cooperation, as we see in the runs under interaction topology FRN. Second, the interaction topologies that preserve context (2DK and FRN) facilitate the emergence of cooperative regimes, thereby validating the earlier findings of Cohen, Riolo, and Axelrod's model. In contrast, when Traditional TFTers are replaced with suspicious ones, increasing world size has no impact on the prospects for societal cooperation, which are essentially obliterated by the introduction of recurrent pessimism to the system at large. In general, the more optimism one can inject into the system (optimism being a defining feature of the standard Traditional TFT strategy), the greater the probability that the pockets of optimism present in the system at the outset will prove contagious, enabling the TFT strategy to dominate all others and emergent cooperation to carry the day. What this little experiment demonstrates, above all, is the absolute criticality of tenacious Traditional TFTers being present at time zero if systemic cooperation is to have a hope of emerging.

The results sketched in this section demonstrate that all of Axelrod's robust and consequential findings are strongly dependent on having 50 percent of the general population willing to cooperate on the first move. In some sense, then, there is a circular nature to the evolution of cooperation. There must be a certain level of cooperative inclination embedded in the very foundations of the iterated Prisoner's Dilemma framework for systemic cooperation based on reciprocity to emerge. Put another way, the seeds of cooperation must be present in the initial inclinations of agents at the onset. Our simple experiment simply draws this basic fact out and forces us to reflect upon it.

Learning and prejudice

The experiments described in the previous section presume that agents are willing to learn from winners, regardless of the strategies they deploy or the histories they embody. At the end of each time step, each player surveys the results of the four-round game, calculates who has done the best (as measured by their average payoff), and adopts the strategy of the fittest without further reflection.

Yet, in the real world, discrimination or frames often figure prominently in the way in which individuals perceive and learn from the world they inhabit. Sometimes humans are more likely to absorb the lessons of life from others they perceive to be "like them," rather than from those with whom they do not share a sense of kinship or commonality. The era of globalization surely diminishes this tendency, but no one would argue that it does not persist in certain regions of the world and even in parts of the United States. What happens in our virtual world when we introduce the possibility of learning that is framed by prejudice, when we remove the difference-blind assumption and replace it with a form of adaptation that is explicitly difference-conscious?

To explore this proposition, we introduce to the basic TopolCon framework the concepts of difference-blind (hereafter DB) and difference-conscious (hereafter DC) learning. We do this by tagging all agents as either black or white and endowing each one with the capacity to perceive whether the opponents with whom he is interacting looks like him or does not. DB learning is simply the standard form of adaptation deployed in previous sections. For DB learning, each player surveys the performance of its opponents at the end of each time step, and adopts the strategy of that round's winner, regardless of whether the fittest does or does not resemble the player in question.

When DC learning pertains, however, each agent surveys its opponents at the end of each round to see who has accumulated the largest average payoff, but if that winner is not of the same group – that is, if it does not look like the player assessing its fitness – the agent simply will not see it. Instead, it will adopt the strategy of the opponent who resembles it whose average payoff exceeds its own. If no such player exists, the agent simply retains its original strategy, even if a player who does not resemble it is actually faring better. Thus, with DC learning, agents will only learn from those they perceive to be like them. When difference exists, they simply do not see the success of those who have in reality bested them.

We start with Cohen, Riolo, and Axelrod's initial conditions (Traditional TFTers, with 25 percent of each strategy type represented in the initial population) and leave everything the same as in the previous section, save for allowing for the possibility of DC learning. We bump the number of players up to 10,000 to maximize the prospects for cooperation, in order to determine better the impact of different forms of learning on those prospects. Figures 7.5–7.11 below capture the results of the simulation. The introduction of DC learning has quite straightforward effects with 2DK interaction, as we can see in Figure 7.5 below. In an artificial society where DC learning pertains, the prospects for robust cooperation are obliterated, but the system quickly settles down to an equilibrium where pockets of the cooperative can coexist in a sea of uncooperative players, but never in sufficient number to take off and produce an all TFT world of cooperation based on reciprocity. In the long run (time step 7 on), DB learning produces a significantly higher societal payoff. Interestingly, from the perspective of society as a whole, prejudice pays in the short run, as demonstrated by the difference in systemic outcomes prior to time step 6.

RWR or the random soup interaction produces its standard nasty and brutish outcome under both learning scenarios (see Figure 7.6 below), but note that, rather counterintuitively, the descent into a world where conflict prevails is slightly more precipitous when DB learning pertains than it is in a difference-conscious world; again, in the short run, for society as a whole prejudice pays. With FRN interaction (see Figure 7.7 below), the results are also noteworthy. With DB learning, the paths to the final destination of cooperation based on reciprocity vary

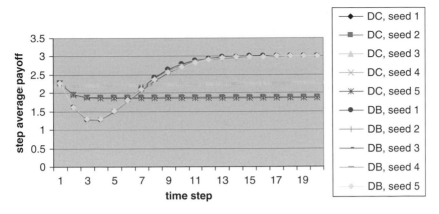

Figure 7.5. Traditional TFT, DC v. DB learning, 2DK 10,000 players

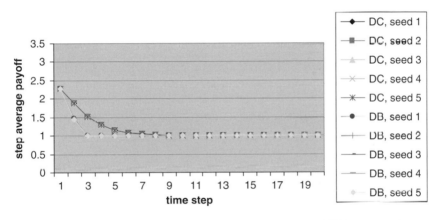

Figure 7.6. Traditional TFT, DC v. DB learning, RWR 10,000 players

significantly across different random seeds, but a TFT world is the ultimate result. Just as they did under 2DK interaction, the DC runs under
FRN wind up hovering around the 2.0 average payoff mark, although at a
slightly lower position. Again, pockets of cooperation manage to keep the
system from descending into a 1.0 average population payoff world, but
they are never of sufficient durability to become contagious. DC learning
effects essentially prevent cooperation from taking off.

Under Traditional TFT and 2DK, comparative systemic outcomes
depend on the time step singled out for viewing, and this effect persists
regardless of world size. In the short run, DC learning is better for society.
In the long run, DB learning prevails. In contrast, under Traditional TFT

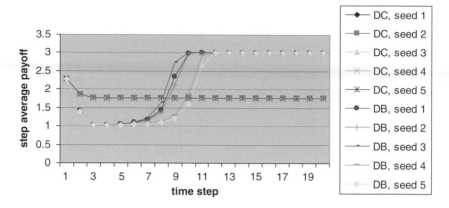

Figure 7.7. Traditional TFT, DC v. DB learning, FRN 10,000 players

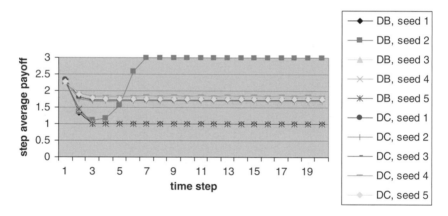

Figure 7.8. Traditional TFT, DB v. DC learning, FRN 256 players

and RWR, from a societal perspective, DC learning outperforms DB learning in the short run, but both functions quickly converge to the nastiest of worlds, and this outcome results regardless of the number of players.

Under Traditional TFT and FRN, however, the number of players in the system proves critical for comparative emergent outcomes. While the same straightforward short run/long run effect pertains at 10,000 players, it is rendered less stable as the number of players falls. At 256 players, for example, DC learning will outperform DB learning in both the short and long run approximately 72 percent of the time. But twenty-eight times out of a hundred, the short run/long run patterns that pertain under 2DK

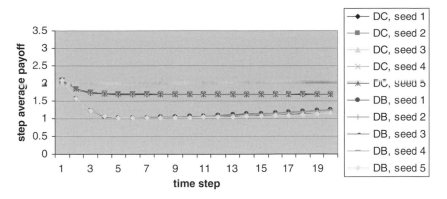

Figure 7.9. Suspicious TFT, DC v. DB learning, 2DK 10,000 players

interaction prevail.[6] With FRN, world size seems to drive the consequences for society, much more so than the interaction topology itself.

Now we tweak the model still further by replacing Traditional TFTers
with Suspicious TFTers and assessing what emerges in both the DC and
DB learning virtual worlds. Under 2DK, the interaction scenario most
likely to produce robust cooperation, the introduction of Suspicious TFT
undermines the prospects for cooperation in dramatic ways, at least in the
short term (first 20 iterations), as seen in Figure 7.9 below. Most interesting is that DC learning with Suspicious TFTers leads to greater systemic
cooperation in the short run than a world with DB learning. In the
Suspicious TFT world, it is better for the population as a whole to learn
in a difference-conscious fashion than it is in a Traditional TFT world, at
least in the opening chapter of the iteration. From Figure 7.9, DB learning
appears to have the potential to take off and facilitate a cooperative regime,
as cooperation is generally on the rise in the system at time step 20. This
apparent effect, however, turns out to be an illusion; the DB learning
function turns out to be certifiably chaotic.

The presence of Suspicious TFTers with RWR interaction produces a
conflict-rich world of ALLDers. Note that descent into such a world is
again more precipitous with DB learning than with DC learning, and this
trajectory is not in the least influenced by world size. Strikingly, the same
pattern pertains under Traditional TFT. In a word, the RWR interaction
topology obliterates the prospects for cooperation, regardless of the number of players or the proportion of optimistic players (first-move cooperators) in the game.

---

[6] Estimates derive from FRN runs over random seeds 1–100.

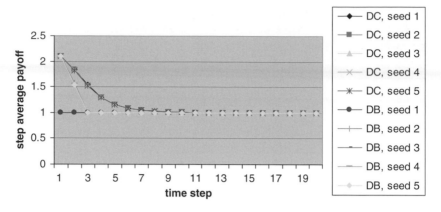

Figure 7.10. Suspicious TFT, DC v. DB learning, RWR 10,000 players

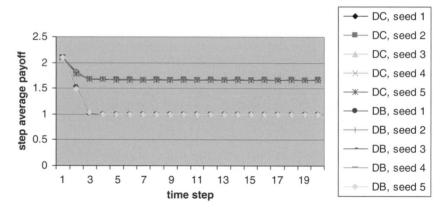

Figure 7.11. Suspicious TFT, DC v. DB learning, FRN 10,000 players

For FRN interaction, an effect parallel to that of 2DK interaction is present; the introduction of Suspicious TFTers makes prejudice on balance pay for society as a whole, but this time consistently across both short and long terms. Varying the number of players does not disrupt this dynamic. While it is slightly better for the system as a whole if DC learning prevails, regardless of world size, both variants of learning put the system in the 1–1.75 step average payoff range, which means that pockets of cooperation are possible, but the general status of the system as a whole is far from sunny.

Stepping back from it all and surveying the broad patterns, under Suspicious TFT, DC learning on balance produces better results for society in both the short run *and* in the long run, regardless of interaction topology or of the number of players. In some instances, it produces equivalent (read equally dismal outcomes), but in no instances, from a societal perspective, does DB learning outperform DC learning when Suspicious TFTers are involved. Put another way, when there is a sufficient level of distrust already in the system (represented by the presence of Suspicious TFTers), prejudice tends to pay for society as a whole.[7]

Conclusion

The thought experiments described in this paper both confirm and challenge our conventional understandings of the origins of conflict and cooperation. That TopolCon can replicate Robert Axelrod's pathbreaking insights about the shadow of the future's role in framing the prospects for cooperation based on reciprocity lends additional support for their validity. Our results confirm his general finding that it is difficult to sustain traditional TFT strategies at the systemic level without context preservation, for "the foundation of cooperation is not trust but the durability of the relationship" (Axelrod 1984, p. 182). As a result, mechanism 1 – a long shadow of the future increases the likelihood of emergent systemic cooperation – gains further authority.

Yet it is quite dramatic that two simple changes in modeling assumptions can effectively obliterate the possibilities for cooperation, and the sensitivity of the general framework to initial conditions motivated the investigations in the previous sections. In the section on "The shadow of the future's fragility," the replacement of Traditional TFTers with Suspicious TFTers in the initial distribution of players suffices to undermine the interactive mechanisms that would otherwise have produced a cooperative regime. The prospects for emergent cooperation rise with the number of players under the FRN interaction topology. The sustainability of cooperation without a central authority would therefore seem to rely quite heavily on where and when the given game begins, which in turn is wholly shaped by the memories players bring to the race's starting line, as well as by the number of individuals lining up in the blocks.

---

[7] There is one curious wrinkle in these findings, and that is the result obtained with a large number of players (10,000), Suspicious TFT, and the 2DK interaction topology. In this instance, the DB function does not converge to any sort of equilibrium but is certifiably chaotic. What renders it so is beyond the scope of this paper; the phenomenon surely merits further investigation.

We might perhaps even go so far as to say that the Axelrod vision of cooperation based on reciprocity, one that has become conventional wisdom in the subfield, inadvertently presupposes an understanding of reciprocity that is inherently culturally bound. It relies on the existence of players in the initial mix with a healthy sense of their own capacity to shape political and social outcomes, which is, after all, what the Traditional TFT orientation presupposes. Pessimists do not lead with cooperation. While world size influences the prospects for cooperative contagion, it only does so when Traditional TFTers are in the mix. When Traditional TFTers were replaced with suspicious ones, world size was not decisive in framing outcomes. What this seems to suggest is that the degree of optimism present in the system at time zero frames the likelihood of emergent cooperation. The more optimists one can inject into the system (an effect of increasing the number of players under the standard 25 percent Traditional TFT parametric assumption), the greater the probability of cooperation taking off and taking hold. Interestingly, as world size goes up under Suspicious TFT, systemic outcomes do not change in any significant way. Thus, from the perspective of society, a few more optimists in the system can affect macro outcomes in strikingly positive ways. In short, mechanism 2 – a long shadow of past discord decreases the likelihood of emergent systemic cooperation – rings true, but to this we might add that a small number of optimists can have an immense societal impact.

Introducing the possibility of difference-conscious learning to the mix in the section on "Learning and prejudice" generates three significant findings. First, DC learning effectively derails the cooperative train that can be driven by DB learning when conditions are right. Second, in a world with Suspicious rather than Traditional TFTers present at the creation, society as a whole fares slightly better on balance when agents allow prejudice to shape what they learn from their social interactions. Just as the critical mass presence of agents who are coded to lead with cooperation facilitates further cooperation, a society where a majority of individuals are inclined to mistrust until given reason to trust sets in motion a dynamic where mistrust and prejudice pay over a range of interactive contexts. Third, even in those scenarios where cooperation does take off, there is a critical distinction between short-run and long-run performance, DB learning usually producing suboptimal results from a systemic perspective in the short run.

What these three findings taken together suggest is that mechanism 3 – the capacity to learn from the "other" increases the likelihood of emergent systemic cooperation – requires further refinement, as DB learning does not always produce the best societal outcomes. In general, DC learning pays for society in the short run, regardless of interaction topology, the initial presence of Traditional or Suspicious TFTers, or the number of players.[8] In the long run, however, DB learning has a large potential payoff when initial conditions are optimal. Again, context matters.

A game theorist might argue that one does not need computer simulation to show that Axelrod's model is sensitive to initial conditions, since the folk theorem of game theory, proved in the early 1950s, demonstrated that full cooperation can be sustained as an equilibrium, often in multiple ways, in some indefinitely repeated games (Fudenberg and Maskin 1990). While this is indisputably true, the folk theorem of game theory can tell us nothing about which equilibrium will prevail when multiple equilibria exist (Binmore 1998, p. 2). It is also mute on multilateral interactive processes involving 256 or more players, the kinds of complex adaptive system on which this paper has focused. And while any equilibrium outcome is logically linked to a certain set of initial conditions, it is precisely how TopolCon responds to changes in initial conditions over time that is most illuminating and has the greatest potential for advancing our understanding of real-world causal mechanisms.

Rather than bracketing the potentially disruptive fact that initial conditions matter, we should instead reflect on just how they matter, especially given the robust finding that context preservation is the key to cooperation. In short, what we need is a "contextual approach to strategy," as Robert Axelrod and Robert Keohane maintained almost twenty years ago (Axelrod and Keohane 1986, p. 228). Theories that "have a one-size-fits-all approach to regions and time periods should be replaced with theories that reflect the highly contingent and context-dependent nature of phenomenon" (Beck, King, and Zeng 2004, pp. 379–80). In this sense, agent-based models such as TopolCon, with their focus on interactive processes at the local level that have global ramifications, provide a new means of contextualizing strategy. Such models "defy classification as either micro or macro in kind but instead provide a theoretical bridge between them" (Macy and Willer 2002, p. 7).

If context matters so profoundly, surely an improved understanding of how our assumptions frame the outcomes of the models we make is a critical component of coming to terms with context. Since initial conditions, at least the ones examined here, are indisputably products of history, it is therefore unwise to detach historical studies from agent-based modeling of the sources of cooperation; the two research agendas are in reality intrinsically intertwined. Because temporal context is

---

[8] One wonders whether this might be a part of the reason why most societies typically first develop with stark attention to difference.

a critical part of getting the puzzle right in the first place, historical knowledge is a precondition for meaningful agent-based models. In turn, agent-based modeling can help students of comparative and international politics to transcend the small-numbers problem of necessity present in serious historically oriented work. We need to think in terms of patterns that can emerge over time, and ask what interactive effects *and* initial conditions produce those patterns, since the shadow of the future, whether our methods acknowledge it explicitly or not, is always very much a prisoner of the past.

8   Chicken dilemmas: crossing the road to cooperation

*Joshua S. Goldstein**

The metaphor of "playing chicken" recurs in both public and policy-elite discussions of international relations (IR). For example, the metaphor was used by *The New Republic*, *Newsweek*, and *Time* to describe the Soviet Union's pressure on independence-minded Lithuania in 1990, the stand-off between Iraqi officials and UN inspectors in 1991, and the US confrontation with North Korea over nuclear weapons in 1994, respectively.[1] In IR scholarship, Chicken has been invoked to describe the 1962 Cuban missile crisis, in which failure to reach agreement could potentially have led to nuclear war (Brams 1975, pp. 39–47; Brams 1985, pp. 48–62), although the preference orderings in that crisis may not actually have conformed with Chicken (see Brams 1994, 130–38; Langlois 1991). Schwartzman (1988) uses the chicken metaphor in discussing Cold War nuclear policies, and humorist Dave Barry (1984) once evocatively described the Cold War as "258 crucial world hotspots, where at this moment the United States and the Soviet Union, each with one hand on the steering wheel and the other on the horn, are simultaneously edging into the same parking space ... "

The chicken metaphor has not, however, played much of a role in the development of IR theory. Rather, mainstream IR theory in the 1980s and the 1990s – specifically neoliberal institutionalism – revolved around the formal model of iterated Prisoner's Dilemma (PD). Keohane's (1984) extremely influential *After Hegemony* exemplifies the approach (see also Oye 1986a; Baldwin 1993). Neoliberalism has developed the theme that reciprocity, reinforced by related norms and institutions, can resolve the

---

* This material is based upon work supported by the National Science Foundation under Grant No. SBR-9617157. For valuable comments on an earlier draft, I thank Barry O'Neill and Steven Brams. For useful suggestions I thank Shibley Telhami, I. William Zartman, Paul Wapner, Louis Goodman, and Nanette Levinson. Elizabeth Kittrell provided research assistance, and American University School of International Service provided research support.

[1] *New Republic*, April 16, 1990, pp. 8–10; *Newsweek*, April 4, 1994, pp. 36–37; *Time*, October 7, 1991, pp. 32–33.

dilemma of the iterated PD game, and hence – by implicit or explicit application – solve many of the world's international conflicts. Axelrod's (1984) work on the "evolution of cooperation," with its "tit for tat" strategy of reciprocity, was aimed squarely at IR as a prime venue for applying the theory (see also Taylor 1976; Keohane 1984; Axelrod and Keohane 1986). IR scholars both inside and outside the formal modeling community have since applied this paradigm to a variety of historical and contemporary contexts, including US–Soviet and US–Soviet–Chinese relations during the Cold War (George, Farley, and Dallin 1988; Goldstein and Freeman 1990), arms races (Downs, Rocke, and Siverson 1986), disarmament (Evangelista 1990), trade wars (Conybeare 1986), monetary coordination (Oye 1986b), and debt negotiations (Lipson 1986b). No equivalent body of work currently exists for Chicken.

Most of the efforts to apply Chicken to IR took place in the 1960s and 1970s. O'Neill (1994, pp. 1010–13) shows that, contrary to myth, game theory in general and Chicken in particular were not influential in the formulation of US nuclear strategy in the 1950s and 1960s. However, Chicken-based models have been used in several studies of escalation (see O'Neill 1994, p. 1015; Kahn 1965, pp. 10–15, 225–26). And by the early 1960s some people interested in nuclear strategy – Bertrand Russell, Thomas Schelling, and Herman Kahn – took an interest in the chicken metaphor (not yet as a formal model). In the 1970s Snyder and Diesing (1977, pp. 107–22; Snyder 1971) used Chicken, along with PD, as one of several game-based categories of international crises, and Jervis (1978) briefly analyzed Chicken dynamics in the context of deterrence under the security dilemma (see also Glaser 1997).

Because Chicken dilemmas regularly confront policymakers, yet remain underdeveloped in IR theory, better understanding of the game would serve scholars and practitioners. This article presents no new formal modeling but discusses the application of Chicken games to IR. It summarizes relevant work in social psychology, game theory, and IR, and offers advice for players of international Chicken.

What is Chicken?

The game of Chicken is both a metaphor in common language and a formal model in game theory. In the original chicken metaphor (of Bertrand Russell), two teenage boys drive cars straight at each other. There is a point of no return after which, if neither has swerved, a collision occurs. The driver who swerves is "chicken" and loses face, while the driver who does not swerve rises in stature. If neither swerves there is a

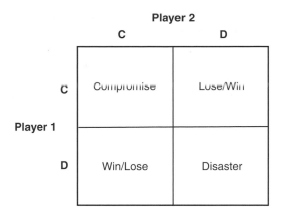

Player 2

	C	D
C	Compromise	Lose/Win
D	Win/Lose	Disaster

Player 1

Notes: C = Concede, D = Don't concede.
Chicken is defined by the ranking of both players' preferences regarding outcomes:
Win > Compromise > Lose > Disaster.
The two equilibrium solutions are Win/Lose and Lose/Win.

Figure 8.1. The structure of Chicken

head-on collision at high speed. Winning at a status competition is a powerful incentive for teenage boys, but not worth dying for.[2]

Chicken is defined formally by an ordering of preferences over four outcomes in a 2 × 2 game. Each driver chooses, at the point of no return, between "concede" (swerve) or "don't concede" (don't swerve),[3] defining the 2 × 2 game with four possible outcomes. The game is Chicken if both players share the following ranking of possible outcomes: each would most like to not concede while the other concedes (make the other player swerve); next best would be for both to concede (both swerve, minimizing loss of face); third best would be to concede unilaterally (becoming a chicken); and worst would be for neither to concede (a head-on collision).

Figure 8.1 shows the outcomes that the players of Chicken associate with each pair of choices. Brams and Kilgour (1987, p. 551) use the terms "disaster," "win," "lose," and "compromise." The game is defined by the combination of each side's preference orderings: to win is best (unilateral

---

[2] The James Dean film *Rebel Without a Cause* features a game in which two teenage boys drive cars over a cliff, trying to jump out in time but not first. The game is not formal Chicken.

[3] These terms are equivalent to the common PD terms, "cooperate" and "defect," or such other terms as "cautious" and "bold," "tough" and "soft," "yield" and "fight," or just A and B.

defection), to compromise is next best (mutual cooperation),[4] to lose is third best (unilateral cooperation), and to experience a "disaster" is worst (mutual defection). Thus in Chicken, as in PD, if both players cooperate each does better than under mutual defection or unilateral cooperation, but not as well as under unilateral defection.[5]

The dilemma of Chicken lies in the formal deduction that the game has two equilibria, the win–lose and lose–win outcomes.[6] At either of these points, both players have no incentive to change their choice to concede or not. But which of these two symmetrical solutions will occur the model does not predict. Rather, in practice, each player tries to make her own preferred equilibrium "stick" – I shall not concede so you must. This leads to battles of will, bluff, and counterbluff, skirting disaster, and other such aspects associated with Chicken in popular metaphorical usage. Since the outcome is not predictable, a Chicken situation is inherently unstable. The chicken metaphor captures a common phenomenon – bargaining for one's best deal without losing the whole deal – in a very simple model that IR policy makers or scholars who are not formal modelers can understand.

The difference between Chicken and PD is that in PD "disaster" is not as bad as "lose" – that is, the worst and next-to-worst outcomes are switched. In Chicken, any deal is better than no deal (Hardin 1982, pp. 168–69). In PD, by contrast, a bad deal is worse than no deal. This seemingly minor difference leads to substantial differences in the dynamics and outcomes of the two games (Snyder 1971, pp. 82–93). Although Chicken reaches cooperation more often than PD, failure to do so is more costly.

Like PD, Chicken presents a dilemma in which eliciting cooperation is problematical. In theory, a repeated Chicken game resembles iterated PD in some ways, and the use of reciprocity to solve the dilemma works in both cases (Axelrod and Keohane 1986, p. 244; see also Keohane 1986; Larson 1988; Leng 1993). As has been noted in a PD-centric context, if players care only about relative gains – how they do compared with

---

[4] Pruitt (1998, p. 479) emphasizes that negotiation may reveal "win–win" solutions which are Pareto-superior to any "simple compromise" between two parties' initial negotiating positions. These are still forms of "compromise," since they reduce utility compared to a "win."

[5] As with PD, Chicken can be played in n-person versions. The main dilemma remains and the issue of coalition formation is added. On the psychological effects of adding players, see Rubin and Brown (1975, p. 64). On the scramble to commit to defection first in an n-person Chicken game, see Ward (1990).

[6] In the formal model there are three such equilibria – the win–lose and lose–win outcomes, and a mixed strategy of choosing randomly with certain probabilities of defecting or cooperating. Maynard Smith (1982, pp. 12, 15–16) develops a game to model animals' competition for resources, which sometimes conforms to Chicken (when $V<C$ in his terms); when this is true, the mixed strategy is an "evolutionary stable strategy."

another player – there is no mutuality of interest (Grieco 1988; Snidal 1991; Powell 1991). International conflicts are then zero-sum games in which neither communication nor reciprocity help. If both absolute and relative gains matter to players, then as the weight given to relative gains (compared with absolute ones) increases, games of Chicken transform into PD at some point, while Coordination and Harmony transform first into Chicken and then into PD (Snidal 1991).

Compared with PD, however, Chicken has somewhat less of a long-term character. For example, Lichbach (1990, p. 51) argues that Chicken seldom describes arms races. This may mean that the shadow of the future is a less important factor in Chicken. The shadow of the future is also complicated in Chicken by the future benefits of establishing a "crazy" reputation today at a cost. It seems doubtful that the strategy of graduated reciprocation in tension reduction (GRIT) – large, sustained, and explicit cooperative gestures to elicit cooperation – recommended by psychologists for players of PD (Osgood 1962; Lindskold, Han, and Betz 1986), would work well in Chicken. The large concession might instead convince the other side that it does not need to compromise. Nonetheless, Myerson (1991, pp. 324–31) shows that the strategy of tit for tat used by both players is an equilibrium solution in repeated Chicken that leads to full mutual cooperation (compromise as a stable outcome). However, he also shows that many other equilibria exist, depending on how much the players discount future payoffs, and these include equilibria that result in the win–lose and lose–win outcomes. Myerson shows that tit for tat is not subgame perfect in Chicken or PD.

A third game type emerges when one player's preference orderings match Chicken and the other's match PD. In this game, named "Called Bluff," the side which values "disaster" more than "lose" can rationally defect without qualms and the other must then rationally cooperate. Perhaps an example of Called Bluff is the 1994 US invasion of Haiti. The military junta could not be sure – in light of a zig-zagging US foreign policy in Somalia and Bosnia – whether President Clinton intended to carry out his threats. But in fact the US side could better absorb the costs of military conflict than could the weak Haitian junta, which retreated without a fight when Clinton called its bluff. Clinton later remarked, "people didn't believe me. When I finally had the planes in the air, they believed me" (Collins 1995).

Chicken situations in international relations

Chicken is not a model of IR in general. Contrary to some claims made on behalf of PD as a general model of IR (or life), what is interesting about

Chicken is that it applies only to certain select cases, notably endgame negotiations. Chicken defines a class of international cases that share structural characteristics. In structured multiple case studies based on game-theoretic models, a fairly small minority of the cases are classified as Chicken games (see Snyder and Diesing 1977 in international security and Aggarwal 1996 in international political economy). Thus, unlike the claims sometimes made for PD, Chicken is not a one-size-fits-all model for IR.

Past applications of Chicken in IR have focused on international security questions, especially on nuclear war as "disaster." But the game also occurs frequently in international political economy (IPE), where "disaster" (no deal) is neither as dramatic nor as costly as nuclear war. Even in the international security contexts, "disaster" is usually a loss that an actor can absorb (painfully), not a mortal blow like a head-on-collision or nuclear war. Lipson (1984) suggests that security contexts may resemble Chicken more often, compared with IPE contexts that resemble PD. However, he seems to base this on the idea that international security presents "sharper conflicts" than IPE, when in fact conflicts in PD are actually sharper than those in Chicken. I would suggest that, if anything, IPE more often resembles Chicken (any deal is better than none) compared with international security with its more intractable dilemmas (notably the security dilemma), which would seem closer to PD.

Aggarwal (1996, pp. 49–50) draws on the insights of Chicken (as well as Called Bluff and PD) in developing a "debt game" to model international debt renegotiations. In a Chicken situation, both debtors and lenders prefer a bad deal to default, which could destabilize both the national economy and the international financial system. If debtors fear a bad deal more, and creditors fear default more, a Called Bluff game results, with creditors giving in to concessionary terms of debt rescheduling. Aggarwal finds that only three of sixty-one cases he examines had the character of Chicken. The case of Mexico in 1985–87 presents a "classic game of Chicken" (Aggarwal 1996, p. 524, also pp. 278–81, 355–60, 425–27, 522–24, 530–32). Both Mexico and its bankers staked out hard-line negotiating positions, raising fears of default, but after US–IMF intervention a compromise was reached. Soon after this episode, bankers took large loan-loss reserves to protect themselves in future such games (by more credibly threatening that they could withstand a default).

Historically, international crises that could escalate to war have fit the Chicken model at least occasionally. Snyder and Diesing (1977, pp. 108–22) classify three such cases as Chicken, but note that each is ambiguous. In the 1938 Munich negotiations over Czechoslovakia, it is unclear whether Hitler really did not mind using military force if the British and French did not concede, whether the latter minded conceding anyway, and whether the players' subjective estimates even roughly corresponded with objective realities (pp. 111–13, 119–21). More plausibly, the 1948 Berlin blockade "was Chicken because both sides would probably have preferred giving up their goals to a serious outbreak of violence" (pp. 113–14, 120–21). The 1958 Lebanon crisis might be called Chicken because the stakes were not worth a superpower confrontation, but in fact the superpowers' goals were not incompatible (pp. 116–17). Snyder and Diesing conclude (pp. 121–22) that no clear-cut cases were found in which Chicken led to either a win by successful bluffing or a compromise after mutual bluffing.

Bargaining in a Chicken game

In a simple formal model, Chicken is a "nonnegotiated game" – one where the players cannot communicate regarding the outcome and therefore cannot make threats or commitments. But Chicken in IR is more often a game of constant and ongoing, though by no means honest, communication. In the original teenaged drivers case, we can imagine them talking with each other on cell phones while driving. We would have to outfit both cars with telephones to approximate how Chicken is played in IR. Indeed, Kahn (1965, p. 12) suggests that Chicken would be a better analogy for escalation if, among other things, drivers were "giving and receiving threats and promises while they approach each other." Misunderstandings about true intentions are a source of mistakes that lead to disasters and although communication does not solve this problem, it often helps.

A related difference between IR Chicken and most formal versions is that in IR there is rarely a predefined "compromise" outcome. Rather, the compromise emerges through a negotiation process (or some kind of protracted bargaining) aimed at bridging the gap defined by the bargaining space between "win" and "lose," with disaster lurking as the cost of failure to reach an agreement. In the Cuban missile crisis, the US and Soviet leaders, after talking on the hotline and sending feelers through back channels, resolved the crisis with an exchange of letters in which the Soviet Union agreed to remove missiles from Cuba and the United States promised not to invade Cuba (provided Cuba stayed on good behavior). This compromise, not predefined by the structure of the crisis at the outset, was how the two sides bridged the gap between a Soviet "win" (keeping missiles in Cuba) and a US "win" (unconditional Soviet withdrawal).

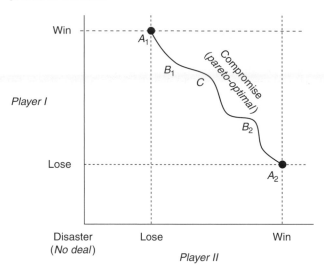

Figure 8.2. The bargaining sequence in Chicken

The compromise outcome thus results from a dynamic process, as bargainers try to close the gap between the two sides' stated "prices." The final agreement may be much closer to one side's bottom line than the other's. We may conceive of this dynamic bargaining process as movement along a scale of utility (value) for both players in Chicken (see Figure 8.2). The bottom left is "disaster" or no deal. Next worst is "lose" (a bad deal). Best is "win" (a good deal). The "compromise" outcome will be negotiated in the bargaining space between "win" and "lose." Each side would rather accept "lose" than have no agreement, yet each prefers its own "win." These win–lose positions, shown on the figure as A1 and A2, are the two equilibrium solutions in Chicken.

In the course of bargaining, one or both sides makes concessions which lower its own utility from the outcome while raising that of the other side (see B1 and B2 on the figure). Eventually, if bargaining succeeds, the parties reach a point (C on the figure) which is the compromise outcome to be achieved if both sides agree to the deal. This compromise point is not an equilibrium solution and is unstable while under negotiation, because each side can rationally think it can move the outcome point closer to its own most desired outcome by holding out for more. Only the "disaster" possibility creates a shared interest in cooperation, because without it, negotiating a compromise point between "win" and "lose" would be a zero-sum game.

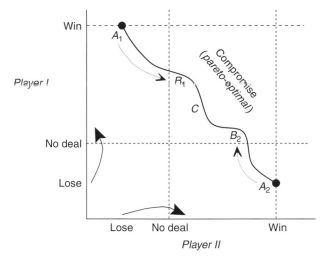

Figure 8.3. Transition from PD to Chicken in bargaining

Chicken often develops in the late stages of negotiations. As Schelling (1960, p. 70) writes, "Most bargaining situations ultimately involve some range of possible outcomes within which each party would rather make a concession than fail to reach agreement at all."

The process of bargaining can transform a game of PD into Chicken, as bargaining positions converge through a process of back-and-forth negotiation. This can be visualized on Figure 8.3. Here initially the "lose" outcome is worse than "no deal" (the disaster is not as disastrous as the bad deal being offered by the other player), creating a PD situation. In the course of negotiations, the two sides may offer terms that are better than no deal for the other player – "lose" shifts past "no deal" as bargaining positions move from A1 and A2 to B1 and B2. (If this shift occurs for one side first, the game passes through Called Bluff.) Thus, as positions converge, negotiations eventually reach a bargaining range in which any solution point is better than no deal to both sides – that is, Chicken.[7] Snyder and Diesing (1977, p. 118) describe a typical IR Chicken crisis as proceeding from mutual defection to bargaining (at which point the "distinctive characteristics of a Chicken crisis begin to appear") and eventually to one or both sides' yielding and a settlement being reached.

---

[7] It is just as possible theoretically, if not in practice, for Chicken to emerge from PD by the "no deal" outcome becoming less attractive to both sides, rather than the bargaining positions becoming more attractive.

The transformation of PD into Chicken through bargaining resonates with Zartman's (2005c) discussion of the "toughness dilemma" faced by a bargainer who must decide when to hang tough (to make an agreement more favorable) and when to soften (to make an agreement more likely). He suggests that a player in a PD-type situation would open soft and then toughen if the other side is not forthcoming (following "tit for tat"). However, in a Chicken-type situation, Zartman suggests, a player would be expected to start tough (to stake out a favorable position) and then soften at some point (to reach a deal). Zartman notes three key time points in a typical negotiation process – when the first concession is made, when negotiations turn to core issues midway, and when closure is at hand. If, as I am suggesting, a PD situation typically passes through a Chicken phase before final agreement is reached, then Zartman's formulations would suggest a bargaining strategy of opening soft and following with reciprocity in the PD phase, but then toughening again as the game reaches a Chicken stage, and finally softening to close the deal and avoid disaster after getting the best terms one can obtain.

Bargaining dynamics have been handled by formal modelers in several ways. As Osborne and Rubinstein (1994, pp. 117–31) note, "models of bargaining lie at the heart of" game theory (p. 117). Rubinstein's (1982) bargaining game of alternating offers resembles Chicken in that "[n]o agreement is worse than disagreement" (Osborne and Rubinstein 1994, p. 119). For example, two people trying to divide a pie (and not receiving any until they agree on a division) face such a situation. Each player's impatience and risk aversion affect the outcome in this model. The structure of the bargaining process also affects outcomes (p. 127).

Time must be valuable, or bargainers would make no progress. Perhaps the pie is made of ice cream which is melting, or perhaps a catastrophe will occur (absent an agreement) at a certain time, or might occur over a certain time period with a certain probability. Alternatively, the lucrative deal that gets pushed into the future by absence of an agreement incurs a cost in short-term benefits not received. Thus time is of the essence in bargaining models.

Rapoport argues that the mutual cooperation outcome (compromise) is the "rational" solution, despite its not being a formal equilibrium. Definitions of rationality affect how one views the game, in Rapoport's (1966, pp. 138–44) view. If a player knows that both players are equally rational, then an asymmetric solution (the formal equilibrium of win–lose or lose–win) does not make much sense. In a "metagame solution" the players adopt a rationality that is, so to speak, up a level from the short-sighted decision to defect unilaterally (Howard 1971). Metagames make mutual cooperation emerge as a logical choice of action in both PD and

Chicken games, more strongly in Chicken than PD. Brams (1994) develops a "theory of moves" in which rational players think about consequences far into the future. Games have "non-myopic equilibria," and in Chicken the mutual cooperation outcome is such an equilibrium, along with the win–lose and lose–win equilibria.

Experimental evidence

Rapoport and Chammah (1969) map the emergence of cooperation in experiments in which hundreds of paired students played Chicken or PD (with equivalent payoffs), without communication, 300 times in a row for small cash rewards.[8] They find two differences in Chicken from PD.

First, the harsher punishment for mutual defection in Chicken produces more cooperation overall as compared with PD. In the student experiments, cooperation overall is somewhat higher in Chicken than PD, and mutual defection only half as common in Chicken as in PD. Second, however, Chicken offers the prospect that one could get away with a long string of defections (since the other side would lock into the lose–win equilibrium) – a prospect absent in PD, where the best strategy in response to a defection is a defection. The experimental results showed some support for this idea. However, the effect of the first difference – higher cooperation in Chicken – is stronger than the more nebulous second effect. Thus, "there is more over-all cooperation in Chicken than in Prisoner's Dilemma …" Rapoport and Chammah (pp. 166–68) suggest that the *magnitude* of the punishment in Chicken outweighs the lower *probability* of actually being punished for defection (the chance that one could win repeatedly and get away with it). To the extent that this finding shows risk aversion to outweigh opportunism in such calculations, it resonates with prospect theory in psychology (see Levy 1992).

Rapoport and Chammah's results are summarized in Figure 8.4. Over the course of 300 rounds, overall cooperative play starts higher in Chicken (65 percent versus 47 percent in PD), experiences less of the downward spiral in the first 30 rounds (when PD players often develop tit-for-tat norms with frequent defection), and remains slightly higher than PD at the end despite the rapid learning curve in PD in rounds 50–200 (when reciprocity leads to more stable cooperation).

---

[8] "In actuality," they note, "the normative prescriptions of game theory are seldom realized in laboratory experiments." For example, in a fixed-length repeated PD game of 300 rounds, the formal equilibrium of constant mutual defection is not found; instead mutual cooperation increases over repeated rounds as students learn to overcome the dilemma.

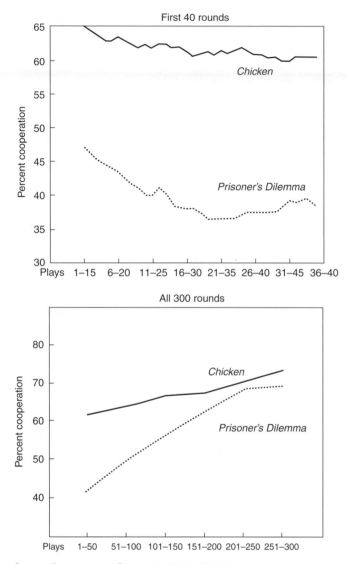

Source: Rapoport and Chammah 1969, 172–73.

Figure 8.4. Trends in cooperation in iterated Chicken and PD psychology experiments

Despite these differences in Chicken from PD, both show a similar learning process in which players first experiment with attempts to gain unilateral advantage, then develop the expectation of reciprocity which makes such attempts unproductive, and finally emerge into a phase of relatively stable and increasing long-term cooperation. Thus, in the experiments summarized in Figure 8.3, Chicken (like PD) shows a decreasing amount of cooperation during the first 40 rounds, followed by a long-term increase over the subsequent 250 rounds. Only after playing the game 100 times in a row do these students get back to their beginning level of cooperation. These results show the importance of individual learning – and presumably, by extension to IR contexts, institutional learning – for the gradual emergence of cooperation in a long iterated game, whether Chicken or PD (see also Komorita, Hilty, and Parks 1991).

Severity of the dilemma

Not all Chickens are created equal. The concept of *severity* or *mildness* of a dilemma, implicit in a given set of payoffs, emerged in the PD literature (Rapoport and Chammah 1965, p. 35; Axelrod 1970; Goldstein 1995, pp. 462–63) but applies to Chicken as well. A severe form of the dilemma is one where payoffs make cooperation especially hard to realize. In the Chicken bargaining context shown in Figure 8.2, severity could be visualized as a bending of the Pareto frontier up to the right (less severe, closer to win–win) or down to the left (more severe).

The presence of audiences can change payoffs, often making dilemmas more severe. To the extent that state leaders look good to their domestic constituencies by standing tough against foreign adversaries, cooperation in IR Chicken is more difficult to achieve. This audience effect drives up the value of "win" and the cost of "lose." In the teenage driver case, the presence of the audience makes it important not to appear "chicken." If a player's standing would be so reduced by losing that "lose" becomes worse than "disaster" – in IR, a leader might be overthrown at home if he capitulated internationally – then the game is PD and not Chicken.

In psychology experiments, players who received (secretly prearranged) derogatory feedback from an audience about their play – like the teenaged boy who is jeered by peers for being a "chicken" – defected more often in subsequent play than players who received praise for their play, for example for "playing fair" (Rubin and Brown 1975, pp. 43–54). Bornstein, Budescu, and Zamir (1997) compare Chicken games involving (i) two individual players; (ii) two teams of two players each (which face internal collective goods problems as well as intergroup ones); and (iii) four individual players (see also Bornstein, Mingelgrin, and Rutte 1996). Based on experiments in a psychology laboratory using student subjects, the authors conclude that cooperation is hardest to achieve in the inter-team setting where players must reach agreement within the team as well as implement a strategy towards the other team.

In territorial disputes the material stakes are typically relatively small compared with the potential costs of "disaster" – usually meaning a war over the territory and potentially a much wider and more costly war. This is especially true of disputes over territories that are not integral to national identity, like European states' nineteenth-century disputes over colonial holdings, or present-day disputes over islands rather than contiguous borders. Despite the low material stakes, however, territories sometimes have high symbolic value for states, and the domestic audience effect can be extremely salient in reducing cooperation in such disputes. This is especially true in cases where disputed territories contain populations with ethnic or religious ties to the inhabitants of a neighboring state. For example, in the Armenia–Azerbaijan dispute over Nagorno-Karabakh, the actual value of the territory by any tangible measure was hardly worth the severe devastation that Armenia suffered as a price for its ultimate military control – control which still does not give Armenia legitimacy or a legal right to the territory. The Armenian and Azeri publics had inflated the value of a "win," however, because the territory contained ethnic Armenians and because it was part of the sovereign territory of Azerbaijan – important identity issues for the two states. These audience effects may have increased the severity of the dilemma.

Territorial disputes are hard to settle quickly, however. When the status quo is disputed, there is always the option of leaving things up in the air, which may be less costly than either fighting or making a substantive compromise. Even when the costs of a hostile and potentially dangerous relationship make it irrational to continue in conflict over small stakes, there is seldom great urgency to the threat. Without an externally imposed deadline, the only push towards a settlement – making disaster loom large – may be a deliberate escalation or threat to use military force by the country not possessing the territory.

Threats and commitments

Players make threats which it would seemingly be irrational to carry out. By hanging tough credibly – ideally with a reputation as a crazy person – a player can nudge the final compromise in the desired direction. For instance, Henry Kissinger reportedly would tell Soviet leaders to take the deal Nixon offered them because Nixon was really a bit unpredictable and irrational. Chicken is a formal model in which *rational* players develop strategies and make choices in light of their expectations about the other player's rational decisions. Yet, in Chicken, the player who feigns irrationality – I would rather die than lose this game – gains a fundamental advantage.

Making such threats credible is a difficult problem. Players may use deception (about true preference orderings). A teenaged driver might yell, "I'm not swerving no matter what" while calculating when to swerve. Far more effective, however, would be to throw the steering wheel out the window in full view of the other driver (and before he thinks of the same plan). Faced with this irrevocable (self-binding) commitment, the other driver must swerve, being a rational actor who prefers swerving to dying (see Rubin, Pruitt, and Kim 1994, pp. 62–67, on "irrevocable commitments"). Thus the popular press invokes the chicken metaphor to describe situations of threat and bluff where two sides in a conflict are in a standoff, each trying not to "blink" first.[9]

Jervis (1978, pp. 77–79) ties Chicken to "the familiar logic of deterrence" in which one actor must convince another that the first will hold firm and therefore the second must back down to avoid disaster. Even when both sides enjoy a cooperative relationship, "the side that can credibly threaten to disrupt the relationship unless its demands are met can exploit the other." He cites the nineteenth-century collapse of the Franco-British entente as an example of a disaster arising from each side's belief that the other would not risk a valued relationship.

The problem of credibility of threats was central to US military strategy during the Cold War. US leaders tried to appear willing to destroy the United States to save Western Europe (an irrational action if actually taken). Assuming that the Soviet leaders really wanted to invade West Germany (which US leaders may have sincerely believed), the ordering of preferences would define a Chicken game in which "disaster" is a nuclear war; a Soviet win (US loss) is a successful invasion of West Germany with no escalation to nuclear war; and a US win (Soviet loss) is the status quo with no invasion of West Germany. A compromise outcome might, for example, cede limited West German territory to Soviet control.

By making it clear to Soviet leaders that the United States *would* escalate to nuclear war in the event of an invasion, the United States could win its preferred outcome by forestalling an invasion and not having to compromise. To make this threat credible despite its apparent irrationality, the US military spread thousands of tactical nuclear weapons among the forces deployed along the East–West border in Europe, preventing any

---

[9] In the world of business, Chicken is often used to describe labor–management relations in a strike situation that could end up damaging both sides. Schelling (1960, p. 12) uses the metaphor of traffic, in which one car must yield for both to avoid a collision. Rubin, Pruitt, and Kim (1994, p. 62) see Chicken as illustrated by a child custody dispute in divorce.

"firewall" from forming between conventional and nuclear war and making it likely that conventional war would automatically escalate to nuclear war. Thus Soviet leaders could not risk invading West Germany because, even though rational US leaders would not lose New York to save Bonn, the US leaders had entered into an irrevocable commitment to escalate and would not exercise control in the heat of the moment. The Soviet "doomsday machine" in the movie *Doctor Strangelove* had the same purpose, except they turned it on before telling the Americans about it!

In this context a player's reputation matters, at least in theory. It is unclear how applicable this really is to repeated Chicken games in IR, however. Jervis (1978, p. 179) argues that a reputation for toughness in Chicken can backfire when players find it hard to consummate beneficial deals with distrustful others. He mentions Bismarck's problems in this regard after 1871 because of his earlier aggressiveness. Ward (1990) analyzes a simulated "pregame" of Chicken, in which players could establish reputations; he finds that most of the time joint benefits are achieved despite a chaotic scramble to commit first.

Mercer (1996) raises more fundamental problems with the idea of reputation in international deterrence. He shows that acts of toughness or softness can be ambiguous and are often misinterpreted; "different people often explain the same behavior differently." Furthermore, when a player "loses" once in a repeated Chicken game, the loss might cause that player either to be expected to become softer in the future (because a norm of win–lose has been established) or to be expected to become tougher in the future (to seek revenge for the loss). Thus, in the real world of IR, there is little evidence of the phenomenon of defecting in an iterated Chicken game in order to establish a reputation so as to win future rounds. "Chicken has no dominant strategy and no determinant outcome. Since defeat may result in a reputation for either resolution or irresolution, it provides a shaky foundation" (Mercer 1996, p. 212).

Similarly, the US–Chinese crisis over Taiwan in 1996 illustrated the difficulty of making "irrational" commitments stick. The crisis itself was an offshoot of a China–Taiwan Chicken game in which Taiwan threatens to declare independence and China threatens to go to war if it does. Since such a war would be a disaster for China, the threat is "irrational," yet China has bound itself so firmly to it that Taiwan can believe it might really be carried out, with devastating consequences for Taiwan (as well as for China). In 1996, China conducted provocative military exercises near Taiwan (before a presidential election there), including firing nuclear-capable ballistic missiles directly over Taipei and into Taiwan's shipping lanes. Although the exercises themselves were very unlikely to be a prelude to an actual invasion, they could test reactions to a future Chinese invasion of Taiwan. Two months before the Chinese exercises, a senior Chinese defense official was told by a visiting former Clinton administration official that a Chinese attack on Taiwan would bring a US military reaction. He replied, "No you won't. We've watched you in Somalia, Haiti, and Bosnia, and you don't have the will." He also mentioned that "in the end, you care a lot more about Los Angeles than Taipei" – a statement which US policy makers apparently took as a nuclear threat should the United States intervene in a China–Taiwan war.

These Chinese postures would be well suited to staking out a tough position in a Chicken game over US defense of Taiwan. When the Chinese exercises began, the three top US foreign-policy makers each repeated to a visiting Chinese official the phrase "grave consequences" – diplomatic code for a military response, and a phrase not heard in US–China discussions in the previous two decades. Two US aircraft carriers sailed around the vicinity (though nowhere near the actual exercises) to underscore the point. Secretary of State Warren Christopher later recalled that "a simple miscalculation or misstep could lead to unintended war" (Gellman 1998). Yet not only did the episode pass peacefully, but it prompted a new effort to improve US–Chinese relations, leading to Clinton's 1998 visit to China in which he promised not to support Taiwanese independence.

The main problem with rational irrationality is that it gives away control and undermines the most central element of the rational choice paradigm – the ability to make deliberate choices in pursuit of one's self-interest. If both players manage to adopt the posture of rational irrationality simultaneously – each perhaps thinking it is throwing the steering wheel just in time to stop the other from throwing *his* steering wheel – disaster ensues.

Thus rational irrationality leaves little room for small mistakes. As Snyder and Diesing (1977, p. 199) note, Chicken crises "allow for less correction of misperceptions" than in PD crises. Yet, indisputably, actions of state leaders fall short of perfect rationality. Certainly communication is imperfect, and the game in IR is what formal modelers call a "noisy" one.[10] The "fog" of war (as Clausewitz described it) extends to some extent into international crises and even normal daily IR. Kahn (1965, pp. 11–12) finds Chicken a flawed strategy for playing international relations for this reason among others. Pruitt (1998, pp. 473–78) reviews the empirical evidence that psychological factors other than a pure

---

[10] "Noisy" PD games have been studied in some detail; the signal distortion makes it more difficult to reach cooperation in such games (Molander 1985; Fudenberg and Maskin 1990).

formal rationality affect outcomes of "social dilemmas." These factors include social values and relationships, trust, social norms, and group size. Jervis (1988) points out some psychological factors that limit the applicability of game models in international relations. And Jones (1998, p. 32) argues that matrix games such as Chicken and PD have contributed little to social psychology, which instead has focused since the mid-1970s on negotiation and bargaining processes not easily captured by simple matrix games.

Because of these vulnerabilities to error, misperception, and accident, extremism is no virtue in Chicken. Up to a point, bluff, bluster, and stubbornness gain the player of Chicken an advantage. However, skating too close to the edge is very risky. Negotiations that stall may be hard to revive. Occasional disasters take a toll. Yet, ironically, disasters *must* occur from time to time in order to motivate players to avoid them.[11] Using a self-binding and rigid defection strategy, although advantageous in the rarified formal modeling context, works less well in the real world. "Good negotiators" are considered good because they can achieve a good deal for their side *without* losing the deal itself.

Because of the advantages gained by seeming irrationality, Chicken produces a strange outcome in terms of IR scholars' understanding of power: the less powerful actor often wins. Paradoxically, if power is defined as the ability to influence outcomes, this makes the less powerful actor more powerful. Weak players may have "less to lose" and therefore fear disaster less than stronger ones. A Chicken player who has "nothing to live for" can more credibly threaten to bring about mutual disaster than can the player who is well-fed, comfortable, and enjoys a high social status. Furthermore, the gap between "win" and "lose" may be a luxury for the powerful player but life-or-death for the weak player. Schelling (1960, p. 37) refers to "cases in which bargaining 'strength' inheres in what is weakness by other standards" (see also pp. 60, 67 n. 5). Schelling invokes the familiar frustration of parents who find punitive threats ineffective against children who cultivate reputations for lapses of self-control (p. 17).

In Chicken, then, sometimes the weak do what they will and the strong suffer what they must. However, weakness is not sufficient to prevail; often weak players feel the "disaster" effects more strongly than strong ones do, and get the short end of the deal in Chicken. Snyder and Diesing

---

[11] This point parallels the observation that after a major war survivors try hard to avoid a repetition, but over a few generations the first-hand experience with the pain of war fades, and new leaders become less cautious about getting into a war (Wright 1965, p. 230; Toynbee 1954, p. 322).

(1977, p. 482, p. 118) argue that "one side capitulates" in a typical Chicken crisis and that the weaker side will do so.[12] So neither power nor weakness predicts outcomes in Chicken.

Advice for players of Chicken

In managing international dynamics that resemble a Chicken game, several strategies may help produce cooperation and avoid disaster. The first step, of course, is to model the situation accurately, to see if it *is* Chicken – each of two players makes one of two moves, which jointly determine a set of outcomes preferred by both players in the order described by Chicken.

Set deadlines

First, Chicken games need deadlines to reach cooperation. Mutual cooperation – at *any* possible compromise solution point – is not stable because there are incentives to defect and dig one's heels in at a more favorable compromise point (or, indeed, at one's most favored outcome). Because of this instability, Chicken games tend to lead to intractable bargaining, in the absence of a firm deadline.

Without the presence of a real deadline beyond which the "disaster" outcome comes into effect definitively, the parties to a Chicken game have little incentive to make final compromises. A kind of statistical deadline might work if the relationship is in an unstable state where an accident or mistake could lead to disaster at any time, as this gives the players an incentive to reach agreement quickly rather than lingering in the dangerous state. But the additional instability does not help in the context of Chicken's indeterminacy. Rubin and Brown (1975, p. 123; and see pp. 120–24) argue that time limits – which may be "explicit or implicit, self-generated or imposed from without, flexible or rigid, and viewed in similar or dissimilar terms by the parties involved" – play a key role in negotiations. "[E]ven when bargaining is begun far in advance of deadlines, these limits are likely to be approached anyway."

---

[12] On power in negotiations generally see Zartman (1997b); Zartman and Rubin eds. (2000). Five other 2×2 games share with Chicken the property that a non-omniscient player does better than an omniscient one (Brams 1994, pp. 178–82). In the context of biological competition, Maynard Smith (1982, pp. 22–23) argues that asymmetries such as preexisting ownership of a territory, even when they do not alter the payoffs, create conventions that lead to settlements of conflicts.

The 1995 Dayton Agreement to end the war in Bosnia offers a good example. With domestic constituencies back home whose members had died for the issues at stake, state leaders had reduced maneuverability. The US government as a third-party mediator used its power to cajole each side into deals that were good for them (but not as good as they hoped to hold out for). The formula of last-minute agreement well describes the Dayton process. Negotiator Richard Holbrooke created a de facto deadline by bringing the participants to a closed air base and negotiating nonstop for three weeks. By the end, with everyone on the brink of total exhaustion, there was no choice but to make a deal or have the entire process collapse in failure. Up until the final moment, however, there was still incentive to hold out for a slightly better deal.

On the final day of negotiation, the entire deal appeared to fall through when the Bosnian government would not give up a final 1 percent of land as part of a last set of negotiations to arrive at a 51–49 split of the country. Secretary of State Warren Christopher (who had not slept in three days) called the Bosnian position "irrational. A great agreement is within their grasp" (Holbrooke 1998, p. 304, also pp. 303–09). Holbrooke used a "drop-dead time limit" and gave the Bosnian president one hour to agree (by midnight) or the conference would be declared a failure and permanently ended at 10:00 a.m. The Bosnians replied, an hour later, that they would cede the land only if they received the town of Brcko – held by the Serb forces – which Serbian President Milosevic was unwilling to give up. A "statement of failure" to be read at 10:00 a.m. was delivered to the participants, and by morning the media were reporting an "absolute crisis" in the negotiations. After 8:00 a.m., with 700 reporters waiting outside for the 10:00 a.m. announcement, Milosevic offered to "walk the final mile for peace" by submitting Brcko for arbitration in a year. The Bosnian side, facing the fact that "time had run out," agreed (Holbrooke 1998, p. 308). Evidently the Bosnians had not been as irrational as Christopher thought; they won an important concession without losing the deal.

In the 1998 Northern Ireland peace agreement, mediator George Mitchell simply declared Good Friday as the deadline, arranging for final negotiations in the preceding days which went around the clock until participants were exhausted and finally ready to sign on the dotted line. It is odd that sleep deprivation and fatigue, which reduce the brain's perceptual, cognitive, and affective abilities, can contribute to the resolution of international conflicts. (Sleep loss is not necessarily a *cause* of deal-making; both may result from "crisis" dynamics.) Yet in Chicken it seems to work; just keep the negotiators in session until they are exhausted, and they will come to a deal with the extra incentive of a good night's sleep. However, to be effective, deadlines must be in some sense real and not merely self-imposed by the parties. For example, the negotiations to implement the Israel–Palestine Oslo accords dragged on in the 1990s in part because self-declared deadlines had been missed often enough that nobody took them seriously any longer.

Use mediation

A second useful strategy in Chicken situations is to use mediation and arbitration to create narrowly focused choices between disaster on the one hand and a mediator or arbitrator's compromise on the other (see Rubin and Brown 1975, pp. 54–64; and Schelling 1960, pp. 143–45, 301–02).

Among other advantages, using mediators or institutions creates what Schelling called *focal points*. When a problem of coordination or bargaining has multiple solutions, participants focus on a solution that is unique and prominent (the prominence being context-dependent). For example, in the coordination problem of meeting someone in the large and busy Grand Central Station, players who could not communicate would tend to meet under the large, prominent clock. Precedent provides one source for focal points (Schelling mentions international debt settlements as an example); so do the "status quo ante" or "natural boundaries," such as rivers (Schelling 1960, pp. 67–68, also pp. 294–95). Psychological research shows that perceived fairness plays an important role in focal-point solutions (Pruitt 1998, p. 484).

Incidentally, although communication usually enhances the ability to find focal points, one can imagine cases where communication could impede cooperation by creating too many solution possibilities instead of forcing the players to a single compromise suggested by norms. For example, imagine the experiment of asking two people to divide a dollar. If they can agree on a division within 30 seconds, they get the dollar (divided as agreed); if not, they get nothing. This is clearly a Chicken game, and with communication allowed, one player may be tempted to say, "75 cents for me, 25 for you, take it or leave it" (at least as an opening negotiating position). Such negotiations might sometimes fail to reach agreement within the time limit. With no communication allowed, and each player required to come up with a solution independently, it is plausible that they would reliably arrive at a 50–50 split, because that is the only logical solution that the other player is likely to come up with independently.

Because of the instability of potential outcomes, it is difficult to find a single "compromise" outcome. As Schelling argues, in a Chicken-like situation:

any potential outcome is one from which at least one of the parties, and probably both, would have been willing to retreat for the sake of agreement, and very often the other party knows it. Somehow, out of this fluid and indeterminate situation ... a decision is reached. These infinitely reflexive expectations must somehow converge on a single point. (Schelling 1960, pp. 70–71)

Convergence on a solution in a Chicken-like situation can happen, Schelling (1960, pp. 111–13) argues, only at outcomes "that enjoy prominence, uniqueness, simplicity, precedent, or some rationale that makes them qualitatively differentiable." A focal-point outcome is one to which a party may retreat without creating an expectation of further retreat to come: "[P]eople have to dig in their heels at a groove." Schelling (1960, pp. 67–68, 111–13, also pp. 294–95) reinforces this point in terms of focal-point solutions, which have certain distinctive qualities. Notably, incremental shifts away from such an outcome are "impossible" (small concessions would only lead to larger ones as a player retreated from a focal point), so such solutions tend to stick. Once a deal is reached, the deal is seldom reopened but rather locked in by both sides. When eaters sit around a table each with a piece of pie, it is much harder to renegotiate a different division of the pie than it was when the whole pie sat in the middle of the table. (If, after arbitration, a state decides it prefers mutual defection to the decision of the arbitrator, this by definition makes the game PD, not Chicken.)

In mediated bargaining in Chicken games, international norms and institutions play an important part in arriving at compromise solutions and thus averting disasters. Norms – shared expectations of social behavior – can help players to mutually define prominent potential solutions and narrow down the bargaining space to a few likely outcomes. Unlike focal points, which are self-enforcing, norms generally must be enforced by members of a group to prevent defection from paying. In IR the relevant norms have something to do with power, something to do with fairness, and something to do with routines, habits, and organizations.

Formally, McGinnis and Williams (1993, pp. 34–38) apply the idea of correlated equilibria to the role of international regimes in Chicken situations such as international crisis escalation. The players correlate (coordinate) their moves by referring to an outside device, which could be a random one like dice or a highly conscious one like an international institution. By following a sequence of moves prescribed by the coordinating mechanism but not known to the other side, the player of Chicken can be sure of receiving higher payoffs on average than by defecting from that sequence. For example, the correlating device could suggest (separately to each player) coordinated moves that result in equal numbers of "win/lose," "lose/win," and "compromise" outcomes but never in disaster. Even in a single-shot Chicken game, a correlated equilibrium can give payoffs superior to the Nash equilibria, though still short of a mutual cooperation payoff, which is not in equilibrium (Myerson 1991, p. 324).[13] McGinnis and Williams (1993) suggest that rival great powers might draw on a kind of correlated equilibrium when they use "spheres of influence" to regulate their decisions on military interventions in local disputes. Kydd and Snidal (1993, pp. 120–23) express both interest and skepticism in this approach. The problem, they conclude, is that international regimes do not appear to have developed such coordinating mechanisms to give states secret instructions. States would not cede such authority, and it is problematical to imagine who would exercise it (the UN? the world's only superpower? the IMF?).[14]

In cases where minor territorial disputes have threatened to hold up the comprehensive settlement of an international conflict, arbitration has proven a viable way to resolve the Chicken game inherent in the final stage of negotiations. For example, in the Dayton Agreement discussed earlier, each side vowed not to sign the accords unless it had control of the strategically located town of Brcko, considered very important by both sides. The "compromise" outcome of submitting the dispute to arbitration let each side retain a possibility for a "win" in the future.

Similarly, to finalize agreement on the Camp David accords, Egypt and Israel had to overcome a conflict over a resort hotel built by Israelis at Taba, just barely over the old border with Egypt. Both sides wanted the hotel, but not enough to break a deal. Submitting such a dispute for arbitration is a straightforward compromise that is prominent and can be accepted by both sides without losing face. The decision ultimately awarded Taba to Egypt. Note that international arbitration can seldom be "binding" – for example, Israel had physical possession of Taba and the arbitrator had no enforcement power to make Israel hand it over. Nonetheless, Israel *did* hand Taba over, because the cost of disaster – a breakdown of the entire peace with Egypt – was hardly worth risking over a resort hotel.

Argentina and Chile nearly fought a war in 1978 over disputed islands. With the prospect of "disaster" thus made real, the two states worked through twenty-two of their twenty-four separate border disputes by 1994, reaching viable "compromise" solutions. The last of these, over a mountainous region between the countries, was submitted to judicial

---

[13] By contrast, such correlation does not help in PD games at all, since the correlated equilibrium is the Nash equilibrium – mutual defection.

[14] On regimes as coordination games see Stein 1982; Snidal 1985. On security regimes as norms of reciprocity, see Jervis 1982.

arbitration. In the Argentina–Chile case, the arbitration panel on a split 3–2 vote awarded the disputed territory to Argentina. Despite the close vote (norms apparently were not very strong), and the fact that the "compromise" here turned out to be close to the "lose" outcome, Chile accepted the decision. In terms of audience effects, the arbitrated loss was not as costly as a voluntary one would be, so the compromise was still better than "lose." Acceptance does not mean quiet acquiescence. Chile protested vigorously, and two months later the Chilean and Argentinean contestants in the Miss World beauty contest carried on the struggle with a hair-pulling fight. Nonetheless, the agreement stood.

Mediation helps in trade disputes as in territorial ones. Several times in the 1990s, trade agreements among the major industrialized countries have been reached at the last moment after approaching the brink of a "trade war" – retaliatory tariffs that would create a downward spiral of the trade relationship. These cases appear to fit the Chicken model fairly well.[15] In trade disputes, the presence of materially interested domestic interest groups (such as industries and labor unions) increases the audience effect, making agreement more difficult. However, the highly developed and detailed norms of trade, and increasingly the third-party role of the World Trade Organization (WTO), make agreements easier.

The most prominent of the 1990s cases was the Uruguay Round GATT agreement, which wrapped up a global trade deal worth an estimated hundreds of billions of dollars to the world economy after seven successive years of failed attempts to conclude the agreement. In these years of intractable bargaining in the absence of a deadline, GATT was often called the "General Agreement to Talk and Talk." In the last stage of negotiations, France dug in its heels on its right to limit US films and television shows, which supposedly endangered French culture but which were a major US export product that mattered to US leaders. France would have been worse off torpedoing the whole GATT agreement than conceding ground on the US films, but it threatened to do just that (rational irrationality). Agreement was reached just a few weeks before an absolute deadline – the expiration of the "fast-track" authority granted by the US Congress to the president, without which he would not be able to approve the GATT deal. After the deadline, the whole deal would fall apart after years of negotiation had brought agreement tantalizingly close. The United States conceded the film issue to France and the deal was done. The entire negotiation made extensive use of established GATT norms and of the GATT negotiating forum as a third-party mediator.

---

[15] Note that the US–European "chicken war" discussed by scholars of trade was a conflict regarding trade in poultry, not a game characterized as Chicken.

Several cases of US–European agricultural disputes, several US–Japanese automobile trade conflicts, and several rounds of US–Chinese disputes regarding intellectual property followed parallel courses in the 1990s. In each case, the United States determined that the European Union, Japan, or China was unfairly excluding US products by using non-tariff barriers. Under the "Section 301" provisions of US law, the United States drew up a list of the offending country's exports to be slapped with large US tariffs in retaliation. There is a set period of time for the country to comply before the US tariffs take effect. Intensive negotiation took place during those weeks and, at the final hour, in each case the two sides came to an agreement. In these cases failure could have caused a downward spiral in trade relations such as occurred in the Smoot–Hawley era in the 1930s. The bargaining made little progress until the credible disaster of a trade war was at hand, marked by the impending imposition of the retaliatory US sanctions. For that to actually happen was in nobody's interest, making the US threat seemingly irrational.

Despite this repeating pattern in the 1990s, historical cases of "trade wars" do not generally seem to conform with Chicken. Conybeare (1986, p. 164; see also Conybeare 1987, pp. 39–47) finds that of the three historical cases of trade wars he considers, none of the three was a Chicken game. The closest was the French–Italian tariff war of 1887–98, which he characterizes as "Called Bluff" (and in which the weak countries ultimately capitulated). Conybeare argues that trade conflicts of the 1980s also had this character, with the United States and other rich countries able to impose terms on poor ones which cannot afford the cost of mutual defection. Conybeare (1987, p. 47) argues that countries with complementary economies are more likely to play Chicken, whereas those with competitive economies will more likely find themselves in PD. Snyder and Diesing (1977, pp. 108, 121) list the autumn 1960 trade dispute between East and West Germany as Chicken, but this was more than purely a trade question.

Conclusion

Classifying preference orderings in international conflicts is somewhat subjective and open to interpretation. The Chicken model as applied to real-world IR is fuzzy around the edges, and connecting the formal model with the real-world situation is not straightforward or merely technical; it is interpretive. Thus the scientific basis of Chicken models and their utility for understanding IR – although real – should not be overstated.

Nonetheless, across substantive issue areas in IR, the basic model of Chicken is an appropriate tool in certain times and places. Many international bargaining processes pass through a Chicken phase just before resolution, even if they began with a different payoff structure. In other contexts, especially where "rational irrationality" comes into play as a strategy for maximizing gains despite high risks, Chicken seems to fit well. Examples of Chicken recur in both international security affairs and international political economy.

Because Chicken appears to be more common in IR than is generally recognized, researchers should think twice before assuming that a mixed-interest game resembles PD. Some of the lessons of the "evolution of cooperation" under PD also apply to Chicken – most importantly the viability of reciprocity as a strategy for eliciting cooperation in a repeated game. In other ways, however, Chicken differs substantially from PD. These differences include, in Chicken, greater incentives for cooperation, unstable bargaining with rational irrationality, the importance of focal-point solutions (enhanced by norms and institutions) and of deadlines, and the stability of final compromise outcomes.

Practitioners in international relations can benefit by incorporating knowledge of the Chicken game into their bargaining strategies. The late stages of bargaining frequently create a nerve-wracking context in which one tries to maximize gains while avoiding failure. Two approaches discussed in this chapter – setting firm deadlines and using outside mediation – can help international negotiators navigate this difficult phase and arrive at the elusive goal of cooperation.

9   Conflict management as cooperation

I. William Zartman

While cooperation and conflict management may often seem to be synonyms, they are in fact parallel concepts with a large but not total overlap. Cooperation refers to a situation where parties agree to work together at some cost to each to produce new gains for each that are unavailable to them by unilateral action. It means combining conflicting interests in order to attain common interests, as developed in Hopmann's chapter, above. Conflict management refers to the reduction of the means of pursuing a conflict from violent to political or, more broadly, to measures to move a conflict toward resolution (elimination of the incompatibilities in the parties' positions on an issue). Conflict management can be accomplished bilaterally or multilaterally, depending on the type of conflict; that is, a party can manage its conflict with its adversary cooperatively,[1] or it can cooperate with other parties to manage someone else's conflict. In a word, it is a matter of negotiation or mediation.[2] So one can say that all cooperation involves some conflict management but not all conflict management involves cooperation.

One may begin with the assumption that states (and most parties in general) prefer to act alone. Cooperation has its costs, as noted, and states in particular prefer unilateral action because they have their own special interests and because they are sovereign. Thus, when faced with a common problem or a conflict, a state (party) has the choice of acting alone, acting with others (cooperatively), or not acting at all. But in dealing with a conflict in which it is involved, it also has a choice of using cooperative or confrontational measures.[3] Consequently, it is assumed as a starting point

---

[1] As will be discussed later, to "conflict cooperatively" is not an oxymoron; it does not mean surrender to the other party, but rather pursuing the conflict by direct communication with the adversary, using carrots rather than sticks to bring it into agreement to end the conflict peaceably with as little change in the ultimate objectives as possible.

[2] "Mediation" is used here to cover all types of third-party diplomatic intervention; see Zartman 2005b; Zartman and Touval 2001.

[3] For a discussion of the attitudinal and negotiatory implications of confrontation (hardliners, warriors) and cooperation (softliners, shopkeepers), see Snyder and Diesing 1977; Nicolson 1963, pp. 24–27.

that a state will prefer to act (or not act) alone when faced with an external conflict and will act confrontationally (by definition) in its own conflict with an outside party. The basic questions for this chapter then become (i) when do parties cooperate with each other to manage other parties' conflicts (mediate) rather than either doing nothing or letting one of their number handle it alone? and (ii) When do parties adopt a cooperative strategy in pursuing their own conflict (negotiate) rather than pursuing a confrontational strategy?

The answer is deceptively simple: when they (perceive that they) have to. Of course that simplicity is enigmatic, since it begs the identification of "having to." So it can be reformulated as, when cooperation has a greater chance of success than unilateral or confrontational measures, and the cost of cooperation does not outweigh the benefits. Thus the answer involves two considerations: success and cost, echoing the definition of cooperation in the first place. Neither is an absolute, both appear in degrees, and the cost element involves, in turn, cost to other interests and costs to the operation itself. The default option is not to act at all.[4] If the conflict or problem is judged serious enough to warrant action, then the first option, as discussed, will be to act alone or to act in confrontation in the two situations; when that fails (in prospect or in fact), a state will act cooperatively, costs permitting.

But another consideration of great importance in making the decision comes into play: the effect of the choice on third parties. This is the special element in the conflict-management/cooperation overlap and the special focus of this analysis. This chapter maintains that the playback effect – the effect that the conduct of conflict through confrontation has on cooperation with one's allies – is a major and analytically neglected consideration in the decision to cooperate (or not) in managing the conflict. It will show that the international community of relevant bystanders will cooperate among themselves to try to induce a conflicting member to shift to cooperation when it gets too confrontational in pursuing its conflict with another party. When it is a question of inducing cooperation into two external parties' conflict, the bystanders often cooperate to induce a policy change away from confrontation. But, contrarily, when one of their members takes on the third-party mediator role of making another state's conflict policy cooperative, the bystanders tend to let it do the job alone,

---

[4] Looked at this way, it is easy to understand why states are slow and reluctant to act at all, whether that reasoning is valid or not in the instance. For discussions of the reasoning and challenges to its validity, see Zartman 2005b.

with minimal backing and lots of criticism, and let it take the rap for any shortcomings.

A countervailing element on a different dimension involves entrapment, affectively or operationally. When a party (state) becomes tied to a policy, it becomes very difficult to reverse course, particularly when the switch involves moving from confrontation to cooperation or the reverse. The party's internal machinery is geared to one course, and a shift often involves shunting aside one part of the bureaucracy in favor of another, an inter-agency infight (Allison 1971). But it also involves turning its back on a part of its public that it enlisted in support of its current course and seeking support from a different sector of opinion.[5] Not only are there operational difficulties; emotional and other affective ties are involved, running from relationships of trust to images of demonizing. In addition, bystanders may conclude from the shift to cooperation that the actor does not have the stamina to confront, and therefore cannot be relied upon as an ally; similarly, a shift from cooperation to confrontation undermines trust and credibility. The bystanders may then hedge their bets. These elements merit – and have received (Höglund 2010) – a separate and full discussion, not engaged here, but they need to be noted lest the following discussion appear to imply frictionless shifts from confrontation to cooperation and back again.

The following analysis is based on a number of salient case studies, briefly recalled. As such, the best it can do is establish that a particular effect or interactional regularity occurs and that a hypothesis is empirically as well as logically supported for further testing and refinement (Zartman 2005a). It cannot establish the fact that the effect occurs more than some other one, or with a particular frequency associated with some other condition. It would be nice to check this occurrence statistically, but, as is not always recognized, the data are notoriously unreliable. They cannot handle such questions as: how many instances are really similar? at what point in the course of events does one measure cooperation or confrontation? how does one handle mixed policies? how much cooperation does it take to outweigh confrontation in a given policy (how many carrots does it take to outweigh a stick?)? Only an analytical narrative of multiple case studies can make the case. But that methodology, in turn, cannot answer the questions, how many? how frequently? Each tool has its purpose, its results, and its limitation. But given the state of the hypotheses and the problem with the data, the multiple case study is chosen as most appropriate.

---

[5] The reactions of President George W Bush's supporters to the shift in policy toward North Korea and Iran is a vociferous illustration.

The playback effect

The playback effect, a cousin of opportunity cost and of the shadow of the future or reciprocation, is the impact of unilateral action on relations with third parties and potential allies in cooperation at other times and on other issues. If a state's unilateral action to manage a conflict is regarded positively or at least neutrally by bystanding states, the state is more likely to make that choice, the other considerations noted above being equal. After all, it is in bystanding states' interests as well not to act and to let someone else bear the costs of handling the problem or managing the conflict, so as not to compromise their own conflicting interests. On the other hand, bystanding states may feel proprietarily toward the problem or conflict, may have interests of their own that they feel the state acting unilaterally is not representing properly, or may not want someone else to reap the benefits of handling the problem or managing the conflict. Even though the unilateral state could handle the conflict or problem by itself, it would not be in its interest to do so if what it gains by conflict management is outweighed by the costs of alienating the third-party bystanders.

These concerns are accentuated in a world order system of limited hegemony such as the present one (Zartman 2009). The hegemon not only prefers to act unilaterally, it also has the means to do so. However, it does not have the means to act unilaterally everywhere every time, but only when success is likely and benefits outweigh costs, the criteria already noted. Bystanding states may be just as happy to free ride and let the hegemon act, except that unilateral action makes them useless, reduces their role and their chance of being consulted, and may well ignore their interests. As a result, the playback effect is even more important in a system of limited hegemony, paradoxically by the very fact that unilateral action is an even greater temptation for the hegemon. Tempted to act alone, a hegemonic state knows – or soon learns – that it needs others, now or the next time, and so needs to take into account the playback cost of unilateralism on future cooperation. It needs cooperation now, when it may not need it, in order to be able to get cooperation later, when it will. This is not just a piece of friendly advice; it is a major theoretical calculation that helps determine the answer to the cooperation question in managing conflicts.

But whose conflicts are to be managed cooperatively? The discussion thus far has been necessarily generic, to pose a base for further distinctions. It faces more difficult problems of practice in distinguishing between two types of conflict management. One concerns the choice of bilateral *cooperation in conflict* between a state and another party (state or not) as an alternative conflict strategy to confrontation – that is, negotiation. The other refers to multilateral third-party *cooperation in management* of a target conflict in which the parties are not one of the protagonists – that is, mediation. While the situations are very different, the above-discussed considerations, and particularly the playback effect, come into play in both cases.

Cooperation in conflict

Decisions to *cooperate in conflict*, using conflict management as a strategy alternative to hostile confrontation, pose a radically different means to the same end, that of achieving one's goals in conflict. In a bilateral conflict between the state and another party, the state is faced with a choice between hostile, confrontational measures and cooperative, conciliatory measures. The choice recalls the old Æsop fable about the contest between the sun and the wind over who could make the man remove his coat. While the intuitive sense of conflict is confrontational, a counter-proposal from the conflict management side is to "work it out" cooperatively to attain the same goal, or to redefine the goal so that it can be achieved while the other side also gains something – the "sun strategy." In the first, the state tries to pursue the conflict unilaterally, seeking to prevail by imposing a solution on the opponent, whereas, in the second, the state tries to achieve its aims bilaterally, through cooperation with the opponent.

The basic question of "which, when, and why?" is crucial – when and why states decide to pursue a bilateral conflict confrontationally, and when and why they decide to shift to a cooperative strategy in pursuing the same conflict. A cooperative strategy does not mean giving in; it means seeking roughly the same goals as in confrontation but seeking the opponent's agreement by giving something to the opponent in return. It means buying agreement with agreement, including compensations and concessions, rather than forcing it with punishments, using carrots or warmth rather than sticks or bluster. Three considerations are involved in the decision – effectiveness, cost-benefit, and playback.

The first consideration, of course, is that of effectiveness in achieving the state's goals or, more specifically, the comparative effectiveness of the confrontational versus the cooperative strategies. Cooperation does not mean giving in or giving up goals, but is an alternative means – as in Æsop's story – of achieving a degree of the same goals; conflict management, it will be remembered, involves changing the means of the conflict, not its ends. An important secondary question, not present in the confrontational strategy choice, is whether the demands of the opponent can be taken into consideration without leading to renewed demands in a stepping-stone process, leading to the appeasement trap. Since the cooperative option has to recognize the legitimacy of the opponent and its interests, even while defending its own concerns and goals, its adoption implies a shift from a zero-sum to a positive-sum view of the conflict and of the other party.

The second consideration is cost-benefit. This includes the operational cost of confronting versus that of cooperating, but it also counts the cost at home and abroad of changing its image and that of the opponent; the state will now be seen as cooperating with the enemy, previously qualified as dangerous, untrustworthy, hostile, and so on.

The third consideration is the playback effect of confronting versus cooperating. The costs of confronting in bystanders' eyes can include the costs of projecting unreasonable hostility, of enforcing secondary sanctions on bystanding states, and of losing a competitive position to cooperating rival bystanders, among others. These costs can be so high that they impel a state to look to other strategies and to pursue its goal through cooperation instead.

Conflicts pursued confrontationally do not frequently undergo a shift in strategies to cooperation, but conflict management specialists often argue that they should. Examples abound, each so idiosyncratic that it would do violence to reality to try to squeeze them into an aggregate data sheet and a statistical test. However, there are enough examples of the shift to provide the basis for an analysis of the elements in the decision. In each case, the story is generally well enough known to render a detailed history unnecessary, so that only the important features need be highlighted, with reference to appropriate literature. Bilateral examples come from Israel, South Africa, Germany, and China and Korea.

Israel's policies toward Arab states in general and Palestine in particular have followed a philosophy of confrontation, mirrored by the Arab side, but interrupted by rare moments of cooperation, a change of means with changes in ends that nonetheless maintained the conflict. If the shift to cooperation is rare, appeals to Israel (and Arabs) to make that shift are much more frequent; critics constantly urge a policy of live-and-let-live and good neighborliness on the states of the region, replacing zero-sum policies and perceptions with positive-sum relations. Of the three considerations involved in making the decision, the chances of success in a shift to cooperation doubtless play the largest role, as Israelis and Arabs mirror each other's perception of the other as untrustworthy and unreliable in holding conciliation agreements and positive-sum perceptions. But when the two sides did engage in cooperation in the pursuit of their conflict, it was because of the playback effect, as a result of bystanding states' pressure on them and assistance in doing so. Most pointedly, on the three occasions when the United States revised its friendly stance toward Israel to apply overt pressure – in 1956 in the Suez Crisis, in 1975 before the second Sinai withdrawal, and in 1991 in the Madrid process – it was to impel a shift from confrontation to cooperative conflict management (Touval 1982; Quandt 2001; Baker 1999). On the other hand, when Israel turned its passive confrontation to an active policy – 1956, 1967, 1982, 2006 – it made sure of a prior green light of various brightnesses from its protectors, whatever the negative playback effect among other bystanders.

The two most significant forays by Israel and its Arab opponents into cooperative ways of pursuing their goals were in the peace process of the 1970s and the Madrid and Oslo process of the 1990s. Both efforts followed a costly war for both sides, leading to a mutually hurting stalemate and a cost-benefit analysis of an alternative course, and both were based on a wary assessment of success. But the crucial consideration in both periods was the playback effect of a confrontation on bystanding states and the strong and patient efforts of external powers, with the United States in the lead, to work for cooperation in a Mideastern peace settlement. Without all three considerations being present, the policy shift would not have taken place, but that is merely to recognize that the effect of confrontation and cooperation on outside states was as important a consideration as the other two. Indeed, President Sadat's policy shift in Egypt was based on a bid for US cooperation, as a preliminary to cooperation with Israel, and the agreement of Israeli Prime Minister Yitzhak Shamir to come to Madrid in the first place was a consequence of a policy of cooperation with the United States, entrapping Israel under Shamir's successor, Ytzhak Rabin, into considering cooperating with the Palestine Liberation Organization (PLO) as a result. It took cooperation with leading states of the international community to make cooperation with the adversary desirable and possible.

Another striking case of turning from confrontation to cooperation was the miracle in *South Africa* in the first half of the 1990s (Sisk 1995). Among the several unique aspects of the settlement process was the fact that it was accomplished unmediated, without outside involvement. Both parties came to feel that a cooperative strategy was feasible – indeed necessary – as a way of achieving their goals, and that the cost was both acceptable and less than that of continued conflict. It is important to note that neither side altered its goals in the conflict – the majority to achieve political equality and therefore state control, and the minority to keep its social and economic privileges even without political power – but only altered their perception of the necessary means: both came to the realization that the only way to the goal was through a pact with the other, in an exchange of goals. But the key to this exchange lay in the hands of the international community, which imposed increasing pressure on and ostracism of both sides. To President F. W. de Klerk, the old regime was no longer able to provide security and prosperity for the minority or to control the dispossessed minority or to maintain its world position and legitimacy, and all these failures were involving steadily mounting costs on the world scene as sanctions mounted (Zartman 1995, p. 148). To the African National Congress (ANC), the fall of the Soviet Union meant the loss of major international support. To both, engagement in a cooperative strategy brought international support and approval. Although neither party's goals changed in their pursuit of their conflict, their means shifted to cooperation, induced by the need for cooperation within the international community, without which the confrontation tactics could and would have continued.

Federal *German* (BRD) Chancellor Willi Brandt's Ostpolitik in the late 1960s and early 1970s marked a notable reversal of the Hallstein Doctrine that refused recognition of and relations with the German Democratic Republic (DDR). By the beginning of the period, the Western allies had turned away from the commitment to a policy aimed at absorbing East Germany into the West (as, ironically, eventually happened three decades later) and began to head toward a policy that was to eventuate in the status quo recognitions of the Conference on Security and Cooperation in Europe (CSCE, the OSCE's predecessor) in half a decade. Only the BRD held out for the old policy (Hanrieder 1989, pp. 176 f.). Policy change actually began in March 1966, before the Grand Coalition government, and then under that government, which preceded Brandt's chancellorship (Haftendorn 2006, p. 210; Hanrieder 1989, pp. 186 f.); the reactions from eastern Europe were a counter-Hallstein (Ulbricht) Doctrine and then the Soviet invasion of Czechoslovakia in 1968, killing the timid démarche. But in the ensuring change in strategy, the BRD did not lose sight of its ultimate goal of a single Germany, even if by other means.

When the socialist government of Brandt took office in October 1969, it launched its own Ostpolitik, exchanging reunification for rapprochement (in Foreign Ministry negotiator Egon Bahr's phrase (Haftendorn 2006, p. 218 n. 30)) within the construction of a European order. (Hanrieder 1989, pp. 196 f.). In so doing, Brandt not only overturned the policy of confrontation but also brought West Germany into line with the rest of the West's policy during the years of detente, despite the immediate reaction of sensitivity and reservations from the West. "The Federal Republic needed the support of its allies," wrote Henry Kissinger (1979, p. 410), and indeed was responding to the playback effect from the West to its previous policy (Hanrieder 1989, pp. 198–200); "the Federal Republic did not want to isolate itself from the West" (Haftendorn 2006, p. 212). There followed treaties with the Soviet Union in August 1970, Poland in December 1970, the DDR in 1971, and Czechoslovakia in 1973, interspersed with a Quadripartite Agreement on Berlin in 1971. The policy lasted through the decade, when it was buried by a return of the Cold War to confrontation, taking the two Germanys with it (Hanrieder 1989, pp. 211–18).

Hanrieder writes,

Détente necessarily entailed a mix of conflict and cooperation: a readiness to show restraint in some areas and ... to compete and enhance one's own power in others, a willingness to draft an acceptable code of conduct on some issues and not on others, an inclination to freeze the status quo in some competitive situations and to accept possible changes in others .... Détente implied a readiness to leave aside the impossible to be able to attempt the possible. (Hanrieder 1989, p. 211)

But that shift from confrontation to détente only made headway within a positive playback effect from the bystanders. In the late 1960s, the BRD's confrontation policy was out of alignment with the new tack from the West and its response from the East, and so it changed to cooperation. Two decades later, continued cooperation left it stranded and alone when the West and East together turned back to confrontation, and Germany returned to a version of the original confrontation that eventually led to reunification on its own terms (Hanrieder 1989, pp. 213 f., 218). It was the playback effect that determined the other criteria, effectiveness and cost/benefit.

These three cases are all instances of smaller states shifting to cooperation (and back to confrontation) in response to playback from stronger allies. But the same effect operates on the great powers, and indeed the superpower, in response to the bystanders around them. US policies toward the People's Republic of China (PRC), the Democratic Peoples Republic of Korea (DPRK) and the Islamic Republic of Iran have taken many swings between confrontation and cooperation. Since the last is still in full swing, the case study will focus on the first two. In all three cases there is a clear conflict between the United States and the opponent, and US policy at least has been characteristically confrontational, with some occasional stabs at cooperation as a means of resolving the conflict (it is more difficult to have a firm grasp on the reality of the opponent's policy). Yet in all three cases the playback element has been so strong that it is impossible to discuss them as simply cooperation-or-not in conflict; they must also be analysed as cooperation in management.

In the *PRC* case, the United States and China were caught in a mutually hurting stalemate in their conflicts on the Asian mainland in 1970, the

United States bogged down in its entrapment in Vietnam and China engaged in military escalation along its border with the Soviet Union (Gibson 2006). The remaining side of the triangle, the conflict between the United States and China, centered primarily on Taiwan but also involving Vietnam, was too costly and dangerous a confrontation for the international bystanders not to be troubled. There was little chance that the substance of the conflict could be resolved but there was a possibility that it be conducted by cooperative rather than confrontational tactics. The bystanding international community stood by, critical above all of the Vietnam war but also of the danger of escalation on the Taiwan issue, with criticism being directed primarily at the United States, making it difficult for the United States to count on international support if either conflict intensified. The new US Nixon administration recognized the risks of its position and made subtle moves from the very first inaugural address to soften one of its conflicts (it then worked later to move to cooperation on the other, in Vietnam). As the Sino-Soviet confrontation heated up, the Sino-US conflict saw tiny delicate pairs of steps toward cooperation, beginning in July 1969. Pakistan, Hong Kong, and Poland were used as communication channels. These steps led to National Security Advisor Henry Kissinger's secret visit to China in July 1971 and then President Nixon's much publicized visit in February 1972 to sign a communiqué that made the basis of the conflict clear but pledged cooperative policies to conduct it.

The policy shift from confrontation to cooperation in the Sino-US conflict at the beginning of the 1970s was undertaken to reduce costs of one conflict within a nest of conflicts. In that sense, one consideration can be considered cost-benefit, the cost of confrontation not outweighed by its benefit. The second consideration, success, had little role to play, as both confrontation and cooperation worked toward a holding position in the conflict, not toward a victory. But the third criterion, playback, completes the causal list. The United States – and China – were concerned about losing support for a continuation of their confrontation, finding greater support for cooperation from a community of relieved, if surprised, bystanders who were concerned about the dangers of escalation and a larger war in the region.

In the *DPRK* case, US policy has taken many swings between confrontation and cooperation, grouped into two major acts, each with many scenes. They will be recalled in greater detail than the preceding cases because of their complicated and controversial nature. Relations in round 1, in the decade after 1984, followed a US policy of seeking cooperative solutions to the conflict; repeated North Korean defections on cooperation led to confrontation between US–UN pressures and escalated defections until a new round of cooperation was inaugurated (Gallucci, Wit, and Poneman 2005; Sigal 2000; Michishita 2003). More immediately than in the China case a decade earlier, the international community was alarmed over the danger of war on the Korean peninsula, and major states of the region – China and Russia – were worried about the dangers of escalation that even sanctions would pose.

Although the story probably should go back to the Korean war or even to the end of World War II and partition, for brevity and focus it will start in 1984, when US intelligence satellites noted the construction at Yongbyon of a second, large-scale reactor capable of producing weapons-grade plutonium (Mazaar 2001). With Soviet help, the United States got North Korea to sign the Nuclear Non-Proliferation Treaty (NPT) in December 1985, but Pyongyang then postponed the required International Atomic Energy Agency (IAEA) inspections and instead began constructing a third, giant facility and conducting nuclear-arms-related tests in 1989. The United States reacted cooperatively, recalling its tactical nuclear weapons from South Korea (ROK), and the DPRK responded by joining the Denuclearization Agreement for the peninsula and signing the IAEA safeguards agreement which opened up North Korea to inspectors. The United States and South Korea then suspended for a year (biennialized) their annual joint military exercise, "Team Spirit," and the United States engaged for the first time in direct talks with the North in 1992. The talks were suspended when the IAEA found its inspections blocked; the United States and the ROK resumed "Team Spirit" to put on pressure for renewed negotiations and inspections, whereupon the DPRK gave its ninety-day notice of withdrawal from the Non-Proliferation Treaty. The United States returned to the table in June and July 1993; the two parties issued a statement in which the DPRK suspended its withdrawal from the NPT and pledged to resume "impartial" inspections, and the United States agreed to support the supply of a light water reactor (LWR) for the North.

For the rest of 1993, the North dragged its feet on inspections, the United States ratcheted up pressure until Super Tuesday at the very end of the year (December 29) when the conflict ratcheted down: the DPRK would allow the IAEA access. The DPRK–ROK talks would resume, then "Team Spirit" would be permanently cancelled, then the DPRK–US talks would resume. Each of these steps in the carefully orchestrated dance proved to be an incitement to distrust rather than a confidence-building measure, giving rise to a new series of US–UN pressures. DPRK blockage of IAEA inspections led to rumors of defensive missile armament of the ROK; the DPRK's flat refusal of access for the IAEA led to threats of sanctions, which the DPRK warned was an act of war, threatening to turn the South into a "sea of fire."

US talks brought about the return of inspectors a year later, which by May 1994 found evidence of spent fuel being removed from Yongbyon, reinforcing the need for challenge inspections. The United States began to explore sanctions, which interested bystanders such as China and Russia opposed and the DPRK called "tantamount to war." Into the mutually (self-)hurting stalemate stepped the *deus ex machina* intervention of the former US president, Jimmy Carter, in June 1994, on the invitation of the then North Korean leader Kim Il-Sung. It saved the scene from consummated crisis and provided a formula – nuclear freeze in exchange for civilian light water reactors – as a face-saving retreat to agreement for both sides. Kim died soon after, but the United States moved to buy compliance on this issue with a package of incentives. On this basis the third round of high-level talks took place in October 1994 and ended in an Agreed Framework spelling out the formula: nuclear non-proliferation in exchange for bilateral political and economic relations. It took repeated retesting of the formula through a ratcheting up and down of relations to make the cooperation path come to fruition. As the US negotiator, Assistant Secretary of State for Political–Military Affairs, Robert Gallucci, summarized,

Looking back, one can indeed find evidence to support the view that the elements of an Agreed Framework could be discerned before the October signing ... The Agreed Framework could not have been achieved on day one of the crisis; the parties first had to traverse the Emerald Forest of exhaustive negotiations, threats of UN Security Council sanctions, military buildups and mounting global pressure in order to lay the groundwork for closing the deal. (Gallucci et al. 2005, p. 163)

Several elements in this act are evident: events rolled up and down the hills and valleys of conflict, the US conflict strategy was cooperation mixed with a threat of confrontation to "rule out extreme option?" (Mazaar 2000, p. 308), and it was coordinated with all other interested bystanders (China, Soviet Union Russia, Europe, even the obstreperous ROK). As highlighted in Gallucci's final sentence, what brought the parties back to renewed cooperation was the disapproval of the impending military confrontation if they kept on their collision course. Institutionally, cooperation was expressed through the UN Security Council, whose members threatened but at the same time refused sanctions and along with the refusal urged the United States to return to a cooperative search for a formula. This is not to say that both sides were equally responsible for walking away from cooperation: the United States merely insisted that the basic agreements of cooperation be implemented for cooperation out of the conflict to continue, whereas the DPRK defected and then reacted to the reactions. But a simple consideration of success and of cost-benefit did not provide the mechanism for returning to cooperation, whatever the conclusions of the analysis might have been.

Act Two began at the end of the decade, when the United States discovered that the North had surreptitiously defected again. Having gotten respite, the DPRK continued its armament program on another tack by testing its long-range Tepodong-1 missile in August 1998. When the United States and Japan threatened to suspend their nuclear power aid, the DPRK increased inspections access, but continued its missile and nuclear programs. The results of a study by the new Bush administration and the ascendancy of hardliners among his advisors brought cooperation under the Agreed Framework to a halt. The United States then decided again on a cooperative strategy of engaging the DPRK, this time incorporating the playback effect in the engagement itself by negotiating along with Russia, China, Japan, and the ROK in six-party talks, while at the same time keeping its ratchets handy. The DPRK began using spent rods for reprocessing into bomb fuel in January 2003, and the six-party talks began. By June 2004 the United States agreed to positive steps in response only to a full nuclear freeze and dismantlement in the North.

The process advanced to produce a Six-Party Agreement, under which the North would give up its nuclear programs in exchange for aid, security assurances, and eventual normalization of relations (i.e., full cooperation). Again, the North defected on the details, and the United States opened a new front of pressure by imposing sanctions on banks laundering DPRK-counterfeited currency. So the DPRK launched a longer-range version of its Taepodong missile. The United States again began a double cooperative strategy – opening discussions with DPRK but conducting them multilaterally, as the six-party talks, including China, Russia, Japan, and the ROK. The talks covered the same mountains and valleys over the following five years, with the valleys marked by continued testing of long-range missiles and finally a claimed nuclear explosion in 2007. But in the end they produced a Joint Statement in the third session of their fifth round on February 13, 2007.

In Act Two, the playback effect was institutionalized in the six-party talks, again dictating the choice between cooperation and confrontation in the conflict. The success and cost-benefit components were ambiguous at best, and were the meat of the negotiations over the playback effect. Cooperation among the five was locked into place by the US desire to avoid a bilateral negotiation while the proliferation issue was unresolved, whereas the DPRK used the proliferation issue to try to gain the equal standing conferred by bilateral talks. In or out of the cooperative attempt to deal with the bilateral conflict, the other four parties imposed determining limits on US and ROK strategies by making the two demands simultaneous instead of conflictingly sequential. The United States followed a mixed cooperative strategy in the conflict under pressure from the bystanders, consistently refusing to engage the DPRK alone – that is, bilaterally, and engaging the bystanders cooperatively in the six-party talks. In this case, *cooperation in conflict* has been embedded in a broader *cooperation in management*, in which the bystanders were involved in collaboration with the major conflicting party.

The five cases examined, chosen for their significance, all illustrate the combined role of the three criteria for the shift from a confrontational to a cooperative conflict policy. Not only effectiveness and a positive cost-benefit balance but also the playback effect from important bystanders brought about a policy change. Cooperation imposes cooperation, lest the lack of it play back as a cost that upsets the cost-benefit balance. The cost is more than a cost in regard to the policy, however. It is a long-term cost regarding relations with significant others, beyond its direct relation to the policy area and much larger than it. Thus attention must turn in this discussion to *cooperation in management*.

Cooperation in management

Deciding to *cooperate in managing* an external conflict in which the states are not direct parties hangs on the ability to decide on a strategy on which other states will cooperate. Again, the three elements determine the answer – estimated effectiveness, cost-benefit calculations, and playback effect on future cooperation. Since all three are matters of degree rather than absolutes, decision is a matter – illustratively – of bringing the three columns to equivalent levels to balance each other, although how much of each is required to balance the others is a subjective, context-dependent judgment. The important point, again, is that there are three columns, one of which is the playback effect. Thus cooperation in prospect is a major determinant of cooperation in practice, but this time cooperation refers to the same parties in both aspects.

Decisions to cooperate or not in managing a conflict external to the international bystanders are major issues in international politics. While states, and particularly a hegemon, often decide to act unilaterally, they often shift to collective means of managing a conflict, that is, to cooperative intervention; the same is more frequently true in the case of problem solving on issues of common international concern, where the failure of unilateral efforts to handle the problem is the basic reason for multilateral cooperation (Hasenclever, Mayer, and Rittberger 1997; Spector and Zartman 2003). When they do decide to act unilaterally, they minimize a negative playback effect by gaining permission and support before proceeding, and they maintain the confidence of the bystanding states by assuring them that their interests are being considered in the proceedings. Both of these aspects require active communication with the bystanders during the operations, effectively conducting cooperation to cover the unilateral action.

The decision among the bystanders to act unilaterally or multilaterally (cooperatively) does not dictate the type of conflict management intervention that will be chosen. Actions can range from the peacemaking mediator to the peace-enforcing bomber, but they must be the basis of group consensus if cooperation among the managers is pursued or multilateral support of unilateral action is achieved. Thus the measure chosen is addressed by the same triple considerations of effectiveness, cost-benefit, and playback. In prominent instances, cooperative conflict management was essayed and repeatedly deadlocked, whereupon a unilateral effort was launched and succeeded. Many of these cases involved cooperation among conflict managers seeking to foster cooperation between protagonists, a combination of cooperation in management and cooperation in conflict. Namibia, Israel, and Yugoslavia can be examined.

The five-member Western Contact Group (WCG) conflict management effort over *Namibia* between South Africa and the South West Africa People's Organization (SWAPO) (and also Angola, and also Cuba) is an example both of cooperation in management and of cooperation in conflict. In 1977 the WCG launched an unusual preventative diplomacy demarche that ran through a drama in six acts over the next five years and failed (Zartman 1989, ch. 5). It was a case of conflict management before the conflict became serious or preventive diplomacy (Zartman 2000), and the WCG members were united in their goals, even if not in their commitment to the necessary measures. The effort collapsed at the end of the fourth phase, in October 1978, when the WCG threatened sanctions (confrontation) on South Africa but instead backed down in favor of continued discussions (cooperation). "It was essential that we convince the new South African government to continue toward an acceptable settlement. The alternative was a bitter confrontation with Pretoria, collapse of the negotiations, and intensification of the guerrilla war," declared US Secretary of State Cyrus Vance, rationalizing the Western retreat.

The second act began with the change in US administrations in the fall of 1982; cooperation within the WCG fell away as the United States assumed the job of mediation, but cooperation with the two antagonists (plus Angola and also Cuba) overcame the confrontation that Vance had feared, producing the Brazzaville–New York Agreement in December 1988 (Crocker 1993; Zartman 1989, ch. 5). The United States was able to take over the conflict management process by maintaining communication with the unemployed members of the WCG and by ignoring their criticisms, as well as the even more vigorous criticisms of the various African states. It was the consideration of success that outweighed the problem of playback. The Reagan administration, through Assistant Secretary of State Chester Crocker, saw that the previous timid confrontation with South Africa produced and was likely to produce no results, despite the cooperation among the CG states, and that a unilateral policy of cooperation with both antagonists had a better chance of success.

The two conflicting groups of parties took a much longer time to see cooperation as an alternative way to achieve their goals. Crocker's strategy took six years of patient, persistent waiting, reminding the parties that the United States was available for and interested in a cooperative solution, before the two sides found themselves in a situation ripe for a policy shift and the opening of negotiations. The standoff at Cuita Carnevale, the return of white body bags to South Africa, the increase in Cuban troops in Angola and their announcement of a hot pursuit policy, all in 1986, told both sides that the cost was high and the benefit unlikely, while the mediator told them that an alternative policy was possible. Interestingly, a cooperative policy would – and did – allow each side to achieve 100 percent of its goals – withdrawal of equal numbers of both Cuban troops from Angola and South African troops from Namibia (and Angola), removing the justification for each other's troops, and then consequently providing for the independence of Namibia. Cooperation with the bystanding parties produced cooperation between the opponents in conflict, and the opponents' cooperation legitimized the mediator's go-it-alone policy in the eyes of the bystanders.

The United States invented the *Mideast* peace process and played a particularly active role in six acts in 1974–75, 1977–79, 1983, 1991–93, 2000, and 2002 (Touval 1982; Quandt 2001). The first round, led by US Secretary of State Henry Kissinger, followed the October War, when the parties found themselves in a mutually hurting stalemate on the West Bank of the Suez Canal. Kissinger felt that the United States, though not a party to the conflict, had interests deeply involved and that it should act alone, without interference from its allies, although a UN conference in Geneva was planned to legitimize the bilateral process, and keep the bystanders busy in their own playpen (Quandt 2001, pp. 131, 132, 135). In the complicated path through three disengagements, two Israeli premiers, and two US presidents, Kissinger remained skillfully true to these two ways of proceeding, with little objection from the bystanders in the light of the results obtained.

The same principles, less explicitly formulated, remained in force to guide the second act of the peace process under President Jimmy Carter. The new administration inherited the multilateral Geneva conference, but it was leapfrogged by Egyptian President Anwar Sadat's visit to Jerusalem in November 1977; the preparation for the Camp David summit in September 1978 was a US operation with Israel and Egypt, without bystander interference. It was consummated, in part, by the Israeli–Egyptian Peace Treaty of 1979, again mediated personally by President Carter's cooperative intervention.

The third act focused on an attempt to create an Israeli–Lebanese peace agreement. The Israeli invasion of Lebanon in June 1982 awakened the new administration to the Mideast conflict. Whatever the color of the light – green or yellow – that Secretary of State Alexander Haig gave to Israel, Israeli refusal to keep its confrontation in bounds provoked a sudden strong reaction from President Reagan. "Your forces moved significantly beyond the objectives that you have described to me," Reagan wrote to Israeli Premier Menachem Begin; "I now call on you to accept a ceasefire" (Quandt 2001, p. 252). He went on to impose a cooperative policy on Israel and Lebanon, producing the ill-fated bilateral peace treaty of May 1983 that Lebanon then abrogated.

The fourth act went back to the Geneva conference idea, opened in Madrid in October 1991, then moved to Washington. It was not a broad-based conference, enjoying only the co-chairmanship of a Soviet Union in full collapse. The states of the Mideast, plus Palestinians, were in attendance, but the invitation to cooperation was a purely unilateral venture on the part of the United States, quite different from the impressive international coalition the administration had amassed for the confrontation in the Gulf the previous year. Both to placate Israel and to keep control of the conference, Secretary of State James Baker refused Syrian demands that all members of the UN Security Council be present at the conference (Baker 1999, p. 195).

The fifth act was the ill-prepared last-minute attempt of President Bill Clinton to pull a rabbit out of his hat at Camp David (Enderlin 2002; Ross 2004). Without going into the reasons for its failure, it suffices to note that this was a purely unilateral initiative, with the bystanders all circled about at a distance, watching incredulously for results. There were none.

The sixth act was quite different. Pressed over its inaction by the other leading bystanders of the international community, the United States joined the United Nations, the European Union and Russia in London to propose the Roadmap for Israeli–Palestine cooperation in their conflict.

The demarche was an exception to the previous rounds and, indeed, to the other, more typical cases examined here. Confronted with US inaction, the bystanders took the initiative and brought the United States to subscribe to a process designed to lead to a final solution. Weak action failed to push the process much further, but at least a set of goals was enunciated for future cooperation, should it later occur.

The six acts of the Mideast case followed a consistent pattern. When the United States took the initiative to move the conflicting parties away from confrontation and into cooperation as a means of conducting their conflict, the international community of bystanders held back, to a greater or lesser degree critically supporting the third-party role. When the United States lagged in that role, cooperation among the bystanders intensified to push it into position to do something; they could push no further, unready and unable to play the conflict management role themselves.

Cooperation in conflict management in the *disintegrating* Yugoslavia followed a reverse pattern. Concerned states made several stabs at acting cooperatively within the international community to introduce cooperative policies into the conflict. When these failed, one of its members – the United States – stepped forward to take over the third-party role itself, reviving international community cooperation when necessary.

In act one, the members of the European Union, after refusing to discuss Yugoslavia at the NATO Council in 1990, sent its troika representatives to Yugoslavia several times between April and July 1991 to mediate the war's end in Slovenia at Brioni, and then at the end of August decided to convene a peace conference at The Hague; the UN joined in with a Special Representative of the Secretary-General (SRSG), Cyrus Vance, two months later. The United States was the bystander in this round, as the European Union tried to induce cooperation and manage the conflict. After a year of operation, the Hague conference became the EU–UN London International Conference on the Former Yugoslavia (ICFY) to begin act two. Its attempts to induce cooperation ran their course by the end of 1993, with the United States still standing by, although the ICFY continued to exist into 1995.

Upon these failures, the United States launched act three in February 1994, by bringing the Bosniac and Croat factions of Bosnia and Herzegovina into cooperation in the Bosnian Federation, and then formed the bystanders into a contact group for support. Over the following eighteen months, the US initiative continued unilaterally, reinforced by NATO air strikes after May, culminating in the mediation with muscle of Assistant Secretary Richard Holbrooke at Dayton in November 1995.

Act four turned to Kosovo. The collapse of the Albanian state in March 1997 and the ensuing flow of arms to the Albanian Kosovar led the independence movement in Kosovo to shift its conflict from the political means of the Kosovar Democratic League (LDK) to the military means of the Kosovar Liberation Army (KLA). The contact group waddled into action early in the following year, but the rump Yugoslav president, Slobodan Milosevic, refused to negotiate with anyone until Holbrooke was appointed special envoy in March. A series of US mediations by Holbrooke and the US ambassador, Christopher Hill, backed by NATO Council action, continued unproductively until the contact group, led by US Secretary of State Madeleine Albright, convened the parties at Rambouillet. When that last attempt to provide a cooperative outcome failed, NATO began its 78-day bombing of Serbia to finally produce an agreement, through the good offices of the Russian prime minister and the Finnish president. The Kosovo Act was a cooperative effort of the contact group at conflict management, led by the United States but buttressed by collective NATO and individual states' efforts. The United States took the lead because previous collective efforts of the bystanders were unproductive and the bystanders then shared the lead because the US efforts were unproductive.

Through three acts on Yugoslavia and then one on Bosnia, the relevant international community of bystanders, organized through the United Nations and the European Union, tried, however impotently, to cooperate in managing the conflicts. In all these efforts the United States was the real bystander, carping at times and barely cooperating at others. When the conflict became too murderous and the cooperating community too impotent, the United States took over, keeping the contact group in name only, as it had in Namibia and the Mideast. When that effort became more than one country could handle in Kosovo, the United States came back into the cooperating community, leading, but as part of a collective effort. To read the internal criticism of the time, one would think that that these sequences were ad hoc and circumstantial. In fact, they were another instance of the established modus operandi of international cooperation in regard to conflict management.

Conclusion: cooperating to manage conflict

These important examples illustrate – they cannot prove – the components of the decision of a state in conflict to shift from a confrontational to a cooperative strategy. When confrontation as a conflict management strategy becomes – or is in danger of becoming – too costly for the international community of bystanders, they press the conflicting state to change strategies, and that pressure is a major consideration in its decision. The cases also illustrate the seemingly reverse action of the bystanders in regard to an external conflict, where they tend to leave conflict management efforts to one of their members, although pressing it to stay on the road, rather than cooperating among themselves to do the job. Only when the designated driver is not doing well enough, because of its own insufficiencies or the resistance of the conflict, do the bystanders activate their cooperation to take up the conflict management process. Why do they leave the dirty work to one of their members, rather than cooperating effectively to manage the conflict? If they want the conflicting parties to cooperate in their conflict, why do the international bystanders not cooperate among themselves to help them do so, and set the example?

Perhaps the answer lies in the qualifier "effectively." Cooperation to induce cooperation is a delicate business, and coordinating state policies is notorious difficult. It is a last resort, when the others' confrontation becomes too dangerous and when the designated driver does not get to the destination. Exercise critical support the international bystanders can do, but to intervene and mediate collectively is more difficult and even contrary to nature (as the Mideast roadmap experience shows). Indeed, more likely – and another reason why cooperative conflict management is unlikely or ineffective – is a number of diverse efforts by individual bystanders to make circumstantial or historic alliances with one party or another in the conflict, to further narrow national interests in case the conflict management fails or while it is going on.

Unilateral action to deal with conflicts and problems is the preferred course, for states as well as other parties including individuals; it cannot be called the default reaction since that choice is reserved for no action at all, the choice all of us make for most things. The decision to cooperate, then, depends on the success and cost-benefit, in practice or in prospect, of unilateral action, and that in turn depends on its playback effect on potentially cooperating bystanders, in addition to the more intuitive considerations of success/failure and cost-benefit. Cooperation depends on its effect on cooperation.

This effect, of course, is a subjective matter. The acting state may consider the playback to be unimportant or may be so sensitive to it that it is totally dependent on the reactions and anticipated reactions of the bystanders. As in so many polar choices, reality is most likely to lie somewhere in the middle, only leaning in one direction or the other. However, it also has an influence on itself over time; there is a learning curve. A state that discounts the playback effect is likely to come to learn of its importance, through experience. Similarly, a state that overemphasizes the playback effect is likely to learn that the two other considerations of success and cost-benefit need to play a role in the decision on unilateral versus cooperative action. The needle will tend to come to rest somewhere in the middle. It may be the realizations of the foreign policy team that bring it back from one side or the other, or it may be public pressure which also comes into play.

Of course, the discussion has its greatest relevance to prime actors, beginning with the hegemon and including other leading states or coalitions of states (such as the European Union). The needle tends more and more towards inaction as one descends through the ranks of actors from powerful to less so, not only because of the playback effect but also because of the two other considerations – success/failure and cost-benefit.

Deborah Welch Larson and Alexei Shevchenko

Since the end of the Cold War, scholars and foreign policy analysts have debated the various strategies of global governance – institutionalized coordination of states' activities to achieve a stable, predictable, controlled, and non-violent international order – a subject that has become urgent since 9/11 and the wars in Afghanistan and Iraq.[1] The key to securing such cooperation is to understand what induces other states to accept and internalize rules and norms proffered by the dominant power. In a system characterized by considerable power asymmetries, weaker states may resist being bullied or dominated by the hegemon.

Primacists have argued that US military and economic preponderance is so great that it is futile for other states to balance against American power, seemingly giving them no other choice but to pursue various accommodationist strategies (Sheetz 1997–98; Lemke 1997; Wohlforth 1999; Brooks and Wohlforth 2002, 2008). On the other hand, history suggests that complacency and imperial hubris are dangerous recipes for a long-term grand strategy in foreign affairs. States can impede the hegemonic power's global governance in numerous ways other than forming an opposing alliance or initiating a large-scale military buildup, including balking, feigned compliance, free riding, binding in international institutions, blackmail, or delegitimation of the hegemonic order (Walt 2005).[2] The US rift with European allies over the war in Iraq suggests that unipolarity does not preclude anti-US collusion on major issues. Whether we refer to opposition as "soft balancing" or use some other term, the result is the same (Paul 2004; Pape 2005).

States' refusal to cooperate is a matter for concern because, as Joseph Nye reminds us, while American power is too great to be challenged by

---

[1] For a typology of different grand strategies, see Posen and Ross 1996–97. For the implications of the September 11, 2001, attacks for US grand strategy, see Posen 2001–02; Walt 2001/02. For a useful collection of articles about US grand strategy published over the last decade, see Brown et al. 2000.

[2] On delegitimation strategies, see also Schweller and Reese 2004.

other states, it is not great enough to handle global problems such as WMD proliferation and terrorism. The United States is not only bound to lead, it is bound to cooperate (Nye 2002). Thus, for those who would design a durable, efficient global governance strategy, a crucial question is, when do states actively cooperate with US hegemony? How can the United States promote effective multilateral cooperation in a unipolar world?

The problem with the most prominent proposals for global governance is that they do not explain how the United States can enlist the cooperation of other states, especially major powers such as China and Russia. Integrating China and Russia into the Western order is one of the most important and challenging tasks facing US policymakers for the foreseeable future (Kissinger 1994). It is crucial for providing a "critical mass" among the major world powers committed to upholding international order and stability and avoiding another dramatic polarization of international politics.[3] China, which in modern times has never been accorded great power status, is rapidly rising in the international system, creating the possibility of an uncertain and destabilizing power transition in the Asia–Pacific region and in world politics. Complicating the situation is the presence of a rival great power in the region, Japan, whose relative economic status has declined dramatically, but not irreversibly, since 2000. Never before have Japan and China pursued active policies in the region at the same time. Russia has recently been resurging in power due to steady economic growth accompanied by rising energy prices, but has not yet found a new place in world politics and may once again be tempted to tilt toward the East if denied acceptance by the West.

The cooperation of China and Russia is essential for maintaining world order, despite threats posed by global terrorism, rogue states, global economic instability, and natural resource shortages. As permanent members of the United Nations Security Council (UNSC), China and Russia can veto any resolutions authorizing intervention or sanctions against rogue states. Because of its previous ties, Russia might be able to mediate with Iran and Syria. China, because of its role as the most important source of economic aid and its geographic proximity, is an essential interlocutor with North Korea. Russia has thousands of nuclear weapons and tons of nuclear materials, both coveted by terrorist groups. As the world's second-largest oil exporter and the holder of the largest gas reserves, Russia could help the United States reduce its dependence on

---

[3] For discussion of the possibility of creating an "encompassing coalition" of great powers in world politics in the twenty-first century, see Rosecrance 2001; Inosemtsev and Karaganov 2005.

Mideastern oil. Russia's geographic location near the Middle East and Central Asia heightens its importance for intelligence sharing and military cooperation. The United States needs China's long-term partnership to stabilize security relationships in the Asia–Pacific region, provide intelligence on fundamentalist Islamist terrorists, and prevent proliferation of weapons of mass destruction.

Successful integration of Russia and China requires understanding the logic behind their post-Cold War grand strategies, evaluating the prospects for their long-term cooperation with the West, and formulating effective policies to achieve this goal. Our paper pursues two goals. The first goal is to present a theoretical framework to explain Russian and Chinese emerging grand strategies in international affairs and to suggest means of enlisting both countries as joiners, not spoilers, in the US-sponsored global governance project. The second (more general and more ambitious) goal is to introduce the broad contours of a new approach to promoting a stable and cooperative international order, an approach that does not rely on shared institutional affiliation, commitment to liberal democratic norms, or the pacifying and cooperative logic of economic interdependence.

Instead, our approach emphasizes states' quest for a positive international identity and how the influence of status and prestige concerns plays out in their foreign policies. In the current international system, states need not compete for military power because their security is not threatened by external attack, and the United States can ultimately be counted on to preserve stability in strategically important regions. But states still contend for status, influence, and prestige – international pecking order. (Mastanduno and Kapstein, 1999; Schweller 1999a). We argue that, properly channeled and adequately recognized, states' concerns for international prestige and status can motivate them to contribute to the dominant power's global governance project and world order. Status incentives should be brought back to scholarly attention as a vital part of a diplomatic strategy to promote cooperation with allies and engage rising powers.

Multilateralism is more effective than unilateral action, in part because it recognizes the status and dignity of other states. Despite asymmetries of power, multilateralism gives states opportunities for meaningful participation. We use John Ruggie's definition of multilateralism as

an institutional form that coordinates relations among three or more states on the basis of generalized principles of conduct: that is, principles which specify appropriate conduct for a class of actions, without regard to the particularistic interests of the parties or the strategic exigencies that may exist in any specific occurrence. (Ruggie 1993b)

We also follow Ruggie in distinguishing between multilateral orders and organizations (Ruggie 1997). Multilateral cooperation need not be restricted to existing international organizations, but can also include coalitions formed to deal with particular problems.

The first section of this chapter identifies some gaps in international relations theories concerning the basis for multilateral efforts at global governance and international order. Section two conceptualizes status concerns in light of related discussions in international relations theories. Section three presents a typology of strategies by which states can improve their international status and indicates appropriate responses by the United States and international institutions. Our argument derives from social identity theory (SIT) in social psychology, which argues that social groups compete for status and predicts that dissatisfied groups will pursue one of three pathways to greater prestige – social mobility, social competition, or social creativity.[4] Finally, we apply our analysis in a case study explaining the paths taken by China and Russia to achieve great power status since the end of the Cold War and evaluating US responses to the course taken by the two major powers. One conclusion from our case study is that knowing when to use multilateral procedures requires understanding the type of strategy pursued by states that wish to improve their relative position in the global pecking order.

Managing international order

Realists, liberals, and constructivists are increasingly converging toward a preference for multilateralism for different reasons. For realists, a standing alliance, such as NATO, and international organizations can help to reduce the burdens placed on the dominant state and avoid "imperial overstretch" (Kissinger 1994; Haass 1997; Art 2003). Realists agree with liberals that consultation and deference to others allows the United States to exercise its power without threatening other states and possibly encouraging "soft balancing." Since states are more likely to form coalitions when a dominant power threatens their sovereignty and security, realists believe that the United States can head off the tendency for other states to align against overwhelming power by acting in a restrained manner and by providing public goods (Mastanduno and Kapstein 1999; Walt 2002; Kupchan 1998; Joffe 2006). Liberals add that diplomacy and multilateral consultation enhance the attractiveness of the United States as a model for

---

[4] Seminal works on social identity theory include Tajfel 1978, 1981; Tajfel and Turner 1979. For applications of social identity theory to international relations, see Mercer 1995; Larson and Shevchenko 2003.

others to emulate, enabling its "soft power" (Nye 2002, 2004). Constructivists maintain that multilateral institutions are more legitimate; consultation with others therefore helps to translate US power into authority (Lebow 2003; Reus-Smit 2004). Legitimacy has two dimensions – procedural and substantive. Decisions are viewed as legitimate if they are made through generally accepted principles of right processes and if they are consistent with international norms (Franck 1990; Clark 2005). Multilateral decisions meet the standard of procedural legitimacy because others are consulted and given an opportunity to express their opinions.

Primacists reject the argument that the United States needs to accommodate or defer to others in order to avoid arousing a hostile coalition. These realists contend that the United States' geographic isolation makes its power less threatening to others, removing the incentives to balance, while the overall size of the US economy and relatively high levels of defense spending and investment in military technology deprive other states of any reasonable prospect of catching up. This does not mean that other states will always agree with the United States, but merely that the balance of theory prediction that states will join together to protect themselves against a superior power no longer applies in the current international system (Brooks and Wohlforth 2005a, 2005b, 2008). That other states may not be able to form a counter-coalition, however, does not imply that they will necessarily cooperate with US efforts at global governance; they can employ other means of resisting US requests (Walt 2005).

How can the United States obtain the cooperation of Russia, China, and other major powers in a unipolar world? Liberal institutionalist John Ikenberry provides a partial answer and an explanation for the durability of the postwar Western international order. As part of an "institutional bargain," the United States provided security and access to its markets to other Western countries in return for their cooperation against Moscow and support for an open economic order. To alleviate fears of abandonment or domination, the United States imposed constraints on its power by adhering to agreed-upon rules of the game and by participating in multilateral institutions that allowed for consultation and joint decision making among allies (Ikenberry 1998–99, 2001).

US policymakers need to renew the post-1945 "institutional bargain" to preserve and strengthen the existing structure of cooperative relations between the United States and other important states. But conditions have changed so that the terms of the post-World War II bargain are no longer applicable. For one thing, the geographic scope of the post-1945 "constitutional order" was limited to western Europe and Japan, states that are democratic (Ikenberry 2001). In order to provide a "critical mass" of major world powers committed to upholding international order and stability, Ikenberry's bargain must not only be refurbished, it must also be extended to include new participants – particularly Russia and China. Neither Russia nor China adheres to liberal democratic norms, and both states resent the United States' lecturing on democracy and human rights. On the other hand, the United States does not have the luxury of waiting until China and Russia become liberal democracies before cooperating with them on such issues as counterterrorism and WMD proliferation.[5]

More generally, the major problem with the pursuit of a liberal international order based on commitment to democratic norms is that it is an extremely ambitious but also costly strategy, a strategy that is likely to lead to a gap between capabilities and commitments so familiar from the history of US foreign policy (Dueck 2004).

We propose an alternative approach to promoting multilateral cooperation – far less ambitious but also less risky – that does not rely on the benefits of US hegemony, institutional affiliation, or liberal democratic values, but relies instead on diplomacy, pluralism, and status concerns in order to motivate compliance with norms and rules. Our approach is informed by social identity theory, which argues that social groups strive for status. Before presenting our suggestions, we need to relate our work to previous scholarship on the effects of status concerns on international stability.

Status and power

Definition and metrics

States may be situated in a rough hierarchy of status and prestige, apart from their military and economic power (Luard 1990; Schweller 1999a). Status refers to the differential regard accorded to an achievement or characteristic of a state (Luard 1990).[6] Despite the sovereignty norm holding that states are juridically equal, great powers have always enjoyed a special, privileged status in the international system. This is obvious even in today's international system, where one of the marks of a true great power is having a permanent seat on the UN Security Council.

---

[5] For a similar critique of imposing a "democratic" test on Russia, see Gvosdev and Simes 2005.

[6] This is also the definition of prestige provided by Barry O'Neill (O'Neill 1999). We do not, however, differentiate prestige from status, as O'Neill does.

Realists have traditionally viewed status as a reflection of military and economic power. Classical realist Hans Morgenthau argues that prestige rests on others' perceptions of a state's military and economic capacity (Morgenthau and Thompson 1985). Similarly, for Robert Gilpin prestige is a state's reputation for power, based on other states' perceptions of its military and economic capabilities and its ability and willingness to use them (Gilpin 1981). A clear hierarchy of prestige linked to military power supposedly contributes to the stability of the system because it reduces uncertainty about the outcome of war, thus, as Hedley Bull stated, "simplifying the pattern of international relations" (Bull 1977, p. 206; Kissinger 1961; Gilpin 1981; Clark 1989).

A state's prestige is most congruent with its relative military power after the end of a war. Over time, changes in relative power can lead to a disjuncture between a state's capabilities and its recognized position in the international system. In addition, a state's self-image of its position and entitlements can diverge from others' perceptions, leading to increased dissatisfaction and conflict (Galtung 1964; East 1972; Wallace 1973). Power cycle theory theorizes that disequilibrium between a state's power and its role in the international system can lead to war (Doran and Parsons 1980; Doran 2000, 1991). Similarly, the original formulation of power transition theory posited that a rising power's dissatisfaction with its relative status was a major contributor to war (Organski 1958).

While status dissatisfaction can lead to instability and war, agreement on the hierarchy of prestige and especially the promise of equal status may facilitate the emergence of a stable, cooperative, international order (Kupchan et al. 2001).Rather than requiring disputes over relative position to be settled by bargaining, for example, the Treaty of Chaumont at the Congress of Vienna in 1815 formalized the hierarchy of status by designating the powers that would in essence run Europe–Britain, Russia, Prussia, Austria, and, later, France (Schroeder 2004).

Effective and flexible readjustment of the international hierarchy of prestige to accommodate rising great powers can hold the key to international peace and stability and may, therefore, be in the hegemonic state's interests.[7] Status incentives are relatively inexpensive. Even more importantly, altering the international pecking order by according more status to a rising state does not upset the governance structures of the system or harm the hegemon's security (Schweller 1999a).

---

[7] Organski 1958. Organski identified the dominant state's flexibility in adjusting to changes in the distribution of power and accommodating the rising challenger through moderate concessions as one of the factors affecting the likelihood that a power transition will result in war. See also Kupchan et al. 2001.

While power and status frequently overlap and have a common basis in military and economic capabilities, status in the international system can also be a more subjective good, with constantly changing and diverse metrics, because it depends on others' recognition and value systems. Even within the same historical era, there has been significant variation in the domains in which states have been able to achieve prestige. For example, during the classic balance of power system, the leading world powers did not pride themselves solely on their military strength. In Europe, from the fourteenth to the sixteenth centuries status depended on the glory of the ruling dynasty, as measured by the number of royal titles, the sumptuousness of royal display, the size of palaces, and the lavishness of entertainment (Luard 1990). While military defeats underlay the French decline in relative power and the dramatic rise of Britain, Prussia, and Austria in the seventeenth and eighteenth centuries, France managed to preserve and improve its status through artistic achievements, the style of its courts and entertainments, and its great writers and thinkers. Britain was known for its philosophers and political system. The Prussians were celebrated for their bureaucratic organization and efficiency (Luard 1992, 1990).

In the contemporary world, states can achieve greater status through multiple routes: their rising regional and international economic role (China), high-technology manufacturing (Japan), provision of generous foreign aid (Norway), possession of a technologically skilled workforce (India), an enlightened social welfare system (Sweden, France), or the provision of diplomatic mediation services (Norway, Canada) (Nye 2002).

The possibility of employing alternative metrics to gain recognition from others means that the quest for status need not be a zero-sum game. As we shall demonstrate below, the availability of multiple status dimensions can be very helpful for designing effective strategies of governance.

Status and identity

According to social identity theory, social groups strive to be distinctive in a positive way – to be not only different, but better besides (Tajfel 1978; Tajfel and Turner 1979). The direction of comparison is upwards, to a social group that is equal or slightly superior. This tendency is apparent in the "reference states" chosen in national discourses on international affairs. The Chinese frequently compare China to Japan or the United States; Pakistanis focus on India; Indians look toward China; and Russians tend to judge their accomplishments relative to the United

States. The outcome of such comparisons significantly affects elite satisfaction with their national identity.[8]

Identity management strategies pursued by states

Social identity theory predicts that group members whose positive identity is threatened by unfavorable comparisons may pursue one of several strategies – social mobility, social competition, or social creativity – to increase their prestige. The choice of strategy depends on the permeability of group boundaries as well as the legitimacy and stability of the status hierarchy (Tajfel 1978; Tajfel and Turner 1979).

If the boundaries of higher-status groups appear to be permeable, members of lower-status groups will pursue a strategy of social mobility, attempting to assimilate or pass into the superior group. Applied to states, the strategy of social mobility tries to gain admission to higher-status groups or clubs through imitation or emulation of elite members (Abrams and Hogg 1990; Ellemers, van Knippenberg, and Wilke 1990; Ellemers, Wilke, and van Knippenberg 1993; van Knippenberg and Ellemers 1993; Lalonde and Silverman 1994).

For example, eastern and central European states have adopted democratic reforms in order to obtain membership in the European Union or NATO. The policy of conditionality – that is, requiring prospective members to adopt new norms – makes use of states' desire for status as well as material benefits (Kelley 2004; Coicaud 2001).

The success of a social mobility strategy critically depends on the dominant members' willingness to accept new members into the great power clubs. Because status is relative, states are sometimes reluctant to yield a place to others (Doran 1991). For example, China strongly opposes Japan's bid for a permanent seat on the UNSC, even though the veto power would protect China from any Japanese action that might harm its material interests.

If the higher-status group's boundaries are impermeable and the status hierarchy is perceived to be illegitimate or unstable, disadvantaged group members may try to improve their relative position by pursuing a strategy of social competition (Tajfel 1981; Tajfel and Turner 1979).[9] In international relations, social competition aims at achieving superior or at least

---

[8] Social psychological experiments have repeatedly demonstrated that groups who rank low on various indices are less satisfied with their identity and are less likely to identify strongly with the group. See, for example, Ellemers and Van Rijswijk 1997.

[9] For evidence from field studies and experiments see Turner and Brown 1978; Ellemers, Wilke, and van Knippenberg 1993; Vennstra and Haslam 2000; Ouwerkerk and Ellemers 2002; Mummendey et al. 1999; Overbeck et al. 2004.

equal status with the dominant group. Indicators of social competition include informal groupings or coalitions that exclude the dominant power, symbolic gestures, rhetoric, military posturing, or ad hoc military exercises aimed at asserting the state's status. To illustrate, after its swift rise to power at the end of the nineteenth century, Japan turned to imperialism in response to the Western powers' refusal to admit it to the club of "great powers," despite its acceptance of international diplomatic norms and rules. This was made clear to Japan by the Triple Intervention of 1895, in which European powers ganged up on Japan to force it to relinquish part of the territory that it had conquered in the Sino-Japanese war. Japan's sense of humiliation and dissatisfaction with its inferior status pushed it eventually to regard military superiority and colonies as a means of combating Western double standards and securing the equal treatment to which it felt entitled (Khong 2001).

Nevertheless, states need not try for social mobility before moving to social competition. A major power may correctly perceive that the boundaries of elite clubs are closed to it and move directly to competitive tactics. For example, from 1945 to 1985, the Soviet Union struggled to achieve political–diplomatic equality vis-à-vis the West, validating Moscow's arrival as a major player on the international scene. The Soviet Union sought to achieve recognition through territorial empire and military strength, yet was never accepted as an equal by the United States, largely because of its "alien" ideology and way of life. "For all its fixation on duopoly," wrote one observer, "American diplomacy has never been willing to offer the Soviets the equal global status they presumably crave."[10]

If they perceive that the status hierarchy is stable, lower-status groups may creatively redefine their relative status by (i) reevaluating the meaning of a negative characteristic, or (ii) finding a new dimension in which their group is superior.[11] This is called a strategy of *social creativity*. An example from domestic politics would be the African-American 1960s slogan "Black is beautiful." Robert Kagan has famously written that "Americans are from Mars, Europeans are from Venus," meaning that Europeans have sought refuge in integration and international law to compensate for military weakness (Kagan 2004).

---

[10] Calleo 1987, quoted in Clark 1989, p. 171. See also the discussion in Larson and Shevchenko 2003.
[11] See, for example, Lemaine 1974; Tajfel and Turner 1986; van Knippenberg 1984; Abrams and Hogg 1990; Jackson et al. 1996; Lalonde 1992; Spears et al. 1997.

Through social creativity, a state can make up for a lagging position in one indicator of status with a superior ranking on another, provided that the leading state accepts the reevaluation of an old trait or acknowledges the value of the new dimension. Because status is based on others' recognition, a group cannot improve its position unilaterally. Achieving a higher status requires social validation. Groups can acknowledge each other's superiority on different attributes, thereby showing *social cooperation* (van Knippenberg 1984; Mummendey and Schreiber 1984; Ellemers et al. 1997). State A can claim to be better on dimension X while acknowledging that state B is stronger on dimension Y. On the other hand, if the higher-status group refuses to accept the outcome of the other group's efforts at social creativity, there is likely to be increased anger and hostility (Tajfel 1979; Brown and Ross 1982). The lower-status group may strike back, with offensive action (Mackie et al., 2000).

Multilateralism and world order

Successful integration of rising powers into elite clubs contributes to world order in several ways. Most obviously, providing a potential challenger with a "seat at the table" demonstrates respect and will help to satisfy its demands for increased prestige (Schweller 1999a).

Inclusion into higher-status groups may be wiser strategy in the long run than containment, which may be counterproductive against a state that is primarily concerned with raising its international profile. It is best to co-opt a state into the "family of nations" early in the process, before the challenger turns to military competition out of frustration as the only available means of improving its relative position (Doran 1991).

Multilateralism facilitates hegemonic order by securing compliance without coercion. A state is more likely to accept principles of order promoted by the hegemon when it is accorded "meaningful participation" in shaping the rules (Khong 2001). In return for being treated as a respected member of the club, states are expected to conform to its rules. International law more closely approximates to social club rules that members feel obliged to observe as a condition of their membership than domestic law which is enforceable by the courts (Franck 1990). As emphasized by Paul Schroeder in his study of the Concert of Europe, fear of being excluded from a valued group can be a powerful deterrent to aggression as, for example, demonstrated by Russian behavior after 1815. In this sense, "[a]ny government is restrained better and more safely by friends and allies than by opponents and enemies" (Schroeder 2004). Similarly, President Franklin D. Roosevelt sought to contain the Soviet Union through "integration" (Gaddis 2005). He wanted to bring it into the "family of nations" by creating an elite "club" to which the Soviet Union could belong. The "four policeman" concept would have created a concert of power composed of Britain, the United States, the Soviet Union, and China that would prevent crises and maintain the peace (Kimball 1991; Ruggie 1993b).

In what follows, we apply these hypotheses to analyze Russia's and China's strategies for achieving great power status since the end of the Cold War. We also argue that US recognition and positive reinforcement of Chinese and Russian attempts at social creativity (granting both countries additional recognition and status) is an effective international order management strategy for encouraging multilateral cooperation in a unipolar world.

Beijing's and Moscow's quest for great power status after the Cold War

Despite pronounced differences in their developmental trajectories in the post-Cold War era (with China swiftly rising in material power and Russia rapidly descending but recently resurging), both countries have followed strikingly similar paths in their quest to improve their relative status and influence in the international system. By the early 1990s, China and Russia experienced significant obstacles to social mobility because of the West's unwillingness to treat them as equals, resulting in a shift to various forms of social competition. However, at the beginning of the new century, both ultimately chose to downplay social competition in favor of a social creativity strategy, striving to establish positive international identities and enhance their status largely outside the traditional balance of power calculus. The United States, however, has taken Russian cooperation for granted, with the result that current Russian foreign policy is in a transitional stage, with some elements of social competition.

Limits to social mobility

Since the late 1970s, Chinese elites have aimed to achieve *social mobility* for China into the ranks of great powers and equality of status with them through economic growth and rising political influence, overcoming a "century of shame and humiliation."[12] While China's economic growth in the reform era was nothing short of astounding, Beijing's quest for increased political influence was less successful.

[12] Bijian 2005; see, *inter alia*, Swaine and Tellis 2000; Kim 2003.

After 1989, China's quest for recognition as a truly great power was jeopardized by several serious challenges to its international position after the end of global bipolarity. The collapse of the Soviet Union led to the obsolescence of the Washington–Beijing–Moscow strategic triangle – the basis for Beijing's claim to strategic importance in international affairs and the foundation for China's "special relationship" with the United States. The onset of US dominance happened to coincide with an acute domestic crisis culminating in bloody suppression by the government, the ensuing harsh criticism of China, and even (albeit rather short-lived) ostracism by major Western countries. The era of seeing China as qualitatively different from other communist regimes (the "so-called communist country," to use President Reagan's memorable 1984 formula) was over. The disappearance of the Soviet threat made it easier for the United States to criticize the authoritarian Chinese political system and the government's human rights record – issues that previously were subordinated to the goal of containing the Soviets. Although China's global strategic presence was visibly reduced, the collapse of the Soviet Union immediately made China a preponderant power in the east Asian region, giving rise to fears among its neighbors of the emerging, arrogant Chinese power. Finally, and perhaps most troubling for Chinese leaders, Taiwan's rapid democratization since the end of the 1980s allowed Taiwanese nationalism to emerge as a crucial factor in domestic politics. Previously unheard-of Taiwanese demands for independence, combined with US support for democratic Taiwan and newfound appreciation of the "China threat," undermined Beijing's project of national unification – the key political and reputational concern for successive generations of Chinese leaders (Goldstein 2005; Ross 1995; Mann 2000; Romberg 2003).

Russia's predicament after the demise of the Soviet Union was even more problematic due to profound internal and external identity crises, exacerbated by the difficulty of adjusting to the rapid decline in its status and position as a superpower (Wallander 1996; Checkel 1995; Valdez 1995; Dawisha and Parrott 1994; Hopf 2002; Trenin 2002). While Russian elites disagreed on their country's orientation, there was one point on which they and the Russian people agreed: despite its temporary weakness, Russia was destined to be a great power, not just a "normal state" (Shlapentokh 2002; Mendelson and Gerber 2005–06). Equally important was the question of Russia's status in its relationship with the United States. Equality and US appreciation of Russia have always been key elements in the domestic legitimacy of both Soviet and post-Soviet rulers (Aron 2006). However, this quest for great power status and equality was hampered by Russian leaders' inability to devise a coherent strategy to arrest and reverse Russia's marginalization in international affairs.

In the early 1990s, Moscow pursued social mobility through a policy of "voluntary dependence" on the West, based on the expectation that Russia would swiftly be integrated into Western clubs (such as the General Agreement on Tariffs and Trade, the International Monetary Fund (IMF), G7, and even NATO) and that Russia would receive large-scale Western aid and technological assistance, enabling the country to make a smooth transition to democracy and free markets.[13] In the long run, however, such "romantic atlanticism" created unrealistic expectations about the magnitude of Western economic aid and support, resulting in widespread disillusionment and a general impression that a pro-Western line encouraged Western countries' attempts to pressure Russia and treat it as a "junior partner" while neglecting its political, security, and commercial interests.

The Clinton administration relied on personal diplomacy and a mix of status and economic incentives for damage control. For example, President Clinton played a decisive role in providing the most significant status incentive of the 1990s – granting Russia's political (as opposed to economic) membership in the G7 in 1997 (Goldgeier and McFaul 2003).

Despite this achievement, in the early 1990s Russia repeatedly and painfully bumped up against Western barriers when it tried to exercise influence on other issues – the former Yugoslavia, NATO enlargement, its relations with the former Soviet republics, the war in Chechnya and Russia's membership in other important international organizations. Periodically orchestrated rounds of international applause and goodwill gestures did not compensate for Russian humiliations on substantive concerns or quell Russian elite resentment at being told that they had to meet externally imposed standards to be accepted into Western clubs (Tsygankov 2006; Trenin 2006).

Failure of social competition

China's and Russia's frustration with Western-imposed barriers to social mobility was initially translated into attempts at direct competition with the United States and its partners, but China's premature efforts at assertion aroused fears in Asia, while Russia could not attract diplomatic partners able to balance the United States.

---

[13] See, for example, "After the Disintegration of the Soviet Union: Russia in the New World" (Report of the Center of International Studies, Moscow State Institute of International Relations) Moscow, February 1992. On NATO membership as a long-term goal of Russian foreign policy see *Diplomaticheskii Vestnik* (Moscow) 1, January 15, 1992, p. 13. See also Light 1996 and Tsygankov 2006.

Emboldened by having survived the collapse of world socialism and by the recent upsurge in the domestic economy (since 1992/93), Jiang Zemin and his followers rather awkwardly attempted to translate China's economic strength into increased international assertiveness and political clout in the Asia–Pacific region. This more forward policy soon provoked a backlash against the perceived "China threat" to the Asia–Pacific region's peace and stability. Chinese military posturing in the South China Sea in 1995, designed to reinforce China's claim on the Spratly Islands, produced collective resistance by ASEAN states to Chinese sovereignty claims. Beijing's decision to heighten tensions around the Taiwan Strait in 1995–96, by conducting missile tests and military maneuvers to curb Lee Deng-hui's pro-independence policies and punish Washington for encouraging them, resulted in the dispatch of two US aircraft carrier groups to the area, a dramatic increase in anti-China rhetoric in the US Congress, academia, and mass media, and ultimately to an upgrading of the US–Japan security relationship, including potential collaboration on a theater missile defense system covering the East China Sea (and possibly Taiwan). China's attempts to frighten the Taiwanese public also backfired dramatically, leading to another term for President Lee and in the long run paving the way for Beijing's ultimate nightmare – the victory in the 2000 presidential elections of a candidate from the openly pro-independence Democratic Progressive Party (Whiting 1997; Mann 2000; Lampton 2001; Ross 2000).[14]

Russia's attempts at social competition did not fare any better. From 1996 to 1999, Foreign Minister Yevgenii Primakov pursued "multipolar" diplomacy aimed at checking the United States' growing power by constructing diplomatic counter-alliances (Pushkov 1998, 2000). This policy of coalition building was primarily symbolic, aimed at restoring Russia's great power status and autonomy rather than balancing a hypothetical future threat from the West (Tsygankov 2006). However, multipolar diplomacy quickly revealed Russia's extreme financial–economic vulnerability and its high degree of economic dependence on the West. Primakov's idea of a possible Moscow–Delhi–Beijing triangle remained in the air, and "strategic partnership" with China did not progress much beyond rhetoric. As the influential Council on Foreign and Defense Policy acknowledged, despite its use of harsh rhetoric, Russia ultimately wound up accepting Western policies on NATO enlargement, Iraq, and Kosovo, becoming an "unwilling partner" of the United States and NATO (Council on Foreign and Defense Policy 2000).

---

[14] For post-crisis alarmist views of China see Bernstein and Munro 1997.

The NATO military strikes against Kosovo in spring 1999 had an immense impact on Russian elites and foreign policy specialists, apparently demonstrating conclusively that Russia's wishes did not matter and that the United States, for all its rhetoric about a cooperative world order, was making geopolitical gains at the expense of Russia (Torkunov 2000). The US unilateral pursuit of national missile defense (NMD) and the imminent approach of a second round of NATO expansion reinforced the image of an increasing rift between the West and Russia (Dobriansky 2000). Coincidentally, the disappointing record of Russian economic reform, culminating in the humiliation of the 1998 financial meltdown, led to scapegoating in Russian domestic politics, with Western aid (or the lack thereof) and advisers the primary suspects.

At the end of the 1990s, Russian efforts to regain international status befitting a great power seemed to be doomed to failure. On top of its economic woes it also faced the risk of falling out of the ranks of "civilized" countries due as a result of harsh Western criticism of its actions in Chechnya (Black 2004).[15] As for Russian elites, they were profoundly disillusioned with their phony "partnership" with the United States and the West (Goldgeier and McFaul 2003; Shevtsova 2003). The preamble to Russia's official Foreign Policy Concept in March 2000 reads like an epitaph for the pro-Western hopes of the 1990s, as it acknowledges that "expectations of equitable, mutually advantageous and partnership relations with the surrounding world" reflected in the previous 1993 concept had not been met (Foreign Policy Concept of the Russian Federation 2000).

Social creativity

The failure of their efforts at social competition prompted both Chinese and Russian elites to modify significantly their strategies in international affairs. The mid-1990s crisis in relations with the United States and its close neighbors pushed Chinese leaders to reevaluate their post-Cold War foreign policy. The fundamental problem, reflected in the mid-1990s fiascos of Chinese foreign policy, was that China had entered the post-Cold War era as a one-dimensional power. While excelling on the economic dimension of international power, Beijing scored quite low on other dimensions such as political or ideological strength.

---

[15] In April 2000, the Parliamentary Assembly of the Council of Europe (PACE) voted to strip Russia of its voting rights and suspend its membership in the Council of Europe because of human rights violations in Chechnya, the first such suspension in fifty years.

In order to attain true great power status while maintaining the benign external environment that was crucial for China's domestic economic development, China had to recast its political role on the international scene. Confronted with the logic of the security dilemma, aggravated by its attempts at international "social competition," beginning in mid-1996 Chinese leaders adopted a new approach to international affairs aimed at establishing a reputation for China as a responsible, cautious, self-restrained, and cooperative player (Goldstein 2001, 2005; Kim 2003). Instead of trying to compete directly with the United States, China would use a *social creativity* strategy of achieving recognition in a new domain – as a constructive member of the international and regional community, guarantor of economic and political stability, and economic role model in the era of globalization.

In the wake of the Taiwan Strait crisis, Jiang formulated the major task of Chinese diplomacy as "enhancing trust, reducing trouble, developing cooperation and refraining from confrontation" (Xinhua 1996). China's 1997 New Security Concept emphasized reassurance based upon cooperative security, dialogue, and mutual economic benefit (Lampton 2005). To reduce the probability that an anti-China coalition might emerge and to advance China's long-standing goal of a multipolar global order, in 1996 Beijing embarked on what Jiang called a "Great Power strategy," aimed at fostering "strategic partnerships" with other major powers – including Russia, the United States, and the European Union – while avoiding firm alignment with any particular state or group of states. China also began to participate actively in multilateral forums designed to solve regional and global conflicts, as well as in bilateral and multilateral confidence-building measures (Goldstein 2005; Shambaugh 2004–05; Zhang and Tang 2005; Gill 2005; Pearson 1999; Johnston and Evans 1999).

Throughout the Asian financial crisis of 1997–98, Beijing – protected from the worst shocks of the regional financial turmoil by its nonconvertible currency, massive foreign currency reserves, and favorable external debt ratio – tried to bolster its image as a reliable and stable world economic power (Moore and Yang 2001). The Chinese strategy for gaining prestige was successful; China was praised for being a responsible regional and international "citizen," an upholder of world economic stability at a crucial moment.

In the aftermath of the crisis, previously ad hoc elements of China's emerging understanding of its regional and global role started to solidify into a more coherent pattern. Chinese leaders decided that China should open even more decisively to global capital, information, and technology flows while simultaneously reconfiguring its domestic and foreign policies to maximize the benefits from new transnational sources of wealth, power, and status (Moore 2000; Kim 2003; Deng and Moore 2004). Beijing also increasingly viewed itself and acted as the leading proponent of Western economic norms (global free trade, open capital flows, and economic transparency) in the Asia–Pacific region and as a champion of regional economic integration, in the process of doing so entering the WTO and exercising leadership in securing an agreement with the Association of South East Asian Nations (ASEAN) to create a free trade area by 2010 (Yang 2002; Wong and Chang 2003).

China has also invested massive efforts in propaganda campaigns aimed at reducing "China threat" perceptions in the Asia–Pacific region and around the world and at presenting itself as a mature force for global stability and security.[16] China's decade-long attempts at social creativity, reinforced by the growing importance of the Chinese economy, have had impressive results, especially at the regional level, where it is increasingly viewed as a constructive partner and a good neighbor (Shambaugh 2005).

China has even exercised social creativity on the Taiwan issue, which is tied to sensitive identity, legitimacy, and status concerns for Beijing. Since the mid-1990s, China's approach to Taipei on average has become increasingly flexible and sophisticated, as demonstrated by Beijing's skillful use of economic and cultural incentives to win the "hearts and minds" of the Taiwanese population. While the possibility of conflict in the Taiwan Strait still exists, there is also the hope that Beijing and Taipei might move toward a political agreement preserving the status quo for the next several decades.[17]

In the aftermath of 9/11, the Chinese leadership quickly seized an opportunity to repair ties with Washington by playing a major role in addressing Washington's new concerns about terrorism, aggressively promoting its image as a power committed to international stability and the fight against Islamic radicalism. Beijing used its leverage over Pakistan to convince President Musharraf to cooperate with Washington's efforts in Afghanistan and provided valuable intelligence information. Beijing supported UN anti-terror resolutions, and in the months prior to the US invasion of Iraq signaled that China would not exercise its veto in the UN Security Council or use the rift in the NATO alliance to engage in anti-Washington coalition building. Despite heightened concerns over

---

[16] Such as the 2003–04 campaign propagating the "peaceful rise theory" or post-2004 "peaceful development" discourse.

[17] This is one of the central findings of a National Committee on American Foreign Policy study group's spring 2006 trip to China and Taiwan. For a summary of the findings see Zagoria 2006.

pro-independence moves by Taiwan's president Chen Shui-bian in 2003–04, Beijing also did not escalate tensions in the Taiwan Strait while Washington was increasingly distracted in Iraq. Finally, China has emerged as a vital player in Washington's efforts to freeze and dismantle North Korea's nuclear program by applying political and economic pressure on Kim Jong-Il's regime to engage in multilateral talks and to give up nuclear weapons (Lampton and Ewing 2003; Swaine 2004; Wu 2005).

As in the Chinese case, having failed to be admitted into Western clubs or to compete effectively, President Vladimir Putin adopted a different strategy for enhancing Russian relative status, a strategy that exhibits *social creativity* in identifying new domains in which Russia can excel, such as guarantor of stability and security in Eurasia, reliable energy supplier for the world economy, intermediary in dealing with rogue states, and vital Western partner in fighting terrorism and extremism. His long-term goal is to turn Russia into a true, not virtual, multidimensional great power, reversing the alarming loss of power, status, and influence suffered throughout the 1990s.[18]

Like his predecessors, Mikhail Gorbachev and Boris Yeltsin, Putin is primarily preoccupied with restoring Russia's great power status. But while Gorbachev attempted to find a shortcut to great power status exclusively through political means, and while Yeltsin largely ignored economic aspects of foreign policy in favor of traditional Russian concerns for the balance of power and spheres of influence, Putin is trying to use foreign policy to achieve economic objectives and to augment Russia's international status and influence through economic instruments. Putin realizes that Russia will need to grow economically at a rate of 7 percent per year to catch up with the West, and that this will require closer integration with the world economy. Understanding that Russia's status is currently based largely on its role as an energy supplier, especially in light of continuing instability in the Middle East, Putin has made active use of oil and gas diplomacy to increase Russian influence in the Western world and the former Soviet space and to put relations with China on a more equal basis. Putin built new pipelines, made deals with European firms giving Russia a majority interest, and applied economic criteria to pricing natural gas for Ukraine and Georgia (Lo 2002; Trenin 2003–04; Legvold 2007; Rieber 2007).

Terrorist attacks against the United States provided Putin with the opportunity and determination to orchestrate a dramatic breakthrough in relations with the West. In the aftermath of 9/11, he discerned and

---

[18] In his 2003 presidential state of the nation address, Putin stressed that his main objective was "returning Russia to the ranks of the rich, developed, powerful and respected states of the world" in the foreseeable future. *RIA Novosti*, May 16, 2003.

effectively grasped a dramatic opportunity to give Russia a distinctive new role in global politics by acting as an indispensable, constructive partner in the war against terrorism. In the wake of 9/11, Russia's cooperation with the United States was extensive, ranging from intelligence sharing and cooperation between the Federal Bureau of Investigation (FBI) and its Russian counterpart, the Federal Security Service, and providing a bridge to the Northern Alliance, to Putin's acquiescence in the US military presence in Central Asia and, later, in Georgia – Russia's former spheres of influence. Putin also successfully used the Bush administration's increased appreciation for the threat of terrorism to mute criticism of Russia's war in Chechnya (Aron 2002; Shevtsova 2003; Malinowski 2003).

Evaluating US responses

Initially, US diplomacy reinforced China's and Russia's search for a new, positive international identity. But the Bush administration subsequently demonstrated a propensity to assume that Russia would cooperate with the United States, without any need to offer a quid pro quo or recognize Russia's special interests. As discussed earlier, the success of a social creativity strategy depends on the higher-status group's willingness to accept the lower-status group's more positive identity, thereby showing social cooperation. The US failure to treat Russia as an equal partner led to a decline in hopes for a strategic partnership and a cooling in US–Russian relations. In contrast, the United States has pursued a steadier policy towards China, avoiding political tensions over Taiwan or excessive criticism of Chinese human rights abuses, and Sino-US relations appear to be solid. In addition, US cooperation with China is buttressed by growing economic trade and interdependence, a factor that is lacking in interactions with Russia.

For China, it was critical that the Clinton administration chose an engagement strategy towards it after the Taiwan Strait crisis rather than containment. Clinton's embrace of "constructive engagement" made possible the Clinton–Jiang summits in 1997 and 1998, agreements to step up joint efforts on nuclear non-proliferation and drug enforcement, the exchange of visits by cabinet-level civilian and military staff personnel, and, ultimately, Clinton's 1998 "3 Nos statement" on Taiwan, designed to address and eliminate Chinese concerns over US support for the island's independence.[19]

---

[19] The three "nos" were that the United States (i) would oppose or resist efforts by Taiwan to gain independence; (ii) would not support the creation of "two Chinas" or one China and a separate Taiwan; and (iii) would not support Taiwan's admission to the United Nations. See the account in Mann 2000; Ross 1999.

The US policy of engagement and the promise of a "constructive strategic partnership" with Beijing encouraged Chinese leaders to stay the course of their "new diplomacy" even when a series of emerging Sino-US disputes of the late 1990s pushed bilateral relations into a tailspin. The Chinese elite's extraordinarily intense 1999 debate on Chinese foreign policy priorities ended with the defeat of attempts to renew competition with the United States (Finkelstein 2000) and allowed the new vision of Chinese international identity to endure in the policies of the "fourth" generation of Chinese leaders presided over by Hu Jintao after they came to power in 2002.

Although the Bush administration came into office criticizing Clinton's policy of "constructive strategic partnership" with China as naïve and labeling Beijing a "competitor," China's impressive record of post-9/11 cooperation led to important shifts in US strategy for managing relations with it. The Bush administration reciprocated by holding meetings with Jiang Zemin and Hu Jintao and by addressing Chinese concerns about Islamic separatist movements on their territory. Even more importantly, Bush reassured Chinese leaders that the US position on Taiwan would remain unchanged. He applied pressure on Chen Shui-bian to tone down his provocative behavior before the 2004 Taiwanese presidential elections, and openly stated that Washington "opposes" (a switch from the previous "does not support" formula) any attempts unilaterally to change the status quo in the Taiwan Strait. With common strategic interests coming to the forefront of Sino–US relations for the first time since the end of the Cold War and with the Bush administration's willingness to address China's vital concerns and to treat Beijing as an important partner, Washington–Beijing ties underwent a remarkable transformation in 2002–04. In December 2003, the then US secretary of state Colin Powell famously characterized relations with China as the "best they have been since President Richard Nixon first visited Beijing more than 30 years ago" (Powell 2004).

US willingness to grant China a special status in the relationship was critical to establishing collaboration. For example, according to Powell, cooperation between the Bush administration and China was significantly facilitated by his and Chinese Foreign Minister Tang Jiaxuan's decision to establish reliable private channels to avoid crises in bilateral relations (Lawrence 2004). In April 2005, Washington further played to China's international prestige aspirations by accepting the Chinese proposal for "strategic dialogue," promising regular, senior-level talks on a wide range of political, security, and economic issues (Kessler 2005).

Although the George W. Bush administration initially deliberately downgraded the importance of Russia, its renewed interest in engaging with Russia beginning in summer 2001 was due in part to Putin's skillful diplomacy, his accommodating attitude to the US security agenda, and good personal chemistry between Putin and Bush. Although Putin did not request any quid pro quo for Russia's assistance after 9/11, the West made several concessions. In May 2002, the NATO–Russia Council was established to give Russia a voice in NATO deliberations, replacing the Permanent Joint Council, established in 1997, which Russia had never taken seriously (Purdum 2002; Sanger 2002). In May–June 2002, the European Union and the United States finally accorded Russia the status of a market economy, ending costly restrictions on Russian products in world markets (Taverniese 2002). At the end of June 2002, the G8 announced its decision to upgrade Russia's status to full membership, although its economy still did not meet the necessary criteria. Russia was invited to become president in 2006 and to host the meeting (*RIA-Novosti* 2002).

But the high expectations for a US–Russian strategic partnership did not last long. Putin apparently expected that in return for his cooperation in the war on terror that Russia would be treated as an equal. This meant that Russia's special interests in states that were formerly part of the Soviet Union would be recognized and that the United States would refrain from interfering in Russia's internal affairs. But the United States had "no intention of making Russia its key partner or even an equal partner" (Shevtsova 2007). The United States disregarded Russia's status concerns by invading Iraq in 2003 without authorization from the UN Security Council, supporting "colored revolutions" in the post-Soviet space, criticizing suppression of dissent in Russia, enlarging NATO even further to include states in Russia's "near abroad," and proceeding with the installation of an antiballistic missile system in Poland and the Czech Republic without Russia's participation. Apart from Putin's belief that Saddam was a containable rather than an imminent threat, the most important reason for Moscow's sharp disapproval of the Iraq war was the US failure to satisfy Putin's expectations that Russia would be accorded the status of a major ally and included at the table in the process of decision making. Status concerns predominated in Putin's decision to oppose the war, because his decision to do so after Bush had already decided on the invasion meant that Russia lost the chance to participate in lucrative contracts for post-war reconstruction (Ambrosio 2005).

From 2003 to 2005, Moscow became increasingly concerned by US efforts to increase its influence at the expense of Russia in countries that were formerly part of the Soviet Union. Putin objected to US support for "colored revolutions" in Georgia, Ukraine, and Kyrgyzstan, areas that Russia has always perceived to be its zone of influence and responsibility (Gvozdev and Simes 2005; Simes, 2007).

Washington's growing criticism of Putin's domestic policies and accusations of backtracking from democratic norms further undermined what had appeared to be an emerging US–Russian strategic partnership. Russians interpret the criticism as evidence that the West cannot tolerate a stronger and more self-confident Russia.[20] An increase in the price of oil from $35 to $72 per barrel in 2004–06 gave Russia the confidence to pursue a more assertive policy toward western Europe and countries in eastern Europe and Central Asia (Legvold 2007).

Putin's displeasure with post-2003 US unilateralism was fully displayed in his February 2007 address to the forty-third annual Munich conference on security policy, where he harshly criticized Washington for overstepping its national borders and imposing its policies on other nations.[21] According to liberal Russian analyst Alexei Arbatov, the speech meant that "Russia wants to be recognized – not only in word, but also in deed – as a great power among great powers." This meant that differences between Russia and the United States should be resolved on the basis of mutual compromise "rather than by pushing the American policy, or by presumptuously suggesting that Moscow interprets its interests in the wrong way" (Arbatov 2007; Migranyan 2008). The US decision in spring 2007 to install a missile defense system introduced unnecessary conflict, as Russians objected to a major European security decision taken without their participation.[22] Even before US–Russian relations dramatically cooled off in the wake of the Russian incursion into Georgia, the prospect of Russian integration in the Western club was viewed as increasingly remote (Trenin 2006, 2007; Aron 2006; Karaganov 2007).

In contrast, while there are a few areas of potential tensions, the relationship between the United States and China continues to be cooperative, largely due to the reaching of a tacit modus vivendi on Taiwan and the Bush administration's relative silence on human rights in China. However, this does not necessarily mean that Washington has finally come up with a coherent power management strategy toward China. The Pentagon continues to attack China's military buildup as strategically threatening, although most experts acknowledge that China is at least two decades behind the United States in military technology and capability (Office of the Secretary of Defense 2008; Council on Foreign

---

[20] The "sovereign democracy" concept developed by deputy head of presidential administration Vladislav Surkov illustrates the Russian elite's concerns about Western interference in Russian affairs. See, for example, Vladislav Surkov's Secret Speech: How Russia Should Fight International Conspiracies 2005, and Surkov 2006.

[21] The full text of the speech is available at www.kremlin.ru/eng/speeches/2007/02/10/0138_type82912type82914type82917type84779_118135.shtml.

[22] For official Russian reactions, see RFE/RL Newsline, February 2, 9, 12, and 20, 2007.

Relations 2007; Ross 2005). Enhanced security cooperation between Washington and Tokyo, especially US efforts to make Japan partially responsible for defending Taiwan, increases the risk of security dilemma dynamics in the Asia–Pacific region (Christensen 1999; Xinbo 2005–06). Finally, Washington's traditionally passive damage-control approach to the Taiwan issue may not be enough to avert an escalation of tension in the Strait, one that could lead to a nightmarish scenario of military confrontation between China and Taiwan involving the United States (Christensen 2002; Lieberthal 2005).

Neither China nor Russia has any expectation of displacing the United States from the top of the status hierarchy. Neither is proposing an alternative ideology to replace liberal democracy or trying to accumulate a network of like-minded allies (Shambaugh 2005). Even if Russia goes ahead with its plan to increase its defense budget by 25 percent in 2009, from $40 billion to $51.3 billion,[23] it will still spend one-tenth of current base US defense expenditures of over $500 billion, apart from the wars in Iraq and Afghanistan.[24] While Chinese military modernization worries US defense officials, its military acquisitions appear to be aimed at deterring Taiwan from declaring independence or preventing the United States from coercing China rather than trying to rival the United States as a global power (Fravel 2008). Yet US relations with Russia and to a lesser extent China continue to experience unnecessary shocks over problems that more skilled diplomacy and more creative statecraft, rooted in a clearer understanding of both countries' strategies for greater status and influence, might have anticipated and preempted. To be sure, neither Russia nor China has the capability to challenge the United States for global supremacy, and this structural constraint may be responsible for their current policy of cooperation with the West. On the other hand, power constraints alone cannot explain why China has devoted diplomatic and material resources to becoming a responsible power, as demonstrated by its involvement in multilateral institutions and strategic dialogue with the United States. Similarly, Putin did not have to engage in extensive cooperation with the United States after 9/11, and most of his advisers at the time recommended that Russia not involve itself in the United States' problems (Pushkov 2007). As former secretaries of state Henry Kissinger and George P. Shultz observe, Russia seeks "acceptance

---

[23] *RIA Novosti* 2008; Johnson's Russia List 2008.

[24] See comparative figures on US and Russian military expenditures at market exchange rates from the Stockholm International Peace Research Institute, available at www.sipri. org/contents/milap/milex.mex_cata_index.html. In purchasing power parity terms, Russia's current military expenditures are about one-seventh of US defense spending.

as equals in a new international system rather than as losers of a Cold War to whom terms could be dictated" (Kissinger and Shultz 2008). Russia and China want respect, not additional territory or military supremacy. China's and Russia's support for Uzbekistan's demand that the United States vacate a military base on its territory and their upgrading of the Sino-Russian military partnership (a warning to Washington to play a more modest role in Russian and Chinese backyards) illustrates the divisions that threaten cooperative efforts at international order and might have been avoided by paying more attention to their status concerns (Badkhen 2005; Magnier and Murphy 2005).

Conclusion

Our case study of the dynamics of Chinese and Russian relationships with the United States since the end of the Cold War suggests that treating both states' status concerns seriously and respectfully and according them positive identities led to major progress in securing their cooperation. If Russia and China pose especially thorny problems because of ideological differences and past enmities, then similar techniques may work with other states. Consulting with other states and inviting them to participate in multilateral forums can be effective tools of influence. Moreover, such efforts by the United States are relatively safe, inexpensive, and efficient, especially compared with the global promotion of democracy. In contrast, US attempts to criticize authoritarian or semi-authoritarian domestic politics or to link benefits to human rights policies will backfire, because Chinese and Russian elites will view US efforts as humiliating and an effort to impose US values on their societies. In this sense, promotion of democracy is not a necessary condition for increased US security (Alexander 2004).

That China and Russia have followed similar paths in trying to establish new identities following the shock of the end of the Cold War highlights the role of status considerations in shaping the foreign policy of major states. SIT suggests that when the status hierarchy is viewed as illegitimate and unstable, members of disadvantaged groups will turn to competition and conflict.

More research is needed to identify specific measures the United States can employ to accommodate the status and prestige concerns of its potential allies. For example, the Clinton administration experience with Yeltsin in the 1990s suggests that purely symbolic status concessions may not outweigh the impact of policies that have the effect of humiliating a major power. Encouraging a division of labor in which other states can specialize in particular functions or sharing leadership roles in international institutions (both formal and informal) are a few of the potentially productive ways to accommodate major powers' desire for acknowledgement of their special talents and capabilities. To provide forums for such symbolic measures, action needs to be taken to overcome the "institutional deficit" in US relations with both China and Russia. China should be admitted to the G8 and the Organization for Economic Cooperation and Development (OECD). Since neither China nor Russia will be admitted to NATO or the European Union, other ways of institutionalizing cooperation must be found, perhaps in a new version of the informal strategic triangle.

As Cold War considerations of the balance of power and nuclear parity recede in importance, Russia, China, and the United States increasingly have shared interests in curbing weapons proliferation and counterterrorism, and dealing with failed states. Both Russia and China are striving to establish positive identities and are willing to cooperate with the United States if they are accepted as important partners and are given real voice on important matters. A comparable effort is needed on the part of the United States to deal with both countries as something other than rivals, junior partners, or reluctant allies and to ensure their ultimate transformation into active maintainers of international order.

11 Asymmetrical cooperation in economic assistance

Jean-Claude Berthélemy

This chapter is about asymmetrical cooperation, as seen in typical foreign aid or official development assistance (ODA), and about the way in which interests rather than reciprocity foster cooperation. It contrasts the effects of proximate (specific) interests and distant (altruistic or general) interests in the choice of bilateral versus multilateral aid recipients, each providing a different basis of cooperation that fits the particular characteristics of the chosen aid recipients. Thus it takes apart the argument that asymmetrical cooperation only serves the stronger party, showing instead that a balance of diverse interests (Udalov 1995) underlies different types of asymmetrical cooperation, much as different values have been shown to constitute the basis of a successful negotiated agreement (Homans 1961; Nash 1950). Thus durable cooperation can come from repeated, matched asymmetrical exchanges, that in turn form the basis of justifying norms that stabilize the instances of cooperation.

The starting point of this chapter, which may appear to be far from these conclusions, is found in the debate opened by the World Bank (Burnside and Dollar 2000, p. 854) on aid efficiency. Its finding was the absence of any "significant tendency for total aid or bilateral aid to favor good policy. On the other hand, aid that is managed multilaterally (about one-third of the total) is allocated in favor of good policy." Burnside and Dollar interpreted bilateral aid allocation decisions as the consequence of a bias toward the self-interest of donors – in particular their geopolitical interests – while multilateral institutions would be more motivated by the needs and merits of potential recipients, and therefore would allocate their development assistance more efficiently.

But this does not mean that bilateral donors make the wrong decisions, only that their cooperation should not be judged on the same basis. Rather, they pursue different goals, which correspond to their own interest. This is, of course, acknowledged by Burnside and Dollar. To take this into account they include as determinants of aid several dummy variables for sub-Saharan Africa, the franc zone, Egypt, and central America. This approach has, however, two shortcomings. First, if aid is given for self-interest motives, this should be tested on a bilateral aid model, while Burnside and Dollar consider only the aggregate amount of aid received by each recipient. For instance, being a franc zone member is relevant for aid received from France, but not from the United States or the United Kingdom; in the multilateral case, France being only one among many other donors, being a franc zone member should not count that much. Second, if aid is given for self-interest reasons, one should also include commercial motives in the analysis. For instance, South Africa receives a significant amount of aid from France because it is a major trading partner of France, not because of any particular geopolitical link.

This chapter is based on an attempt to correct these two limitations, and with them probe deeper into an understanding of asymmetrical cooperation. In other words, what is the basis of asymmetrical economic cooperation if it does not improve the economic condition of the weaker recipient and does not respond to the geopolitical interests of the stronger donor? To this end, the whole information on bilateral aid flows is considered – that is, for each year the observations include aid commitments granted by the different bilateral donors to the different recipients. Second, it introduces not only geopolitical variables to capture the donor self-interest motives, but also economic variables such as the intensity of bilateral trade between the different donors and the different recipients.

The core results of this paper are based on econometric estimates of an aid allocation equation. In this exercise, variables that capture the donor self-interest motives are used to define a "bilateralism effect" in aid allocation decisions – that is, the shift in aid allocation that would be theoretically observed if all bilateral preference variables were neutralized in the aid allocation decision rules implicitly implemented by the donors.

Observing this bilateralism effect can then be used to compare the pattern of assistance that the different recipients would receive in the absence of bilateral preferences with what they actually receive, and with what they receive from multilateral donors. The end result is that the pattern of distribution of bilateral aid exhibits the same correlation with economic performances (measured by economic growth) as the pattern of distribution of multilateral aid. Moreover, the correlation of bilateral aid distribution with economic growth is entirely due to the component that is associated with the bilateralism effect. This result suggests that pursuing self-interested bilateral goals does not necessarily undermine the efficiency of the aid allocation system. When donors target countries with high trade-intensity linkages, they target also on averagely good performers, given that economic performance is generally linked to openness and therefore also to trade intensity.

In the chapter, the next section, section 2, assesses variables that can be introduced to capture the effect on bilateral aid allocation patterns of both the donor's self-interest and the recipient's needs and merits. Section 3 reviews some econometric issues underlying the estimates of the aid allocation equation. Such estimates are used in section 4 to evaluate the bilateralism effect, to discuss its consequences on overall aid patterns, and to compare such patterns with multilateral aid distribution. Section 5 returns to the general topic of asymmetric cooperation and concludes with some considerations of the architecture of the international aid system.

Self-interest of donor and recipient needs/merits variables

Since the contributions of Dudley and Montmarquette (1976) and McKinley and Little (1977), there has been a long debate in the development finance literature on the question of the true motives of asymmetrical cooperation through development assistance: do bilateral donors grant their assistance with a view to improving the development perspectives of recipients, or is this assistance driven by self-interest motives? There is a growing consensus in the most recent literature (see, e.g., Berthélemy 2005; and, for a recent survey, Neumayer 2003) that both types of variables contribute to explaining aid allocation decisions. Conversely, multilateral agencies are often viewed as free from self-interested behavior – although their decisions may be so influenced by some of their members.

Donors may pursue several objectives. One of them is geopolitical. It is usually assumed that a donor provides assistance to recipients who are like-minded, or at any rate who are potential political allies. Alesina and Dollar (2000) use data on votes at the United Nations to measure such a political alliance effect. However, political alliance may be a result as well as a determinant of aid allocation. Other possibilities are to link this political alliance factor to the colonial past of the donors, or to common interests due to geographical proximity. In this chapter I try to capture these effects through a combination of dummy variables for former colonial ties and for other broad geopolitical interests of the donors:

> Dummy variables for former colonies of Belgium, France, Portugal, Spain and the United Kingdom.
> A dummy variable for the pair United States–Egypt, because Egypt has received large amounts of assistance from the United States since its peace accords with Israel. Were Israel to be in our database, we would obviously need to introduce a similar dummy variable for its link with the United States, but

> Israel is no longer a developing country, and therefore does not belong to our database.
> A dummy variable capturing the close ties that exist between the United States and Latin American countries.
> A dummy variable capturing the geopolitical interest of Japan in assisting Asian developing countries.

I have also tested whether EU countries were giving more assistance across the board to ACP countries (associated states of Africa, the Caribbean and the Pacific Ocean), to which the European Community has granted since 1963 a preferential treatment, but this variable is never significant in my regressions.

Aid may also be used to deepen commercial linkages, not only political alliances. Not all donors have strong geopolitical interests, but all of them have trade interests. A donor's foreign assistance policy based on self-interest will typically be biased toward recipients who tend naturally to have more trade with it. This is, after all, the clear motive of tied aid, which persists in spite of continuous efforts from the OECD Development Assistance Committee (DAC) to reduce it. Therefore I have also introduced commercial interest motives in the analysis of aid allocation, as measured by the flow of exports to the recipient country, expressed as a percentage of the donor GDP. There might be a simultaneity bias when aid is tied, since more tied aid implies more imports from the donor. However, the risk is limited since I am working on aid commitment flows, and aid disbursements usually lag behind commitments, particularly for project loans or grants, which require building new equipment. In order to be on the safe side, I have lagged this variable by one year. The combination of the geopolitical dummies and of the trade intensity variable just described will define what I call the "bilateralism effect" in my aid allocation equations.

As a complement, it is useful to consider financial motives, particularly for my period of observation, during which a large number of recipients has been affected by a debt crisis. In the debt crisis literature (Birdsall, Claessens, and Diwan 2003), this is known as the "defensive lending" argument. Donors could be locked in a "debt game," in which they have to provide new resources to highly indebted countries simply to avoid these debtors falling in arrears. However, it is not possible to include this argument in the bilateralism effect, for two reasons: first, theoretically speaking a donor cannot protect its own financial interest alone through defensive lending, because refinancing and other financial relief mechanisms are usually subjected to burden-sharing rules, for instance under the auspices of the Paris Club; second, bilateral debt data are hardly accessible, when they exist. Nevertheless, the aggregate debt burden of a recipient, defined as the ratio of net present value of debt over export, may be a significant explanatory variable of aid allocation.

Let me turn now to the development motives of aid. These development motives are, of course, according to the usual donor political statements, the actual motives for their assistance programs. Such motives can be captured by the introduction of two different categories of variables. A first set is based on the argument that aid is granted to the neediest countries, for the sake of poverty alleviation. A second set takes into account the issue of aid efficiency: to some extent, aid should be given to recipients where it can have an impact on poverty, which depends on the quality of their economic policies and of their governance.

The most straightforward indicator of beneficiary needs is income per capita, measured at international prices (in purchasing power parity terms). If aid is to be allocated on the basis of recipient needs, the poorest countries should receive more and the richest countries less.

The quality of economic policies is more difficult to measure. I have tried several policy variables similar to those introduced by Burnside and Dollar, such as openness, government deficit, and inflation. None of these variables was significant. I have also tried social outcome variables, such as life expectancy at birth, child mortality, literacy rate, and school enrolment ratios, but none of these variables showed any robust correlation with aid allocation, possibly because their introduction reduces drastically the number of available observations, for lack of complete data.

Concerning governance, I have introduced a dummy variable that separates democratic and non-democratic regimes, based on the civil liberty and political freedom evaluation provided by Freedom House. I have in addition introduced dummy variables for internal and interstate conflicts, based on the database built by PRIO (International Peace Research Institute, Oslo). The methodological aspects of construction of these governance-related variables are discussed in Berthélemy (2005).

Another variable that can be used to check whether aid is granted to recipients considered to be well governed is the per capita amount of assistance that they receive from multilateral donors, given that multilateral assistance acts very often as a catalyst for bilateral assistance. Such multilateral assistance is usually conditional on the implementation of structural adjustment or reform programs, and it is therefore frequently used by bilateral donors as a signal that the recipient is committed to put to good use the external resources that it receives.

In the same spirit, I have also entered the total aid commitments (per capita) provided by other bilateral donors. This variable, utilized for instance by Tarp et al. (1999), is introduced to test whether donors are complementary to or substitute for each other. This variable must, however, be considered with caution, due to risks of simultaneity biases.

Econometric estimation

All the previously mentioned variables have been introduced in the estimation of an aid allocation equation. An original feature of this exercise is that the estimation is performed on a very large three-dimensional panel dataset, covering yearly data for the 1980s and the 1990s, and 22 donors and 137 recipients. The dependent variable is the amount of aid commitment per capita received yearly by each recipient from each donor, converted in constant US dollars at 1985 prices, using the OECD GDP deflator. The explanatory variables are those introduced in the previous section, augmented by two auxiliary variables, as discussed below.

Following the previous literature, the population of the recipient has been included in the list of explanatory variables. The size of the recipient is not neutral, as initially shown by Dudley and Montmarquette (1976), because there are aid administrative costs, which are not proportional to the amount of aid granted. As a consequence of the presence of fixed costs in aid administration, per capita aid granted to a recipient may depend positively or negatively on its population, depending on the elasticity of administrative costs with respect to the amount of aid granted, and on the elasticity of the expected aid impact with respect to the recipient's population. Empirically, one usually observes that small countries receive more assistance per capita than large countries.

The total amount of aid granted by the donor in the year of observation has also been entered as a variable. This provides a way to take into account the fact that some donors have larger aid budgets than others, and that such aid budgets fluctuate over time. I do not attempt here to explain the size of donors' aid budgets, which is usually a decision made prior to aid allocation per se.

The definition of all variables and their sources is provided in Appendix 1.

Once explanatory variables have been identified, an important step is to choose an appropriate specification and method of estimation. Technical issues, related notably to the treatment of the censored nature of the dependant variable, and to the use of a panel data set, are discussed in Berthélemy (2005). Appendix 2 provides a summary of this discussion and different estimates that I have performed for robustness check.

Most estimates are very significant and robust to changes in method of estimation. They are also very robust to changes in the list of explanatory variables. To summarize, I find that the per capita aid commitment

Table 11.1. *Summary of estimation results (final equation)*

Explanatory variable	Sign	Comments for interpretation
Self-interest of donor variables		
Bilateral trade/donor GDP (lagged one year)	>0	Commercial interest
Pot-colonial dummies	>0	Geopolitical ties
USA – Egypt dummy	>0	Geopolitical ties
USA – Latin America dummy	>0	Geopolitical ties
Japan – Asia dummy	>0	Geopolitical ties
Net present value of debt-to-export ratio (non-bilateral variable)	>0	Defensive lending
Recipients' needs and merits		
Real GDP per capita (lagged one year)	<0	Recipients need
Civil liberty and political freedom dummy (lagged one year)	>0	Recipient governance
Dummy for non-minor internal conflict (lagged one year)	<0	Recipient governance
Dummy for non-minor interstate conflict (lagged one year)	<0	Recipient governance
Per capita multilateral aid commitment	>0	Catalyst of bilateral aid
Per capita aid commitment granted by the other bilateral donors	<0	substitute to one's aid
Auxiliary variables		
Donor total aid commitment budget	>0	Parameter close to 1
Population of recipient	<0	Fixed effects also depend on population (see note)

Source: Appendix 11.2.
The parameter for recipient population cannot be directly interpreted because (i) at least one explanatory variable depends on the size of the recipient (the trade intensity variable); and (ii) fixed effects are also correlated with population. All in all, however, our estimations confirm the usual finding that larger countries receive less assistance per capita than smaller countries.

patterns is influenced by the different explanatory variables as reported in Table 11.1.

Using these estimates, the pattern of the bilateralism effects can be studied, with the results reported in the next section.

Assessment of the impact of bilateralism in aid allocation

A simple examination of estimated parameters suggests a very large impact of bilateralism. Given that my specification in log-linear, my parameters define multipliers on aid commitment. As shown in Table 11.2, all these multipliers are of very large magnitude. In this

Table 11.2. *Multiplier effect of bilateral variables on aid received by recipients*

Explanatory variable	Multiplier of aid commitment
Former Spanish colony	15.9
Former Belgian colony	6.4
Former French colony	5.8
Former Portuguese colony	4.9
Former British colony	3.5
Egypt–USA ties	24.7
Asia–Japan ties	3.3
Latin America–USA ties	1.8
Trade: + 1 standard deviation of explanatory variable	2.6

Source: Appendix 2.

table the multipliers associated with geopolitical dummy variables indicate by how much a bilateral aid flow is multiplied when the observed recipient and donor belong to the specified category. For the trade intensity variable, which is not a dummy variable, I consider by how much aid is multiplied when the explanatory variable increases by one standard deviation.

It should be noted that Table 11.2 may underestimate the actual impact of the bilateral variables, because most (but not all) of them have an impact on the probability of being selected as an aid recipient by a donor. For example, former French colonies have a higher probability than other developing countries of being selected as an aid recipient by France. Appraising the magnitude of the influence of bilateralism on the selection of aid recipients is, however, impossible here, for technical reasons. For several dummy variables (concerning former French and Belgian colonies, and the specific ties between the United States and Egypt and between Japan and Asian recipients), it is impossible to estimate properly the corresponding parameters (see Berthélemy 2005).

The next step is to compute the aggregate influence of bilateral variables on the bilateral aid pattern. To define this, I first compute the notional amount of aid that recipients would receive assuming that the trade intensity variable is equal to its average, and that the bilateral dummy variables are equal to zero. However, the sum of these notional aid flows is not equal to the sum of actual aid flows. This is essentially due to the non-linearity of my equation, where the impacts of bilateral variables on

Table 11.3. *Implicit shift of aid resources due to bilateralism: the "bilateralism effect" (US$ billion per year)*

	Number of countries	Aid actually received	Aid that would be received without bilateral factor
Countries with negative bilateral effect			
Asia	14	0.8	1.8
Latin America	16	0.9	1.4
Middle East and North Africa	6	0.4	0.8
Sub-Saharan Africa	39	5.6	10.6
Others	16	0.4	1.3
Total	91	8.1	15.9
Countries with positive bilateral effect			
Asia	11	8.2	3.4
Latin America	14	1.7	1.3
Middle East & North Africa	9	3.7	1.4
Sub-Saharan Africa	9	1.2	0.9
Others	0	0.0	0.0
Total	43	14.8	7.0

Source: Author's estimates based on Appendix 11.2 and aid data.
All aid flows considered here are yearly averages over the 1980–99 period.

aid allocation are multiplicative instead of additive. Moreover, there are indirect effects, given that neutralizing the effect of bilateral variables changes also the total aid assistance received from other donors. To correct all this, I make the assumption that total aid flows should not be affected by the neutralization of bilateral variables. This simply amounts to multiplying all notional aid flows by the same scalar, determined so as to ensure that the total flow of aid net of the bilateralism effect is equal to the total actual aid flows. The result is what I call the aid commitments that would be received in absence of bilateralism. The final step consists in computing the bilateralism effect as the difference between actual aid commitments and the commitments that would be received in the absence of bilateralism.

The results suggest that large amounts of aid are linked to decisions based on purely bilateral criteria. Some countries would receive much more assistance in absence of bilateralism, other would receive less. The common received wisdom is that former colonies would receive less assistance. However, as shown by Table 11.3, this is not necessarily the case.

The main result of this exercise is that it shows that aid allocation based on bilateralism is biased against sub-Saharan Africa, instead of in favor of this region. Conversely, it is favorable to Asia and the Middle East and

Table 11.4. *Implicit shift of aid resources due to geopolitical factors (US$ billion per year)*

	Number of countries	Aid actually received	Aid that would be received without geopolitical factor
Countries with negative geopolitical effect			
Asia	13	2.1	2.2
Latin America	22	2.1	2.5
Middle East and North Africa	14	2.0	2.4
Sub-Saharan Africa	41	6.1	7.4
Others	16	0.4	0.5
Total	106	12.7	15.0
Countries with positive geopolitical effect			
Asia	12	6.9	5.6
Latin America	8	0.5	0.4
Middle East and North Africa	1	2.2	1.0
Sub-Saharan Africa	7	0.7	0.6
Others	0	0.0	0.0
Total	28	10.3	7.6

Source: Author's estimates based on Appendix 11.2 and aid data.
All aid flows considered here are yearly averages over the 1980–99 period.

North Africa (MENA) region. This stems from the fact that geopolitical ties such as postcolonial relations are quantitatively a much less significant component of the bilateralism effect than the trade intensity: sub-Saharan African countries enjoy favorable treatment from the former colonial powers, but the fact that they are very small trading partners has in the end a much more significant negative influence than the positive influence of postcolonial ties. Moreover, even though the multipliers attached to former colonial dummy variables are very large, most of them apply to relatively small aid flows, and this reduces significantly their influence on the aggregate result. In addition, virtually all recipients have a privileged linkage with one donor, be it because of history (former colonies) or of geography (regional dummies for Asia and Latin America), implying that in the aggregate these effects cancel out to some extent. As a consequence, the trade component of the bilateralism effect has for all practical purposes a much higher influence on aid allocation patterns than its geopolitical component.

This is confirmed in Table 11.4, where I have replicated the previous exercise without taking into account the trade intensity variable. In Table 11.4, the shift in aid allocation that is attributable to geopolitical

Table 11.5. *Correlation between the two components of bilateral aid and multilateral aid*

Region	Correlation between bilateralism effect and multilateral aid		Correlation between bilateral aid net of the bilateralism effect and multilateral aid		Correlation between bilateral aid & multilateral aid	
Asia	0.52	***	0.74	***	0.68	***
Latin America	−0.33	*	0.84	***	0.80	***
Middle East and North Africa	0.79	***	0.85	***	0.79	***
Sub-Saharan Africa	−0.34	**	0.65	***	0.77	***
Others	−0.37	***	0.30	***	0.09	***
All countries	0.3633	***	0.5792	***	0.6545	***

Source: Author's estimates based on Appendix 11.2 and aid data.
All aid flows considered here are yearly averages over the 1980–99 period.
***(**,*) = significant at 1 percent (5 percent, 10 percent) level.

factors is relatively small, accounting for a little more than 10 percent of aid flows, as compared with over one third in Table 11.3, where all bilateral variables are taken into account.

An indirect way of controlling the relevance of the proposed measure of the effect of bilateralism is to check that the aid that would be allocated to countries in the absence of bilateralism is correlated with multilateral aid that they receive. This is the case, as reported in Table 11.5, both for the whole sample and for regional sub-samples. This in fact explains most of the correlation that is observed (last column of Table 11.5) between the bilateral and multilateral aid patterns. This suggests that my decomposition of bilateral aid into its two components actually describes well the pattern of bilateral behaviors, which for one part depends purely on motives of self-interest and for the other part follows a pattern consistent with multilateral aid allocation.

Of course, there are still differences between the patterns of allocation of multilateral aid and of bilateral aid net of the bilateralism effect. The principal difference is that Asia receives more assistance from the multilateral donors than it would receive from the bilateral donors in absence of the bilateralism effect (Figure 11.1). Within Asia, China and the three large South Asian countries (India, Bangladesh, and Pakistan) receive relatively more assistance than other recipients (Figure 11.2), which explains the relatively favorable treatment of Asia by the multilateral

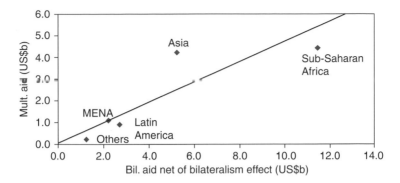

Figure 11.1. Comparison by region of multilateral aid with bilateral aid net of the bilateralism effect (author estimates based on Appendix 2 and aid data)

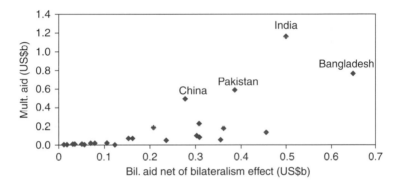

Figure 11.2. Comparison within Asian region of multilateral aid with bilateral aid net of the bilateralism effect (author estimates based on Appendix 2 and aid data)

donors suggested by Figure 11.1. Of course, there are other differences in treatment of some countries within other regions, but these differences have less impact on regional aggregate outcomes. For instance, within sub-Saharan Africa, the multilaterals favor Ethiopia, while the bilateral donors favor Senegal (a relatively small and not so poor country, compared with Ethiopia, but a very large recipient of bilateral aid), even after elimination of the bilateralism effect (Figure 11.3).

A comparison of the pattern of distribution of total bilateral aid over the whole period with the distribution of multilateral aid shows that both aid patterns exhibit on average comparable modest but positive correlations with economic growth (Table 11.6).

Table 11.6. *Correlation between the bilateralism effect and growth (averages over 1980s and 1990s)*

	Correlation between bilateral aid and growth		Correlation between bilateral aid net of bilateralism effect and growth		Correlation between bilateralism effect and growth		Correlation between multilateral aid and growth	
Asia	0.65	***	0.47	**	0.60	**	0.48	**
Latin America	−0.29		−0.41	*	0.29		−0.44	*
Middle East and North Africa	0.28		0.03		0.25		0.23	
Sub-Saharan Africa	−0.12		−0.04		−0.08		0.01	
Others	0.01		0.01		−0.01		−0.17	
All countries	0.34	***	0.13		0.31	***	0.28	***

Source: author's estimates based on Appendix 11.2 and aid data.
All aid flows considered here are yearly averages over the 1980–99 period.
***(**,*) = significant at 1 percent (5 percent, 10 percent) level.

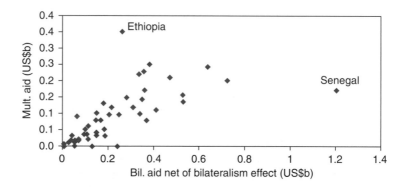

Figure 11.3. Comparison within sub-Saharan African region of multilateral aid with bilateral aid net of the bilateralism effect (author estimates based on Appendix 2 and aid data)

Of course, this correlation is purely a descriptive statistic, and does not mean anything in terms of causality. However, it suggests that, for all practical purposes, multilateral and bilateral aid flows are equally poorly "efficient," in terms of growth promotion. Moreover, when one decomposes bilateral aid flows between the bilateralism effect and aid commitments that would be received in the absence of bilateralism, the former is on average significantly correlated with growth, while the latter is not. This observation, which runs against common received wisdom, suggests that the bilateralism effect cannot be considered as the principal explanation of the poor efficiency of bilateral assistance. Its lack of selectivity should rather be linked to the existence of common biases in aid allocation, independent of the donor, such as, for example, the fact that Senegal is a major aid recipient in Africa in spite of modest economic performance and smaller needs than other countries. To some extent, the bilateralism effect appears paradoxically favorable to selectivity, simply because openness is good for growth and has also a catalytic effect on aid flows. When one computes correlations within regions, a similar pattern of results appears for Asian countries and, partially, for Latin America (where multilateral aid is negatively correlated with growth). For the other regions there is no correlation whatsoever between growth performances and our different aid aggregates.

Conclusion

This chapter has examined the motives of asymmetric cooperation through bilateral aid allocation decisions as they are revealed by data on bilateral aid commitments. Both self-interest motives of the stronger party and need and merit motives of the weaker recipient have been identified. Bilateral variables that describe self-interest motives are related to economic and political ties between donors and recipients. These variables have been used to define what is termed the "bilateralism effect" in aid allocation decisions, which appears to be a significant factor influencing bilateral aid patterns. In turn, these estimates have been used to compute what would have been, on average over the past two decades, the amount of aid commitments granted to each recipient in the absence of this bilateralism effect. Unsurprisingly, this aid allocation net of the bilateralism effect is highly correlated with multilateral aid commitments received by the different recipients. Perhaps more surprisingly, it appears that the bilateralism effect is adverse in the sub-Saharan African region, in spite of its strong post-colonial ties with European donors, and is favorable to Asia and the Middle East. This result stems from the fact that, in self-interest aid allocation motives, trade linkages actually play the principal role. On average, bilateral donors tend to provide more aid not only to their political allies, but also, and even more so, to their main trading partners.

The results suggest as a consequence that, contrary to the common received wisdom that has been reinforced by Burnside and Dollar (2000), bilateral cooperation through aid policies is not necessarily adverse to aid selectivity after all. The recipients who benefit the most from the bilateralism effect are major trading partners of donor countries, and this is on average positively related to their economic performances.

Such results suggest some interesting conclusions regarding the architecture of the international aid system. The self-interest motive of bilateral donors provides after all a good basis for asymmetric cooperation with relatively good performers as a stimulus to bilateral official development assistance. This is, of course, only a second best, because bilateralism in aid allocation is unavoidably blended with purely geopolitical motives, which possibly have nothing to do with economic development. Such geopolitical motives cannot be prevented if one relies on a bilateral aid system, because they are part and parcel of the reasons why the principal bilateral donors provide assistance to developing countries.

In such a system, asymmetric cooperation with multilaterals should concentrate their efforts on assistance to the neediest recipients, instead of the good performers, as the basis for their exchange of interests, to correct the bias of bilateral aid in favor of major trading partners and of geopolitical allies. Too much focus on aid efficiency by multilateral agencies as a criterion for cooperation would leave the potential recipients that are not significant political allies or trading partners of the bilateral donors excluded from all aid sources. The employment of two different bases of asymmetrical cooperation corresponding to the division of responsibilities between the bilateral and multilateral donors has the merit of avoiding a too heavy concentration of aid on a few good performers and of arriving at a Nash point or Homans exchange, which would be impossible if all donors adopted the same pattern of aid allocation as the multilateral agencies. Thus asymmetric cooperation can reside in a complementarity rather than reciprocity.

Appendix 11.1. List and sources of variables

Variable	Definition	Source
ODA	Real ODA (OA) commitments divided by the population of the recipient country, using the OECD GDP deflator	OECD DAC database (international development statistics) and OECD national account statistics
Total ODA of donor	Total real ODA of the donor (totaled over the 137 recipients)	Author's own calculation
Other donors' ODA	Total of ODA given by other donors to the recipient country	Author's own calculation

Multilateral ODA per capita	Real ODA (OA) commitments of multilateral donors divided by the population of the recipient country, using the OECD GDP deflator	OECD DAC database (international development statistics) and OECD national account statistics
GDP per capita	Real GDP per capita in constant dollars (international prices, base year 1985) of the recipient countries	Penn World Tables
Population	Population, total	World Bank's World Development Indicators
Trade	Bilateral exports to recipient in % of donor's GDP	OECD trade database
Growth	GDP growth (annual %) of the recipient lagged one period	World Bank's World Development Indicators
Global freedom	Mean of civil liberties and political right indexes, ranging from 1 (most free countries) to 7 (less free countries)	Freedom House website. See Berthélemy (2005) for transformation in a dummy variable
Interstate conflict	Dummy variable for non-minor interstate conflict	International Peace Research Institute, Oslo
Internal conflict	Dummy variable for non-minor internal conflict	International Peace Research Institute, Oslo
NPV of debt/ export	Ratio of net present value of debt over export	Data provided by Bill Easterly (Easterly 2001)

Appendix 11.2. Determinants of bilateral ODA per capita commitment (in logarithm)

Column (1) in the table below reports the estimates of the aid allocation equation using a standard one-step Heckman maximum likelihood method. It fits parameters of the joint system:

$Y = bX + u$

Y observed if $cZ + v > 0$

Where u and v are normally distributed error terms, with $cov(u,v)=\rho$, and

Y = the dependent variable, i.e., the log of aid commitment per capita (ODA)

X = explanatory variables

Z = explanatory variables for the selection equation. Here $Z=X$

In this equation, the pseudo-student statistics are computed using correction for cluster autocorrelation of residuals (cluster being defined here on recipients).

Column (2) provides similar estimates, with Z defined as level instead of logarithm variables for all variables that may have null values. This saves

	(1)Heckman	(2)Heckman	(3)OLS	(4)Fixed effects	(5)Fixed effects
ln(GDP per cap) (lagged)	-0.646 ***	-0.593 ***	-0.610 ***	-0.721 ***	-0.719 ***
	(5.71)	(5.49)	(5.56)	(7.51)	(7.49)
ln(population)	-0.474 ***	-0.495 ***	-0.486 ***	-1.124 ***	-1.125 ***
	(7.59)	(8.05)	(7.97)	(10.24)	(10.25)
Global freedom<=4 (lagged)	0.191 *	0.152	0.169 *	0.182 ***	0.183 ***
	(2.21)	(1.89)	(2.03)	(4.78)	(4.82)
Interstate conflict (lagged)	-0.373 **	-0.330 *	-0.344 *	-0.114	-0.209 ***
	(2.65)	(2.25)	(2.41)	(1.33)	(5.11)
Internal conflict (lagged)	0.190 *	0.184	0.183	-0.242 ***	-0.209 ***
	(1.89)	(1.90)	(1.88)	(4.99)	(5.11)
ln(NPV of debt/export)	0.099	0.087	0.091	0.208 ***	0.205 ***
	(1.44)	(1.32)	(1.37)	(6.69)	(6.62)
ln(total ODA of donor i)	0.992 ***	0.931 ***	0.951 ***	0.974 ***	0.974 ***
	(28.37)	(24.31)	(27.49)	(111.20)	(111.19)
ln(oth. donors ODA per cap)	0.288 ***	0.281 ***	0.281 ***	-0.143 ***	-0.143 ***
	(4.66)	(4.63)	(4.61)	(6.15)	(6.15)
ln(multilateral ODA per cap)	0.235 ***	0.228 ***	0.229 ***	0.183 ***	0.183 ***
	(5.77)	(5.81)	(5.84)	(9.87)	(9.85)
ln(trade) (lagged)	0.313 ***	0.297 ***	0.298 ***	0.367 ***	0.367 ***
	(6.39)	(6.34)	(6.35)	(39.06)	(39.06)
Former French colony	1.851 ***	1.804 ***	1.839 ***	1.756 ***	1.756 ***
	(7.49)	(7.35)	(7.54)	(18.63)	(18.63)
Former British colony	1.466 ***	1.366 ***	1.414 ***	1.262 ***	1.262 ***
	(8.64)	(8.34)	(8.75)	(16.04)	(16.04)
Former Portuguese colony	2.158 ***	2.216 ***	2.187 ***	1.579 ***	1.580 ***
	(3.68)	(4.04)	(3.93)	(4.96)	(4.96)
Fomer Spanish colony	2.769 ***	2.889 ***	2.825 ***	2.765 ***	2.767 ***
	(16.08)	(16.35)	(17.15)	(13.00)	(13.01)

	(1)	(2)	(3)	(4)	(5)
Former Belgian colony	2.570 ***	2.411 ***	2.486 ***	1.850 ***	1.850 ***
	(10.21)	(9.75)	(10.15)	(6.06)	(6.06)
USA–Egypt tie	3.399 ***	3.418 ***	3.431 ***	3.209 ***	3.208 ***
	(33.77)	(34.37)	(33.65)	(8.18)	(8.18)
USA–Latin America tie	0.725 *	0.759 *	0.751 *	0.588 ***	0.589 ***
	(2.29)	(2.48)	(2.42)	(6.15)	(6.16)
Japan–Asia tie	1.663 ***	1.674 ***	1.681 ***	1.183 ***	1.183 ***
	(7.50)	(7.63)	(7.60)	(10.80)	(10.80)
Intercept	-7.930 ***	-6.707 ***	-7.204 ***	5.274 **	5.273 **
	(3.54)	(2.98)	(3.29)	(2.74)	(2.74)
Number of observation	27542	33836	19983	19983	19983
Uncensored observations	19983	19983			
ρ	0.139 ***	-0.067			
R^2			0.547		
Hausman test				235.81 ***	250.09 ***

(1) Standard Heckman maximum-likelihood model.
(2) Heckman maximum-likelihood model without logarithm for trade, other donors' aid and multilateral aid in the selection equation.
(3) OLS without sample selection correction.
(4) Fixed-effect model.
(5) Fixed-effect model with same parameter for interstate and internal t- or z-statistics between brackets (estimated with robust recipient cluster method whenever relevant).
*** (**, *) significant at 1 percent (5 percent, 10 percent) level.

some 6,400 censored observations for the selection equation. With this improvement of the selection equation, the correlation between u and v becomes non-significant, suggesting that the aid allocation equation can be estimated independently of the selection equation. Pseudo-student statistics are estimated using the correction for cluster auto-correlation.

Column (3) reports ordinary least square estimates of the same aid allocation equation and, consistently with the previous finding, exhibits parameter estimates very close to those obtained in column (2). Student statistics are estimated using the correction for cluster auto-correlation.

Column (4) provides estimates of the same equation, augmented with a random effect for recipient, that is:

$$Y_{ijt} = bX_{ijt} + e_i + u_{ijt}$$

Where i stands for the recipient, j the donor and t the year of observation, and e_i and u_{ijt} are normally distributed random variables.

Column (5) reports estimates obtained with the fixed-effect method, that is the same as above, but where e_i is not a random variable but a deterministic parameter, which is estimated together with the b parameters (estimates not reported). The Hausman specification test suggests that this fixed-effect method is preferable to the random-effect method.

Column (6) is the same as column (5), but where the parameters for internal and interstate conflicts have been constrained to be equal (they were not significantly different in the previous estimation. These column (6) estimates are used to produce results reported in Tables 11.2 to 11.6.

12   Conclusion: improving knowledge
of cooperation

Saadia Touval and I. William Zartman

We seem to be living in an era of elusive cooperation after the Cold War, not exactly unilateralism but still a pervasive tendency to grasp for policies that depend on one or few actors (Zartman 2009). Of course, the George W. Bush administration – now past – is often cited as the prime example, and although in reality its single-shooting was more a matter of aggressive packaging during the first administration than effective action, it had a real predilection for small groups, such as the six-power talks on Korea or the quartet on Israel or the G4+1 on Iran. But other leading states in the early twenty-first century have followed a policy of limited cooperation or minilateralism. Russia has embarked on a single-handed revival of Cold War attitudes, with the Shanghai Cooperation Organization as company; the major powers of Asia – China, Japan, and India – focus on their own position and policy rather than on broad cooperative ventures; Iran and North Korea, too, have sought security in unilateral nuclear action; and Venezuela embarked on an attitude of sticking it to its Big Brother in the hemisphere, picking up a few friends along the way. Only Europe in its Union suit has adopted an official policy of cooperation, but it, too, is not only ragged but operating inward within a limited group. The major multilateralist cooperative ventures such as the Doha Round of trade talks or the post-Kyoto plans on climate change have been neither efficient nor effective, as Touval's chapter signals. The twenty-first century has not opened up as an era of cooperation, and has not brought much support to the theory that cooperation is innate and future-shadowed.

Yet of course multilateral cooperation is alive and well as an option, even if not as a characteristic. This collection of essays has brought some important insights into the phenomenon and they can be gathered together into a deeper meaning for the concept. The contributors to this volume examined what IR scholars mean by "cooperation," what are its dynamics, and what is the relationship between "cooperation" and its extended policy, "multilateralism." They go some way to clarifying the picture, revealing both a wide area of consensus and some significant differences. There is broad agreement on the meaning of cooperation; the contributors' use of the term is consistent with the definition offered in the introduction: "a situation where parties agree to work together to produce new gains for each of the participants unavailable to them by unilateral action, at some cost."

Depth of cooperation

To return to the basic question underlying this examination – when and why do states cooperate? – the initial cut of the answer is found to be in the definition itself: when they agree to work together to produce new gains for each of the participants unavailable to them by unilateral action, at some cost.[1] Cooperation is not altruism, a subject of much current research, and therein lies the analytical challenge. Altruism is giving or costing, with no (apparent) expectation of reward. Cooperation is giving at a cost, but with expectation of reward. It involves a decision, not just an innate proclivity. So the basic question that invites further research refers to the balance of cost and reward: how much reward is needed to outweigh the cost of producing it?

States cooperate when they can achieve gains through pooling efforts and through trade, an economic concept that has equal meaning in politics and that encapsulates the basic notion of negotiation. The historical overview by Keller that plots the development of ideas on the nature of states and their relations since the birth of the state system in the Peaces of Westphalia of 1648 brings out the importance of seeing the system as a market and therefore counting competition as cooperation. Indeed, the period covered was the same time when the French term *négoce* (business) was being transformed into *négociation* (diplomacy) (de Callières 2005 [1716]; deFelice 1976 [1778]), whose basic idea is giving something to get something, the definition of trade on which subsequent prescriptions for negotiation are founded (Nash 1950; Homans 1961), as the chapters by Hopmann and Touval then develop. The prospect of sustained gains based on expected reciprocity is the core notion underlying cooperation, whether long- or short-term.

Yet reciprocity is not enough as an explanation for cooperation, as the preceding chapters show. If it were, the wave of large multilateral cooperation would have swept further and faster than it has, as states (that is, statesmen and their publics) came to realize the compound benefits of

---

[1] Recent evolutionary research indicates that the cooperation has to produce benefits above ten times the cost (Boyd 2006), but that is high for interstate relations. Nigeria joined the African-Caribbean-Pacific agreement with the then European Economic Community for a benefit that was estimated at less than the cost of the negotiations. Bloom 1966, cited in Zartman 1976.

enlightened self-interest. Instead, the problems of inefficiency and ineffectiveness highlighted by Doran, Hampson, Hopmann, and Touval, as well as the undermining effects of sideline observation, free riding and free viewing explored in these and Zartman's chapters, limit cooperation and weigh in on the decision to cooperate. Yet, as all the chapters underscore, they do not eliminate it. What, then, determines the dimensions of cooperation?

Neither Realism nor Liberalism give an answer, and whether cooperation is "in us" or "for us" only tells our predilections, not what triggers them or what makes them last, although, as noted, they last less long for the Realists than for the Liberals in any case. Furthermore, recognizing the true nature of the general predilection does not explain the current tendency for limited rather than global cooperation, or how to make cooperation either broader or longer-lasting. For these answers one has to look outside the contending approaches and then consult the findings of the previous chapters that reach beyond the initial problem of cooperate-or-not to focus on the enabling conditions of the cooperation decision.

Along with the international relations and social science studies, and at the same time, growing scholarship on evolutionary studies in behavioral science has focused on the same question of cooperation, often working through game theory and its Prisoners' Dilemma game (Axelrod and Hamilton 1981; Maynard Smith 1982; Clements and Stephens 1995; Dugatkin 1997; Hammerstein 2003). While the analysis has dealt with human evolution, it comes to a conclusion similar to that of international relations, even though with *mutatis mutandis* of significance. A significant, if secondary, explanation of cooperation in evolution turns to the same concept as in international relations – reciprocity (Trivers 1971). The variously refined strategies of tit for tat, tit for double-tat (Axelrod 1984) and win–stay/lose–shift (Nowak and Sigmund 1993) and the looser notion of reputation (Nowak and Sigmund 1998) all operationalize the shadow of the future.[2]

But the primary evolutionary answer regarding reasons for cooperation is found elsewhere, in kinship (Hamilton 1964). Kin selection or inclusive fitness does not depend on reciprocity, but rather draws on a special kind of altruism, in which the individual does not benefit but the group does.[3] While it might seem that this explanation based on "social altruism" would be outside the definition of cooperation and would not apply to

---

[2] Two further refinements of network or spatial reciprocity (Nowak and Sigmund 1992) and group selection (Traulsen and Nowak 2006) do not seem to apply to interstate relations.

[3] Presumably this does not cover certain parts of kinship such as sibling rivalry or certain rounds of segmented society.

states, in fact it does. Kinship does not have to be "real," whatever that would mean in communities as large as states. States seek to establish their "families" ethnically, regionally, or ideologically in order to promote cooperation, solidarity, and support based on imagined kinship (Anderson 1983). The individual actor benefits indirectly, through the group, as well as directly. Since states are above all responsible to their people, they cannot be expected to be altruistic in the same sense as individuals. In fact, ethnic and regional cooperation is often based on "protection of the species," and cooperation among ideological kin can even be seen to foster not only "kin" protection but expansion.

Reciprocity in the extended sense is too broad, providing too great a dilution of the benefits. Instead, states cooperate with others "like them," whether it be geographically, ideologically, or socially (ethnically or in other identity terms). Imagined kinship holds cooperation together in "social altruism," so that benefits can be shared among those who hold the same values and identities. Values and identities, as Hopmann emphasizes, are the necessary glue for cooperation, not simply costed benefits; they identify not only the purpose of the cooperation but also the shared kinship of those included in the cooperation. This finding does not derive from constructivism but, in reverse, brings an important emphasis to it, and reaches over the contending explanations of Realism and Liberalism.

Unfortunately, there is a negative as well as positive side to the solidarizing element of kinship. Cooperation is most solid when parties cooperate not only for something but against something, and more powerfully against someone. Nothing helps cooperation like an external enemy. Enemies promote internal solidarity around a common purpose; they help the parties identify themselves, by identifying who they are not, as an aid to identifying who they are. The lesson is apposite to the understanding of the limits of cooperation in the post-Cold War (and postcolonial) era. The external enemy was obvious in both periods and was useful in fostering defensive solidarity; indeed, unity under decolonization was best expressed in who the colony was not (the colonizer) in order to overcome divisions that might arise among cooperating components in trying to identify who the colony was. NATO after the Cold War accomplished a monumental feat by holding together when the external enemy had disappeared, but then runs into a clash between the negative (anti-Qaeda but also anti-Russian) and positive (pro-democratic) basis of its cooperation on issues of expansion. (Europe, too, runs into a clash between past – Christian – and future – modernized development – aspects of its imagined kinship in regard to its expansion.) Larson and Shevchenko carry this aspect one step further by emphasizing the importance of not turning external parties into external enemies but including them under the cloak of cooperation. The fact that China and Russia have a potential opponents' role makes the call for the manipulation of social identities more necessary but more difficult. The absence of a clear external enemy in the case of anti-protectionist cooperation in the Doha Round and anti-pollution cooperation in the Kyoto negotiations has a powerful weakening effect.

Imagined kinship, however, merely sets up the situation for a set of decision challenges, analyzed by Hopmann as the Dilemmas of Common Interests (and how to get there) and of Common Aversions (and how to avoid them). The first dilemma is illustrated by the Prisoners' Dilemma, in which the search for a jointly beneficial agreement is overshadowed by the danger of defection to a unilaterally better outcome and, in the end, by inevitable mutual deadlock. The second is pictured in the Chicken Dilemma Game (CDG), where the search to avoid that deadlock as the worst outcome shows no clear strategy as to how to either achieve that goal or reach a jointly beneficial agreement. In this light, states cooperate when, and only when, they have established relations of trust or punishment, through negotiation. Interstate analysis shows that negotiation can build trust as the means to reaching an agreement, neither as a precondition nor as a result, but as a necessary part of the process, required for its end but not for its beginning.

Yet a reproduction of the original PD experiment in building trust, in Stanger's chapter, refines that preliminary conclusion. Not only is the shadow of the future a powerful motivation for parties to build a reputation for themselves and a relationship with others as a reason for cooperating; the shadow of the past also operates. This should not be surprising; it is the same type of reasoning, *mutatis mutandis*, that has characterized evolutionary studies of cooperation: cooperation results from expectations of reciprocation, the future shadow (Trivers 1971), or from kinship, the past shadow, that provide a reason to trust. States attempt to propagate a notion of "their own kind" as imagined kinship among allies to strengthen solidarity, whether that kind be defined in terms of ideology, region, or ethnicity. In sum, states' decisions to cooperate differ according to their past prejudices and relations with each other as well as their prospect of future relations (shadows of the past and future).

On the other hand, the Chickens in their Dilemma as analysed by Goldstein tell that cooperation comes when deadlock is the worst outcome, worse even than giving in to the opponent's own position. While most of the use of game theory in international relations has been based on the "other" big dilemma, the PD, the arguably more helpful scenario of a CDG produces insights of positive policy usefulness. In other words, states reach out toward cooperation when they realize that they are in a mutually hurting stalemate (Zartman 2000). Such a situation does not tell when the parties will achieve that realization, or more specifically where they will end up, but it does indicate that in the absence of a dominant solution they will begin to think, and eventually seek to define a way out of the stalemate. In game-theoretic terms, in the presence of two Nash equilibria they will seek to create a new outcome at the Nash Point that turns the game into an Angels' Project (northwest corner high), a situation of mutual cooperation that avoids the risk of individual defection, if only through free riding, and it does so by means of longer-range cooperative thinking embodied in a relationship. Such efforts are outside the CDG scenario, game theorists are quick to point out, but they can be read into the scenario or into the uncomfortable situation it portrays. CDG also points to useful strategies in building cooperation, notably those that emphasize the painful unacceptability of non-agreement and those that identify a focal point or salient solution as a Nash Point to win parties away from their unilateral preferences.

Size of cooperation

The other limitation on cooperation can be expressed as a search for a minimum effective coalition (MEC). Earlier work on coalitions (Riker 1962; Lawler and Young 1975; Murnigham 1978; Shapley and Shubik 1954; Brams 1990) emphasized the importance of the minimum winning coalition (MWC) and then the minimum contiguous winning coalition (MCWC), particularly in regard to voting. All were based on the crucial concept of "minimum," that is, coalitions would be no larger than necessary because superfluous members would claim their shares of the benefits of winning and diminish the shares of the others. While these concepts are relevant to multilateral cooperation in regime-building, where winning votes or more usually consensus is important to the definition of the cooperative terms, they need to be modified to be applicable to other types of cooperation (Brams, Kilgour, and Sanver 2007). In security matters, trade cooperation, and other areas where universal cooperation carries the terms of agreement down to the lowest common denominator or, worse, to inaction – Seyom Brown's (2008, 2009) "balking" – all that is needed is cooperation among the few necessary to build capability for the chosen policy – Hampson's minilateralism. The result is coalitions of the willing, regional and bilateral free trade agreements, and other cases of cooperation limited to the minimum number necessary for effective action, overcoming the reluctant, the competing orientations, the lowest common denominators, the free riders and free viewers, and the claims of those who would add nothing significant to the capabilities of a smaller group. The MEC overcomes Touval's critique of cooperation ineffectiveness and even inefficiency by limiting cooperation to its highest common denominator.

Minimum effectiveness is also seen to be a decision criterion in cooperation for conflict management. When the situation involves the conflict of a member of the international community with an outside party, the community of bystanders passively or actively supports their member in conflict, but it urges cooperation and a policy of negotiation and moderation – conflict management – when the conflict begins to hurt them, in Zartman's analysis. But when the situation is one where both parties to the conflict are external to the cooperating community, the international community lets one of its members intervene to manage conflict as mediator, reinforcing their position as often-critical bystander. The common element for the international community's decision to cooperate among themselves is that in both cases they seek to reduce their risk of loss, whether it be a loss of present gain from relations with parties of the conflict or loss of present comfort by avoiding the battle scars of mediation. The first situation is understandable; the second may also be understandable, even though more active support for the mediating member would increase its effectiveness and reduce the danger of wounds. Instead, individual bystanders often benefit from their own relations with one of the conflicting parties, despite the need for solidarity behind the mediation. It would be interesting to test these conclusions in greater depth in regard to a restricted "kin" community such as the European Union.

Behavior under cooperation also depends on the size of the states, as analysed by Doran and by Larson and Shevchenko. Small states cooperate in order to influence and even restrain large states, reversing the logic of bandwagoning, whereas large states cooperate when multiple participation is more important for effectiveness than its terms. Both approaches mean that cooperation is often thereby reduced to the lowest common denominator or, in other words, many is more important than much. The trap, or fallacy, of each strategy is that small states risk finding themselves sitting powerless on the bandwagon that the larger partners drive, whereas the larger state faces the choice between weak policies or alienating states whose cooperation it will need at some other time.

Large states of the international community increase their effectiveness by returning to a basic notion of negotiation theory, that parties reach agreement most efficiently and effectively when they cultivate the impression of equality (Zartman and Rubin 2000). Recognizing that true equality does not exist outside the laboratory, social identity theory emphasizes the costliness of near-equality (or minor asymmetry), which demands position-equalizing efforts and underscores the importance of apparently equalizing efforts. Status and prestige concerns are aspects of imagined kinship and provide the affective basis of cooperation, the bed on which it lies, and it works best when the lumps are smoothed out. When the number of potential partners is limited and cooperation demands broad participation, building positive identity in an imagined kinship rather than exclusion is the key to effectiveness.

The large asymmetry of the economic assistance situation analyzed by Berthélemy provides a different answer from a different angle: states decide to cooperate when their interests match, that is, when they achieve complementary rather than simply common payoffs from complementary activities, looking at both political self-interest and economic need and merit motives in aid allocation. Privileged economic and political ties between donors and recipients are highly correlated with the multilateral aid pattern. Yet, in the sub-Saharan African region examined, trade linkages actually play a greater role than political ties. A consequence of the major role played by trade linkages is that self-interest motives are not necessarily adverse to aid selectivity, given that major trading partners are also on average open and relatively well-performing economies. In sum, unequal states cooperate for "sound," complementary advantages (the shadow of the "present"?) as well as out of habit, because they know each other and so are "of the same kind" (the shadow of the past).

Questions

The focus on cooperation as a decision and not merely as a proclivity and the introduction of the two ideas of imagined kinship and minimum effective coalitions focus the concept of cooperation beyond the basic idea of reciprocity to indicate additional elements important for solidarity and durability and for efficiency and effectiveness. They stem from conceptual approaches beyond those normally considered in international relations discussions, and in turn they enter in various ways into different aspects of the subject discussed in the contributions to this book.

The contributions to this volume have expanded our knowledge about cooperation and multilateralism. But the more we know, the more questions present themselves. Our interest has been drawn especially to two issues – the impact of time horizons on cooperation, and the relationship between external and domestic factors.

The impact of time horizons

It has become widely accepted that long-term time horizons tend to encourage the emergence of cooperative relationships between players embodied in the shadow of the future effect (Axelrod, Keohane, Goldstein). The empirical evidence to support this view comes in part from reiterated game simulations. When parties play a single game, they tend to resort to exploitative strategies. Everything seems to depend on that single game. Therefore they try to protect themselves against losing and perhaps improve their chances of winning, by playing "defect" rather than "cooperate." But if they expect the game to extend indefinitely into the future, players tend to adopt cooperative strategies. The phenomenon is usually explained as stemming from the realization that cooperative strategies will yield to each higher gains in the long run than other strategies. Construal level theory in social psychology also confirms that immediate events will be conceived in concrete, specific terms, whereas distant events will be perceived in generalized, abstract terms (Liberman, Trope, and Stephan 2007), making long-term cooperation a matter of negotiated formulas and short-term cooperation bedeviled by details. The long view favors cooperation; the short view (myopia?) favors conflict, making it hard to get to the long view.

However, this hypothesis does not stand well when tested against the record of international history. States (or their leaders) have always been aware that they are "condemned" to live and interact with other states forever; that their relationships with other states are likely to extend into an indefinite future. This was especially true of neighbors (Kautilya 1960). Yet relationships between states tended to fluctuate – being sometimes cooperative and sometimes hostile, and relations with neighbors are more conflictual than any other types of pair. It would be hard to demonstrate that the turn toward cooperation was induced by a discovery of a common future. Germany and France dropped their hostile history after World War II and cooperated on a common project of building Europe, but that was the same Germany and France whose only use of the shadow of the future, earlier, was to make sure that the other side would not find an occasion to defect and get back at them. Similarly, were the leaders of England and France unaware during the centuries that they fought each other that their relationship would extend far into the future? And what about Germany and Russia, and others? In fact, for whom is cooperation innate and for whom is it learned, sporadically or durably?

One can also turn the argument around and claim that the shadow of the future encourages conflict, as Stanger's chapter also suggests, under defined conditions. If one enters into a regime, or an agreement committing oneself to a long period of a cooperative relationship with others, a likely reaction would be making an effort to establish rules and precedents that are favorable to oneself. Status is likely to become important. Whoever thinks that its own status is inferior or that the rules of the game favor the other, will likely try to change this and improve its own situation, while the party that holds an advantage will want to protect it. Thus we may observe competitive interactions within an overall cooperative relationship between states that maintain such a regime, as is indeed evident between the United States and Canada (Winham and DeBoer-Ashworth 2000; Stein 1995). But what makes people think long or short when they consider cooperation is still unexplored.

The role of domestic factors

Several contributions to this volume discuss the dynamics of interaction between parties – the factors encouraging cooperation or the resort to multilateral strategies. The contributions address mainly external factors – the interactions with other actors in the international system. There is very little explicit reference to the role of domestic factors.

Yet the critical role played by domestic factors and their interaction with external considerations is quite obvious. Understanding how domestic and international factors interact to produce conflictual or cooperative moves, to shape cooperative relationships, to pursue multilateral or bilateral negotiation strategies, is quite central for understanding both cooperation and multilateralism. If we view calculations of costs and benefits as shaping cooperation, we need to know *whose* costs and benefits, and how the interests of actors within the state combine with their perceptions of the external environment. In referring to time horizons then, we probably need to be aware of an array of actors' expectations; not only whether the state will be interacting with another state, but also leaders' domestic timetables and deadlines. When states choose whether to pursue their goals unilaterally, or by working with single partners bilaterally, or by negotiating multilaterally, again both internal and external considerations mesh together to produce a choice.

The relationship between internal politics and international relations has recently attracted renewed attention. Much work has been done about the influence of domestic factors upon international negotiations, as well as on international regimes (e.g. Putnam 1998, Spector and Zartman 2003). Some of this seems relevant to the dynamics of cooperation. Some is relevant also to understanding multilateralism. It would be particularly rewarding to investigate how deep cooperation must be to be durable, either in the learned or the innate sense, and therefore how easily it can be reversed. Current work highlights the importance of audience costs (Fearon 1995), but the notion should be carried further to establish whether it is a temporary issue-of-the-moment phenomenon, in an extended realism or momentary reciprocity, or a internalized shadow of the past on the future, in a deepened liberalism or exploited kinship. When governance was shallow and the right of kings and the world was big and cut up into many small pieces, the inquiry would quickly run into land and water boundaries and irresponsible foreign policies, but now that the world has shrunk into becoming a single mental landmass and people, the question of how deep cooperation runs is pertinent (Harles 2008). Besides the obvious policy considerations, there is also interest in whether (and if so how) the two sub-disciplines of comparative politics and international relations might be linked through some overarching theoretical structures. In a word, we know more about cooperation but we also know there is more to know.

Bibliography

Abrams, Dominic and Michael A. Hogg. 1990. An Introduction to the Social Identity Approach. In Abrams and Hogg, eds., *Social Identity Theory: Constructive and Critical Advances.* New York: Harvester Wheatsheaf.

Adler, Emanuel and Michael Barnett, eds. 1998. *Security Communities.* Cambridge University Press.

Aggarwal, Vinod K. 1996. *Debt Games: Strategic Interaction in International Debt Rescheduling.* Cambridge University Press.

Albin, Cecilia. 2001. *Justice and Fairness in International Negotiation.* Cambridge University Press.

Alesina, Alberto and David Dollar. 2000. Who Gives Foreign Aid to Whom and Why? *Journal of Economic Growth,* 5: 33–63.

Alexander, Gerard. 2004. The Authoritarian Illusion. *The National Interest,* fall: 79–83.

Allison, Graham. 1971. *Essence of Decision: Explaining the Cuban Missile Crisis.* New York: Little, Brown.

Ambrosio, Thomas. 2005. The Russo-American Dispute over the Invasion of Iraq: International Status and the Role of Positional Goods. *Europe-Asia Studies,* 57 (8): 1189–210.

Anderson, Benedict. 1983. *Imagined Communities.* New York: Verso.

Arbatov, Alexei. 2007. Is a New World War Imminent? *Russia in Global Affairs,* July–September, available at http://eng.globalaffairs.ru/numbers/20/1130/html.

Arneil, Barbara. 1996. *John Locke and America: The Defence of English Colonialism.* Oxford: Clarendon Press.

Aron, Leon. 2002. Russia's Choice. *Russian Outlook,* winter, available at www.aeg.org/publication13639/.

2006. The United States and Russia: Ideologies, Policies, and Relations. *Russian Outlook,* summer, available at www.aei.org/publications/pubID.24606/pub_detail.asp.

Arrow, Kenneth. 1951. *Social Choice and Individual Values.* New York: John Wiley.

Art, Robert J. 2003. *A Grand Strategy for America.* Ithaca, NY: Cornell University Press.

Artlow, Joshua P. 2008. At Brazil Conference, G–20 Urges Swifter Action on Financial Crisis. *Washington Post,* 10 November, available at www.washingtonpost.com/wp-dyn/content/article/2008/11/09/AR2008110902499.html.

Avenhaus, Rudolf. 2007. Nash's Bargaining Solution. *PINPoints,* 29: 7–9.

Axelrod, Robert. 1970. *Conflict of Interest: A Theory of Divergent Goals with Applications to Politics*. Chicago: Markham.

1984. *The Evolution of Cooperation*. New York: Basic Books.

1997. *The Complexity of Cooperation: Agent-Based Models of Competition and Collaboration, Princeton Studies in Complexity*. Princeton University Press.

Axelrod, Robert and Robert O. Keohane. 1986. Achieving Cooperation under Anarchy: Strategies and institutions. In Kenneth A. Oye, ed., *Cooperation under Anarchy*. Princeton University Press, 226–54.

Axelrod, Robert and W. D. Hamilton. 1981. The Evolution of Cooperation. *Science*, 211: 1390–96.

Axtell, Robert. 2000. *Why Agents? On the Varied Motivations for Agent Computing in the Social Sciences*. Working Paper Series. Washington, DC: Center on Social and Economic Dynamics.

Axtell, Robert, Robert Axelrod, Joshua Epstein, and Michael Cohen. 1996. Aligning Simulation Models: A Case Study and Results. *Computational and Mathematical Organization Theory*, 1: 123–41.

Badkhen, Anna. 2005. US, Russia Descend into Mutual Distrust; Divisions Threaten Anti-Terror Efforts. *San Francisco Chronicle*, July 21.

Baker, James. 1999. The Road to Madrid. In Chester Crocker, Fen Osler Hampson, and Pamela Aall, eds., *Herding Cats: Multiparty Mediation in a Complex World*. Washington, DC: US Institute of Peace Press.

Baker, Keith M. 1990. *Inventing the French Revolution*. Cambridge University Press.

Baldwin, David A., ed. 1993. *Neorealism and Neoliberalism: The Contemporary Debate*. New York: Columbia University Press.

Barry, Dave. 1984. Macho Diplomacy: Maybe US Foreign Policy Needs the Feminine Touch. *Boston Globe*, May 30: 57.

Bernard, Jessie. 1949. *American Community Behavior*. New York: Dryden.

1957. The Sociological Study of Conflict. In Bernard et al., *The Nature of Conflict*. New York: UNESCO.

Bernstein, Richard and Ross H. Munro. 1997. *The Coming Conflict with China*. New York: Alfred A. Knopf.

Berthélemy, Jean-Claude. 2005 Bilateral Donors' Interest vs. Recipients' Development Motives in Aid Allocation: Do All Donors Behave the Same? *Review of Development Economics*, 10 (2): 179–95.

Bijian, Zheng. 2005. China's "Peaceful Rise" to Great-Power Status. *Foreign Affairs*, 84 (5): 18–24.

Binmore, Ken. 1997. Book Review of Robert Axelrod's *The Complexity of Cooperation: Agent-Based Models of Competition and Collaboration*. *Journal of Artificial Societies and Social Simulation (JASSS)*, http://iasss.soc.survey.ac.uk/1/1/2.html.

Birdsall, Nancy, Stijn Claessens, and Ishac Diwan. 2003. Policy Selectivity Forgone: Debt and Donor Behavior in Africa. *World Bank Economic Review*, 17 (3): 409–36.

Black, J. L. 2004. *Vladimir Putin and the New World Order. Looking East, Looking West?* Lanham, MD: Rowman & Littlefield.

Blechman, Barry M. 1996. Emerging from the Intervention Dilemma. In Chester A. Crocker, Fen Osler Hampson, and Pamela Aall, eds., *Managing Global Chaos:*

Sources of and Responses to International Conflict. Washington, DC: United States Institute of Peace Press, 287–96.

Bloom, Bridget. 1966. Unpublished paper, NISER, August 25.

Bornstein, Gary, Danny Mingelgrin, and Christel Rutte. 1996. The Effects of Within-group Communication on Group Decision and Individual Choice in the Assurance and Chicken Team Games. *Journal of Conflict Resolution*, 40: 486–501.

Bornstein, Gary, David Budescu, and Shmuel Zamir. 1997. Cooperation in Intergroup, N-person, and Two-person Games of Chicken. *Journal of Conflict Resolution*, 41: 384–406.

Boucher, David. 1998. *Political Theories of International Relations*. Oxford University Press.

Bourhis, R. Y. and P. Hill. 1982. Intergroup Perceptions in Higher Education: A Field Study. In Henri Tajfel, ed., *Social Identity and Intergroup Relations*. Cambridge University Press.

Bowles, Samuel. 2006. Group Competition, Reproductive Leveling, and the Evolution of Human Altruism. *Science*, 314: 1569–72.

Bowles, Samuel and Herbert Gintis. 2003. Origins of Human Cooperation. In Peter Hammerstein, ed., *The Genetic and Cultural Origins of Cooperation*. Cambridge, MA: MIT Press.

Boyd, Robert. 2006. The Puzzle of Human Sociality. *Science*, 214 (Dec. 8).

Bradford, Colin and Johannes Linn. 2007. *Policy Briefing #163: Reform of Global Governance: Priorities for Action*. Brookings Institute, available at www.brookings.edu/~/media/Files/rc/papers/2007/10global%20governance/pb163.pdf.

Brams, Steven J. 1975. *Game Theory and Politics*. New York: Free Press.

1985. *Superpower Games: Applying Game Theory to Superpower Conflict*. New Haven: Yale University Press.

1990. *Negotiation Games*. London: Routledge and Kegan Paul.

1994. *Theory of Moves*. Cambridge University Press.

Brams, Steven J. and D. Marc Kilgour. 1987. Winding Down if Preemption or Escalation Occurs: A Game-Theoretic Analysis. *Journal of Conflict Resolution*, 31: 547–72.

Brams, Steven J., D. Marc Kilgour, and M. Renzi Sanver. 2007. A Minimax Procedure for Negotiating Multilateral Treaties. In Rudolf Avenhaus and I. William Zartman, eds., *Diplomacy Games: Formal Models and International Negotiations*. Springer.

Brooks, Stephen G., and William C. Wohlforth. 2002. American Primacy in Perspective. *Foreign Affairs* 81 (4): 20–33.

2005a. Hard Times for Soft Balancing. *International Security* 30 (1): 72–108.

2005b. International Relations Theory and the Case against Unilateralism. *Perspectives on Politics* 3 (September).

2008. *World Out of Balance: International Relations and the Challenge of American Primacy*. Princeton University Press.

Brown, Chris. 2002. *Sovereignty, Rights and Justice: International Political Theory Today*. Cambridge: Polity Press.

Brown, Michael E., Owen R. Coté, Jr., Sean M. Lynn-Jones, and Steven E. Miller, eds. 2000. *America's Strategic Choices*. Rev. ed. Cambridge, MA: MIT Press.

Brown, Rupert J. and Gordon F. Ross. 1982. The Battle for Acceptance: An Investigation into the Dynamics of Intergroup Behavior. In Henri Tajfel, ed., *Social Identity and Intergroup Relations*. Cambridge University Press, 155–78.

Brown, Seyom. 2008. *Higher Realism: A New Foreign Policy for the United States*. Paradigm.

2009. Adapting to the Evolving Polyarchy, In I. William Zartman, ed., *Imbalance of Power: The Post-bipolar System of World Order*. Boulder, CO: Lynn Rienner.

Brzezinski, Zbigniew. 2004. *The Choice: Global Domination or Global Leadership*. New York: Basic Books.

Bueno de Mesquita, Ethan. 2004 Conciliation, Counterterrorism, and Patterns of Terrorist Violence. *International Organization*, 59 (1): 145–76.

Bull, Hedley. 1977. *The Anarchical Society: A Study of Order in World Politics*. London: Macmillan.

Burnside, Craig and David Dollar. 2000. Aid, Policies and Growth. *American Economic Review XC*, 4: 847–68.

Byers, J. Michael and Georg Nolte, eds. 2003. *United States Hegemony and the Foundations of International Law*. Cambridge University Press.

Calleo, David P. 1987. *Beyond American Hegemony: The Future of the Western Alliance*. Brighton: Wheatsheaf.

Campbell, T. D. 1971. *Adam Smith's Science of Morals*. London: George Allen & Unwin.

Caporaso, James A. 1993. International Relations Theory and Multilateralism. In J. G. Ruggie, ed., *Multilateralism Matters*. New York: Columbia University Press.

Cederman, Lars-Erik. 1997. *Emergent Actors in World Politics: How States and Nations Develop and Dissolve*. Princeton University Press.

2001a. Agent-Based Modeling in Political Science. *Political Methodologist*, 10 (1):16–22.

2001b. Modeling the Democratic Peace as a Kantian Selection Process. *Journal of Conflict Resolution*, 45: 470–502.

2005. Computational Models of Social Forms: Advancing Generative Macro Theory. *American Journal of Sociology*, 110 (4): 864–93.

Checkel, Jeffrey. 1995. Structure, Institutions, and Process: Russia's Changing Foreign Policy. In Adeed Dawisha and Karen Dawisha, eds., *The Making of Foreign Policy in Russia and the New States of Eurasia*. Armonk, NY: M. E. Sharpe.

Chicago Council on Foreign Relations. 2006. US Role in the World: Multilateral Cooperation and International Institutions, available at http://worldpublicopinion.org.

Chiu, Daniel Y. 2003. International Alliances in the Power Cycle Theory of State Behavior. *International Political Science Review*, 24 (1): 123–36.

Choi, J. K. and S. Bowles, 2007. The Coevolution of Parochial Altruism and War. *Science*, 318: 636–40.

Christensen, Thomas J. 1999. China, the US–Japan Alliance, and the Security Dilemma in East Asia. *International Security*, 23 (4): 49–80.

2002. The Contemporary Security Dilemma: Deterring a Taiwan Conflict. *Washington Quarterly*, 25 (4): 7–21.

Chua, Amy. 2007. *Day of Empire: How Hyperpowers Rise to Global Dominance – and Why They Fail*. New York: Doubleday.

Clark, Ian. 1989. *The Hierarchy of States: Reform and Resistance in the International Order*. Cambridge University Press.

2005. *Legitimacy in International Society*. Oxford University Press.

Clément, Sophia. 2003. The United States and NATO: A Selective Approach to Multilateralism. In David M. Malone and Yuen Foong Khong, eds., *Unilateralism and US Foreign Policy: International Perspectives*. Boulder: Lynne Rienner, 399–420.

Clements, K. C. and D. W. Stephens. 1995. Mutualism and the Prisoner's Dilemma. *Animal Behavior*, 50: 527–35.

Clough, Emily. 2001. Computational Modeling from a Graduate Student Perspective. *Political Methodologist*, 10 (1): 26–28.

Cohen, Michael, Rick L. Riolo, and Robert Axelrod. 1999. *The Emergence of Social Organization in the Prisoner's Dilemma: How Context-Preservation and other Factors Promote Cooperation*. Santa Fe: Santa Fe Institute.

2001. The Role of Social Structure in the Maintenance of Cooperative Regimes. *Rationality and Society*, 13 (1): 5–32.

Coicaud, Jean-Marc. 2001. Legitimacy, Socialization and Social Change. In C. Kupchan et al., eds., *Power in Transition: The Peaceful Change of International Order*. Tokyo: United Nations University Press, 68–100.

Collins, Nancy. 1995. A Legacy of Strength and Love [interview with President Clinton]. *Good Housekeeping*, 221 (5): 113–15.

Commission on Human Security. 2003. *Human Security Now: Protecting and Empowering People*, final report, New York.

Constant, Benjamin. 1988 [1819]. *Political Writings*, ed. Biancamaria Fontana. Cambridge University Press.

Conybeare, John. 1986. Trade wars: A Comparative Study of Anglo-Hanse, Franco-Italian, and Hawley-Smoot conflicts. In Kenneth A. Oye, ed., *Cooperation Under Anarchy*, Princeton University Press, 147–72.

Conybeare, John. 1987. *Trade Wars: The Theory and Practice of International Commercial Rivalry*. New York: Columbia University Press.

Cooper, Andrew F. 1995. In Search of Niches: Saying "Yes" and Saying "No" in Canada's International Relations. *Canadian Foreign Policy*, Winter: 1–14.

Coser, Lewis, 1956. *The Social Functions of Conflict*. New York: Free.

Council on Foreign and Defense Policy (Russia). 2000. *Strategiya dlya Rosii: Povestka Dnya dlya Presidenta-2000* [*The Strategy for Russia. The Agenda for the President-2000*] Moscow: Vagrius.

Council on Foreign Relations. 2007. US–China Relations: An Affirmative Agenda, A Responsible Course, available at www.cfr.org/content/publications/attachments/ ChinaTaskForce.pdf.

Cox, Robert W., ed. 1997. *The New Realism: Perspectives on Multilateralism and World Order*. Tokyo: United Nations University Press.

Crane, David. 2008. Paul Martin's Prescient Idea Takes Hold. *Embassy*, November 12, available at www.embassymag.ca/page/view/crane-11–12–2008.

Crocker, Chester A. 1992. *High Noon in Southern Africa*. New York: Norton.

Crawford, Neta. 2002. *Argument and Change in World Politics: Ethics, Decolonization, and Humanitarian Intervention*. Cambridge University Press.

Dahrendorf, Ralph and Timothy Garten Ash. 2003. L'Europe et l'Amérique que nous voulons. *Le Monde*, September 7, available at http://watch.windsofchange. net/themes_62.htm.

Dawisha, Karen and Bruce Parrott. 1994. *Russia and the New States of Eurasia*. Cambridge University Press.

Dean, Jeffrey S., George J. Gumerman, Joshua M. Epstein, Robert Axtell, and Allan C. Swedlund. 1998. *Understanding Anasazi Culture Change through Agent-Based Modeling*. Working paper. Santa Fe: Santa Fe Institute.

De Callières, François. 2005 [1716]. *On the Manner of Negotiating with Sovereigns*. Washington: Institute for the Study of Diplomacy, Georgetown University.

De Felice, F. B. 1976 [1778]. Negotiations, or the Art of Negotiating. In I. William Zartman, ed. *The 50% Solution*. New York: Doubleday Anchor.

Deng, Yong and Thomas G. Moore. 2004. China Views Globalization: Toward a New Great Power Politics? *Washington Quarterly*, 27 (3): 117–36.

Denton, Russ and Rachael Solomon. 2004. Bush's Multilateralism. *Chronicle Online*, September 21, available at www.chronicle.duke.edu/vnews/display. v/ART/2004/09/21/415017b0e507.

Denver Post. 2008. Reform Pledged at Summit. 15 November, available at www. denverpost.com/newsheadlines/ci_10993435.

Deutsch, Karl W. et al. 1957. *Political Community and the North Atlantic Area*. Princeton University Press.

de Waal, F. B. M. 1992. *Chimpanzee Politics*. London: Cape.

Dobriansky, Paula J. 2000. Russian Foreign Policy: Promise or Peril? *Washington Quarterly*, 23 (1): 135–44.

Doran, Charles F. 1991. *Systems in Crisis: New Imperatives of High Politics at Century's End*. Cambridge University Press.

2000. Confronting the Principles of the Power Cycle: Changing Systems Structure, Expectations, and War. In Manus I. Midlarsky, ed., *Handbook of War Studies II*. Ann Arbor: University of Michigan Press.

2001. *Why Canadian Unity Matters and Why Americans Care: Democratic Pluralism at Risk*. Toronto: University of Toronto Press.

Doran, Charles F. and Wes Parsons. 1980. War and the Cycle of Relative Power. *American Political Science Review*, 74 (4): 947–65.

Downs, George W., David M. Rocke, and Randolph M. Siverson. 1986. Arms Races and Cooperation. In Kenneth A. Oye, ed., *Cooperation Under Anarchy*. Princeton University Press, 118–46.

Drahos, Peter. 2003. When the Weak Bargain With the Strong: Negotiations in the World Trade Organization. *International Negotiation*, 8 (1): 79–109.

Dresner, Daniel W. 2008. The Future of US Foreign Policy. *Internationale Politik und Gessellschaft*, 1: 11–35.

Dudley, Leonard and Claude Montmarquette. 1976. A Model of the Supply of Bilateral Foreign Aid. *American Economic Review*, 66 (1): 132–42.

Dueck, Colin. 2004. New Perspectives on American Grand Strategy. *International Security*, 28 (4): 197–216.

Dufour, A. 1984. Grotius et le droit naturel du dix-septième siècle. In Royal Netherlands Academy of Arts and Sciences, ed., *The World of Hugo Grotius (1583–1645)*. Amsterdam: Holland University Press, 15–41.

2003. Economics, Philosophy of History, and the "Single Dynamic" of Power Cycle Theory: Expectations, Competition and Statecraft. *International Political Science Review*, 24 (1): 13–49.

Dugatkin, L. A. 1997. *Cooperation among Animals*. Oxford University Press.

Dutt, Sagarika. 2002. *UNESCO and a Just World Order*. New York: Nova Science Publishers.

Dyer, Geoff. 2008. China lectures US on economy. *Financial Times*, December 4, available at www.ft.com/cms/s/0/48ac15fc-c1bc-11dd-831e-000077b07658. html.

East, Maurice A. 1972. Status Discrepancy and Violence in the International System: An Empirical Analysis. In James N. Rosenau, Vincent Davis, and Maurice A. East, eds., *The Analysis of International Politics*. New York: Free Press.

Easterly, William, 2001. *Growth Implosions, Debt Explosions, and My Aunt Marilyn: Do Growth Slowdowns Cause Public Debt Crises?* Policy Research Working Paper 2531. Washington, DC: World Bank.

The Economist. 2004. The Bush Presidency: Je ne regrette rien. August 26.

Ellemers, Naomi and Wendy Van Rijswijk. 1997. Identity Needs Versus Social Opportunities: The Use of Group-Level and Individual-Level Identity Management Strategies. *Social Psychology Quarterly*, 60 (1): 52–65.

Ellemers, Naomi, Ad van Knippenberg, and Henk Wilke. 1990. The Influence of Permeability of Group Boundaries and Stability of Group Status on Strategies of Individual Mobility and Social Change. *British Journal of Social Psychology*, 29: 233–46.

Ellemers, Naomi, Henk Wilke, and Ad van Knippenberg. 1993. Effects of the Legitimacy of Low Group or Individual Status on Individual and Collective Status-Enhancement Strategies. *Journal of Personality and Social Psychology*, 64 (5): 766–78.

Ellemers, Naomi, Wendy Van Rijswijk, Marlene Roefs, and Catrien Simons. 1997. Bias in Intergroup Perceptions: Balancing Group Identity with Social Reality. *Personality and Social Psychology Bulletin*, 23 (2): 186–98.

Elster, Jon. 1998. A Plea for Mechanisms. In R. Swedberg, ed., *Social Mechanisms: An Analytical Approach to Social Theory*. Cambridge University Press.

Enderlin, Charles. 2002. *Le rêve brisé*. Paris: Fayard.

Epstein, Joshua, and Robert Axtell. 1996. *Growing Artificial Societies: Social Science from the Bottom Up*. Washington, DC: Brookings Institution Press.

Evangelista, Matthew. 1990. Cooperation Theory and Disarmament Negotiations in the 1950s. *World Politics*, 42: 502–28.

Evans, Gareth and Mohamed Sahnoun, eds. 2001. *The Responsibilty to Protect*. Ottawa: International Commission on State Sovereignty.

Fearon, James D. 1995. Signaling Foreign Policy Interests: Tying Hands versus Sinking Costs. *Journal of Conflict Resolution*, 41 (1): 68–90.

Feinberg, Richard. 2008. Voluntary Multilateralism and institutional Modification: The First Two Decades of Asia Pacific Economic Cooperation (APEC). *Review of International Organizations*, 3 (3): 239–58.

Finkelstein, David M. 2000. *China Reconsiders Its National Security: The Great Peace and Development Debate of 1999*. Alexandria, VA: CAN Corporation.

Fisher, Roger and William Ury. 1982. *Getting to Yes*. New York: Houghton & Mifflin.

Foreign Policy Concept of the Russian Federation. 2000. *Nezavisimaya Gazeta*, July 11.

Franck, Thomas M. 1990. *The Power of Legitimacy Among Nations*. New York: Oxford University Press.

Fravel, M. Taylor. 2008. China's Search for Military Power. *Washington Quarterly*, 31 (3): 125–41,

Fudenberg, Drew, and Eric Maskin. 1990. Evolution and Cooperation in Noisy Repeated Games. *American Economic Review*, 80 (2): 274–79.

Gaddis, John Lewis. 2005. *Strategies of Containment: A Critical Appraisal of American National Security Policy During the Cold War*, rev. and expanded ed. New York: Oxford University Press.

Gallucci, Robert, Joel Wit, and Daniel Poneman. 2005. *Going Critical: The First North Korean Nuclear Crisis*. Washington, DC: Brookings Institution Press.

Galtung, J. 1964. A Structural Theory of Aggression. *Journal of Peace Research*, 1 (2): 95–119.

Gellman, Barton. 1998. US and China Nearly Came to Blows in 1996. *Washington Post*, 21 June: A1.

George, Alexander L., Philip J. Farley, and Alexander Dallin, eds. 1988. *US–Soviet Security Cooperation: Achievements, Failures, Lessons*. New York: Oxford University Press.

Gibson, Neil. 2006. *The Shanghai Communiqué*. Washington, DC: SAIS-The Johns Hopkins University.

Gill, Bates. 2005. China's Evolving Regional Security Strategy. In David Shambaugh, ed., *Power Shift: China and Asia's New Dynamics*. Berkeley: University of California Press.

Gilpin, Robert. 1981. *War and Change in World Politics*. Cambridge University Press.

Glaser, Charles L. 1997. The Security Dilemma Revisited. *World Politics*, 50: 171–201.

Glennon, Michael J. 2003. *Limits of Law, Prerogatives of Power: Intervention after Kosovo*. London: Palgrave Macmillan.

Goldgeier, James M. and Michael McFaul. 2003. *Power and Purpose: US Policy toward Russia after the Cold War*. Washington, DC: Brookings Institution.

Goldstein, Avery. 2001. The Diplomatic Face of China's Grand Strategy: A Rising Power's Emerging Choice. *China Quarterly*, 168: 835–64.

   2005. *Rising to the Challenge: China's Grand Strategy and International Security*. Stanford University Press.

Goldstein, Joshua S. 1995. Great Power Cooperation under Conditions of Limited Reciprocity: From Empirical to Formal Analysis. *International Studies Quarterly*, 39: 453–78.

Goldstein, Joshua S. and John R. Freeman. 1990. *Three-Way Street: Strategic Reciprocity in World Politics*. Chicago: University of Chicago Press.

Grant, Charles with Tomas Valasek. 2007. *Preparing for the Multipolar World: European Foreign and Security Policy in 2020*. London: Centre for European Reform.

Grieco, Joseph M. 1988. Anarchy and the Limits of Cooperation: A Realist Critique of the Newest Liberal Institutionalism. *International Organization*, 42: 485–507.

Grotius, H. 1925 [1625]. *De Jure Belli ac Pacis*, ed. James Brown Scott, trans. Francis W. Kelsey. Classics of International Law. Oxford: Clarendon Press.

Gunaratana, Rohan. 2002. *Inside Al Quaeda: Global Network of Terror*. New York: Columbia University Press.

Gvosdev, Nikolas K. and Dimitri K. Simes. 2005. Rejecting Russia? *National Interest*, Summer.

Haakonssen, Knud. 1983. *The Science of a Legislator: The Natural Jurisprudence of David Hume and Adam Smith*. Cambridge University Press.

1996. *Natural Law and Moral Philosophy. From Grotius to the Scottish Enlightenment*. Cambridge University Press.

Haas, Ernst B. 1966. *International Integration: The European and the Universal Process in International Political Communities*. New York: Doubleday.

Haass, Richard N. 1997. *The Reluctant Sheriff: The United States after the Cold War*. New York: Council on Foreign Relations.

Habermas, Jürgen. 1998. *Between Facts and Norms: Contributions to a Discourse Theory of Law and Democracy*, trans. William Rehg. Cambridge, MA: MIT Press.

Haftendorn, Helga. 2006. *German Ostpolitik in a Mutilateral Setting*. In Helga Haftendorn, Georges-Henri Soutou, Stephen Szabo, and Samuel Wells, Jr., eds., *The Strategic Triangle: France, Germany and the US in the Shaping of the New Europe*. Washington, DC: Woodrow Wilson Center Press/The Johns Hopkins University Press.

Hamilton, W. D. 1964. The Genetic Evolution of Social Behavior. *Journal of Theoretical Biology*, 7 (1): 1–16.

Hammerstein, Peter. 2003. *Genetic and Cultural Evolution of Cooperation*. Cambridge, MA: MIT Press.

Hampson, Fen Osler and Stephen Flanagan, eds. 1986. *Securing Europe's Future: Changing Elements of European Security*. Boston, MA: Auburn House.

Hampson, Fen Osler. 1995. *Multilateral Negotiations*. Baltimore: Johns Hopkins University Press.

Hampson, Fen Osler with Holly Reid. 2003. Coalition Diversity and Normative Legitimacy in Human Security Negotiations. *International Negotiation*, 8 (1): 7–42.

Hanrieder, Wolfram 1989. *Two Decades of German Foreign Policy*. New York: Harper Row.

Hardin, Russell. 1982. *Collective Action*. Baltimore: Johns Hopkins Press.

Harles, John. 2008. Health Care. In David Thomas and Barbara Boyle Torrey, eds., *Canada and the United States: Differences that Count*, 3rd ed. Peterborough: Broadview.

Hasenclever, Andreas, Peter Mayer and Volker Rittberger. 1997. *Theories of International Regimes*. Cambridge University Press.

Heinbecker, Paul. 2004. Washington's Exceptionalism and the United Nations. *Global Governance: A Review of Multilateralism and International Organizations*, 10 (3): 273–80.

Held, David, Anthony G. McGrew, David Glodblatt, and Jonathan Perraton. 1999. *Global Transformations: Politics, Economics, Culture*. Stanford University Press.

Hemmer, Christopher and Peter J. Katzenstein. 2002. Why Is There No NATO in Asia? Collective Identity, Regionalism, and the Origins of Multilateralism. *International Organization*, 56 (3): 575–607.

Hobbes, Thomas. 1996 [1651]. *Leviathan*, ed. Richard Tuck. Cambridge University Press.

Hoffmann, Stanley. 1998. *World Disorders: Troubled Peace in the Post-Cold War Era*. Lanham, MD: Rowman & Littlefield.

Höglund, Christine. 2010. Tactics in Negotiations between States and Extremists. In I. William Zartman and Guy Olivier Faure, eds, *Engaging Extremists*. Washington, DC: United States Institute of Peace Press.

Holbrooke, Richard. 1998. *To End a War*. New York: Random House.

Holzgrefe, L. and Robert O. Keohane, eds. 2003. *Humanitarian Intervention: Ethical, Legal, and Political Dilemmas*. Cambridge University Press.

Homans, G. C. 1961. *Social behavior*. New York: Harcourt, Brace & World.

Hont, Istvan. 2005. *Jealousy of Trade. International Competition and the Nation-State in Historical Perspective*. Cambridge, MA: Harvard University Press.

Hont, Istvan and Michael Ignatieff, eds. 1983. *Wealth and Virtue: The Shaping of Political Economy in the Scottish Enlightenment*. Cambridge University Press.

Hopf, Ted. 2002. *Social Origins of International Politics: Identities and Foreign Policies, Moscow 1955 and 1999*. Ithaca, NY: Cornell University Press.

Hopmann, P. Terrence. 1996. *The Negotiation Process and the Resolution of International Conflicts*. Columbia, SC: University of South Carolina Press.

2001. Bargaining and Problem-Solving: Two Perspectives on International Negotiation. In Chester A. Crocker, Fen Osler Hampson, and Pamela Aall, eds., *Turbulent Peace: The Challenges of Managing International Conflict* Washington, DC: US Institute of Peace Press, 445–68.

Howard, Nigel. 1971. *Paradoxes of Rationality: Theory of Metagames and Political Behavior*. Cambridge, MA: MIT Press.

Hume, David. 1985 [1742]. Of the Balance of Power. In *Essays Moral, Political and Literary*, ed. Eugene F. Miller. Indianapolis: Liberty Fund.

Ikenberry, G. John. 1998–99. Institutions, Strategic Restraint, and the Persistence of American Postwar Order. *International Security*, 23 (3): 45–78.

2001. *After Victory: Institutions, Strategic Restraint, and the Rebuilding of Order After Major Wars*. Princeton University Press.

Ikle, Fred Charles, 1964. *How Nations Negotiate*. New York: Harper & Row.

Inosemtsev, Vladislav and Sergei Karaganov. 2005. Imperialism of the Fittest. *National Interest*, summer: 74–81.

Jackson, Linda A., Linda A. Sullivan, Richard Harnish, and Carole N. Hodge. 1996. Achieving Positive Social Identity: Social Mobility, Social Creativity, and Permeability of Group Boundaries. *Journal of Personality and Social Psychology*, 70 (2): 241–54.

James, Patrick and Lui Hebron. 1997. Great Powers: Cycles of Relative Cabability and Crises in World Politics. *International Interactions*, 23: 145–73.

Jervis, Robert. 1978. Cooperation Under the Security Dilemma. *World Politics*, 30: 167–214.

1982. Security Regimes. *International Organization*, 36: 357–78.

1988. Realism, Game Theory, and Cooperation. *World Politics*, 40: 317–49.

Job, Brian. 1997. Multilateralism: The Relevance of the Concept to Regional Conflict Management. In David Lake and Patrick Morgan, eds., *Regional Orders: Building Security in a New World*. University Park: Pennsylvania State University Press.

Joffe, Josef. 2006. *Überpower: The Imperial Temptation of America*. New York: W. W. Norton.

Johnson's Russia List. 2008. 177, September 30.

Johnston, Alastair Iain and Paul Evans. 1999. *China's Engagement with Multilateral Security Institutions*. In Johnston and Robert S. Ross eds. *Engaging China the Management of an Emerging Power*. New York: Routledge.

Jones, Edward E. 1998. Major Developments in Five Decades of Social Psychology. In Daniel T. Gilbert, Susan T. Fiske, and Gardner Lindzey, eds., *The Handbook of Social Psychology*, 4th ed., Boston: McGraw-Hill (repr. from 1985 ed.), I, 3–57.

Kagan, Robert. 2004. *Of Paradise and Power: America and Europe in the New World Order*. New York: Random House, Vintage Books.

Kahler, Miles. 1992. Multilateralism with Small and Large Numbers. *International Organization*, 46: 681–708.

   1993. Multilateralism with Small and Large Numbers. In J. G. Ruggie, ed., *Multilateralism Matters*. New York: Columbia University Press, 295–326.

Kahn, Herman. 1965. *On Escalation: Metaphors and Scenarios*. New York: Praeger.

Kaiser, Karl. 2007. However, There Is Something New in the West. *Internationale Politik*, 62 (7–8): 120–21.

Kaldor, Mary, Mary Martin, and Sabine Selchow. 2007. Human Security: A New Strategic Narrative for Europe. *International Affairs*, 83: 273.

Kane, Thomas. 2006. *Theoretical Roots of US Foreign Policy: Machiavelli and American Unilateralism*. London: Routledge.

Kanet, Roger and Edward Kolodziej, eds. 1991. *The Cold War as Cooperation*. Baltimore: Johns Hopkins University Press.

Kant, I. 1991. *Political Writings*, ed. Hans Reiss. Cambridge University Press.

Karaganov, Sergei. 2007. Cold Peace is More Dangerous than Cold War. *Rossiyskaya Gazeta*, March 7, available at www.rg.ru/2007/03/07/karaganov.html.

Kaul, Inge, Pedro Conceicão, Ketell Le Goulven, and Ronald U. Mendoza, eds. 2003. *Providing Global Public Goods: Managing Gloablization*. New York: Oxford University Press.

Kautilya. 1960. *Arthasastra*. Mysore Publishing House.

Keck, Margaret E., and Kathryn Sikkink. 1998. *Activists Beyond Borders: Advocacy Networks in International Politics*. Ithaca, NY: Cornell University Press.

Keene, Edward. 2002. *Beyond the Anarchical Society. Grotius Colonialism and Order in World Politics*. Cambridge University Press.

Kegley, Charles W., and Gregory A. Raymond. 2002. *Exorcising the Ghost of Westphalia: Building World Order in the New Millennium*. Upper Saddle River, NJ: Prentice Hall.

Kelley, Judith. 2004. International Actors on the Domestic Scene: Membership Conditionality and Socialization by International Institutions. *International Organization*, 58 (3): 425–58.

Kennedy, David. 1986. Primitive Legal Scholarship. *Harvard International Law Journal*, 27: 1–98.

Keohane, Robert O. 1983. The Demand for International Regimes. In Stephen D. Krasner, ed., *International Regimes*. Ithaca: Cornell University Press.

1984. *After Hegemony: Cooperation and Discord in the World Political Economy*. Princeton, NJ: Princeton University Press.

1986. Reciprocity in International Relations. *International Organization*, 40: 1–27.

1989. *International Institutions and State Power. Essays in International Relations Theory*. Boulder: Westview.

2002. *Power and Governance in a Partially Globalized World*. London: Routledge.

Keohane, Robert and Joseph Nye. 1977. *Power and Interdependence: World Politics in Transition*. Boston: Little, Brown.

Keohane, Robert O. and Joseph S. Nye, Jr. 2000. Introduction. In Nye and John D. Donahue, eds., *Governance in a Globalizing World*. Washington, DC: Brookings, 1–44.

Kessler, Glenn. 2005. US, China Agree to Regular Talks. *Washington Post*, April 8: A14.

Khong, Yuen Foong. 2001. Negotiating "Order" During Power Transitions. In C. Kupchan et al., eds., *Power in Transition: The Peaceful Change of International Order*. Tokyo: United Nations University Press, 39–44.

Kim, Samuel S. 2003. China's Path to Great Power Status in the Globalization Era. *Asian Perspective*, 27 (1): 35–75.

Kimball, Warren F. 1991. *The Juggler: Franklin Roosevelt as Wartime Statesman*. Princeton: Princeton University Press.

Kirton, John J. and Radoslava Stefanova, eds. 2004. *The G8, the United Nations and Conflict Prevention*. London: Ashgate.

Kissinger, Henry. 1961. *The Necessity for Choice – Prospects of American Foreign Policy*. New York: Harper Row.

1979. *The White House Years*. New York: Little, Brown.

1994. *Diplomacy*. New York: Simon & Schuster.

Kissinger, Henry A. and George P. Shultz. 2008. Building on Common Ground with Russia. *Washington Post*, October 8.

Knippenberg, Ad van. 1984. Intergroup Differences in Group Perceptions. In Henri Tajfel, ed., *The Social Dimension: European Developments in Social Psychology*, Vol. 2. Cambridge University Press.

Knippenberg, Ad van and Naomi Ellemers. 1993. Strategies in Intergroup Relations. In Michael A. Hogg and Dominic Abrams, eds., *Group Motivation: Social Psychological Perspectives*. London: Harvester Wheatsheaf.

Kolb, Robert. 2000. *La bonne foi en droit international public: contribution à l'étude des principes généraux de droit*. Paris: Presses universitaires de France.

Komorita, S. S., J. A. Hilty, and C. D. Parks. 1991. Reciprocity and Cooperation in Social Dilemmas. *Journal of Conflict Resolution*, 35: 494–518.

Krauthammer, Charles. 2002. American Unilateralism, Hillsdale College Churchill Dinner, Mayflower Hotel, Washington, DC, December 4.

Kuglanski, A. W. and E. T. Higgins, eds. 1996. *Social Psychology: A Handbook of Basic Principles*. New York: Guilford.

Kupchan, Charles A. 1998. After Pax Americana: Benign Power, Regional Integration, and the Sources of a Stable Multipolarity. *International Security* 23 (2): 40–80.

Kupchan, Charles A., Emanuel Adler, Jean-Marc Coicaud, and Yuen Foong Khong, eds. 2001. *Power in Transition: The Peaceful Change of International Order.* Tokyo: United Nations University Press.

Kydd, Andrew and Duncan Snidal. 1993. Progress in Game-Theoretical Analysis of International Regimes. In Volker Rittberger, ed., *Regime Theory and International Relations*, New York: Oxford University Press, 112–35.

Lalonde, Richard N. 1992. The Dynamics of Group Differentiation in the Face of Defeat. *Personality and Social Psychology Bulletin*, 18 (3): 336–42.

Lalonde, R. N. and R. A. Silverman. 1994. Behavioral Preferences in Response to Social Injustice: The Effects of Group Permeability and Social Identity Salience. *Journal of Personality and Social Psychology*, 66: 78–85.

Lampton, David M. 2001. *Same Bed, Different Dreams: Managing US–China Relations, 1989–2000*. Berkeley: University of California Press.

2005. China's Rise in Asia Need Not Be at America's Expense. In David Shambaugh, ed., *Power Shift: China and Asia's New Dynamics*. Berkeley: University of California Press, 306–26.

Lampton, David M. and Richard Daniel Ewing. 2003. *The US–China Relationship Facing International Security Crises: Three Case Studies in Post-9/11 Bilateral Relations*. Washington, DC: Nixon Center.

Langlois, Jean-Pierre P. 1991. Rational Deterrence and Crisis Stability. *American Journal of Political Science*, 35: 801–32.

Laqueur, Walter. 1999. *The New Terrorism: Fanaticism and the Arms of Mass Destruction*. Oxford University Press.

Larrère, Catherine. 1992. *L'invention de l'économie au XVIIIe siècle*. Paris: PUF.

1999. Le stoïcisme dans les œuvres de jeunesse de Montesquieu. In Catherine Volpilhac-Auger, ed., *Montesquieu. Les années de formation (1689–1720)*. Naples: Liguori Editore, 163–83.

2001. Montesquieu on Economics and Commerce. In David W. Carrithers, Michael A. Mosher and Paul Rahe, eds., *Montesquieu's Science of Politics. Essays on The Spirit of the Laws*. New York: Rowman & Littlefield, 335–73.

Larson, Deborah Welch. 1988. The Psychology of Reciprocity in International Relations. *Negotiation Journal*, 4: 281–301.

Larson, Deborah Welch and Alexei Shevchenko. 2003. Shortcut to Greatness: The New Thinking and the Revolution in Soviet Foreign Policy. *International Organization*, 57 (1): 77–109.

Lawler, E. J. and G. A. Young. 1975. Coalition Formation: An Integrative Model. *Sociometry*, 38 (1): 1–17.

Lawrence, Susan V. 2004. US Diplomat Stands Firm: How China Relations Improved: An Insider View. *Far Eastern Economic Review*, October 28.

Lax, David and James Sebenius. 1986. *The Manager as Negotiator*. New York: Free Press.

Lebow, Richard Ned. 2003. *The Tragic Vision of Politics: Ethics, Interests, and Orders*. Cambridge University Press.

Legvold, Robert. 2007. Russian Foreign Policy during Periods of Great State Transformation. In Legvold, ed., *Russian Foreign Policy in the Twenty-first Century and the Shadow of the Past*. New York: Columbia University Press.

Lemaine, Gerard. 1974. Social Differentiation and Social Originality. *European Journal of Social Psychology*, 4 (1): 17–52.

Lemke, Douglas. 1997. The Continuation of History: Power Transition Theory and the End of the Cold War. *Journal of Peace Research*, 34: 23–36.

Leng, Russell J. 1993. Reciprocating Influence Strategies in Interstate Crisis Bargaining. *Journal of Conflict Resolution*, 37. 3–41.

Lennon, Alexander T. J., and Camille Eiss, eds. 2004. *Reshaping Rogue States: Preemption, Regime Change, and US Policy toward Iran, Iraq, and North Korea.* Cambridge, MA: MIT Press.

Lesaffer, Randall. 2000. The Medieval Canon Law of Contract and Early Modern Treaty Law. *Journal of the History of International Law*, 2 (2): 178–98.

Lesage, Dries. 2007. Globalisation, Multipolarity and the L20 as an Alternative to the G8. *Global Society* 20 (3): 343–61.

Lesser, Ian O., Bruce Hoffman, John Arquilla, David Ronfeldt, and Michele Zanini. 1999. *The New Terrorism.* Santa Monica, CA: Rand Corporation.

Levy, Jack. 1992. Prospect Theory and International Relations. *Political Psychology*, 13: 283–310.

Liberman, Nira, Yaakov Trope, and Stephan, E. 2007. In E. T. Higgins and A. W. Kuglanski, eds., *Social Psychology: A Handbook of Basic Principles.* New York: Guilford.

Lichbach, Mark Irving. 1990. When Is an Arms Rivalry a Prisoner's Dilemma? Richardson's Models and 2 x 2 Games. *Journal of Conflict Resolution*, 34: 29–56.

Lieberthal, Kenneth. 2005. Preventing a War Over Taiwan. *Foreign Affairs*, 84: 53–63.

Light, Margot. 1996. Foreign Policy Thinking. In Neil Malcolm, Alex Pravda, Roy Allison and Margot Light, eds., *Internal Factors in Russian Foreign Policy.* Oxford University Press, 44–45.

Lindskold, Svenn, Gyuseog Han, and Brian Betz. 1986. The Essential Elements of Communication in the GRIT Strategy. *Personality and Social Psychology Bulletin*, 12: 179–86.

Lipson, Charles. 1984. International Cooperation in Economic and Security Affairs. *World Politics*, 37: 1–23.

   1986. Bankers' Dilemmas: Private Cooperation in Rescheduling Sovereign Debts. In Kenneth A. Oye, ed., *Cooperation Under Anarchy.* Princeton: Princeton University Press, 200–25.

Lipson, Michael. 2004. Transaction Costs Estimation and International Regimes. *International Studies Review*, 6 (1): 1–20.

List, Friedrich. 1857. *Système national d'économie politique.* Paris.

Lo, Bobo. 2002. *Russian Foreign Policy in the Post-Soviet Era: Reality, Illusion and Mythmaking.* New York: Palgrave Macmillan.

   2003. *Vladimir Putin and the Evolution of Russian Foreign Policy.* London: Blackwell Publishing.

Locke, John. 1988 [1690]. The Second Treatise of Government. In Locke, *Two Treatises of Government*, ed. Peter Laslett: Cambridge University Press.

Luard, Evan. 1990. *International Society.* London: Macmillan.

   1992. *The Balance of Power: The System of International Relations, 1648–1815.* New York: St. Martin's Press.

Lustick, Ian. 2000. Agent-Based Modeling of Collective Identity: Testing Constructivist Theory. *Journal of Artificial Societies and Social Simulation (JASSS)*, 3: 1–19.

Lustick, Ian S., Dan Miodownik, and Roy J. Eidelson. 2004. Secessionism in Multicultural States: Does Sharing Power Prevent or Encourage It? *American Political Science Review*, 98 (2):209–29.

Lyons, Gene M. 2007. Rethinking American Foreign Policy: Towards Realistic Multilateralism. *American Foreign Policy Interests*, 29 (1): 73–86.

Lyons, Gene M. and Michael Mastanduno, eds. 2001. *Beyond Westphalia? State Sovereignty and International Intervention*. Baltimore: Johns Hopkins University Press.

McCrisken, Trevor. 2004. *American Exceptionalism and the Legacy of Vietnam: US Foreign Policy since 1974*. London: Palgrave Macmillan.

McGinnis, Michael D. and John T. Williams. 1993. Policy Uncertainty in Two-Level Games: Examples of Correlated Equilibria. *International Studies Quarterly*, 37: 29–54.

Mackie, Diane M., Thierry Devos, and Eliot R. Smith. 2000. Intergroup Emotions: Explaining Offensive Action Tendencies in an Intergroup Context. *Journal of Personality and Social Psychology*, 79: 602–16.

McKinley, Robert D., and Richard Little. 1977. A Foreign Policy Model of US Bilateral Aid Allocation. *World Politics*, 30 (1): 58–86.

Macy, Michael and Robert Willer. 2002. From Factors to Actors: Computational Sociology and Agent-Based Modeling. In Karen S. Cook and John Hagan, eds., *Annual Review of Sociology*, 28. Palo Alto, CA: Annual Reviews.

Magnier, Mark and Kim Murphy. 2005. An Exercise Fit for Sending US a Message. *Los Angles Times*, August 17: A5.

Magnusson, Lars. The Controversy on Free Trade and Protection–An Introduction. In Magnusson, ed., *Free Trade 1793–1866, 2* vols. London: Routledge, 1993.

Maier, Charles. 2006. *Among Empires: American Ascendancy and its Predecessors*. Cambridge, MA: Harvard University Press.

Malinowski, Tom. 2003. Overlooking Chechen Terror. *Washington Post*, editorial, March 1: A19.

Malone, David M. and Yuen Foong Khong, eds. 2003.*Unilateralism and US Foreign Policy: International Perspectives*. Boulder: Lynne Rienner.

Mann, James. 2000. *About Face: A History of America's Curious Relationship with China, from Nixon to Clinton*. New York: Vintage Books.

Martens, Jens. 2007. *Multistakeholder Partnerships – Future Models of Multilateralism?* Dialogue on Globalization Occasional Paper 29. Berlin: Friedrich Ebert Stiftung.

Martin, Lisa. 1999. Interests, Power and Multilateralism. In Charles Lipson, and Benjamin J. Cohen, eds., *Theory and Structure in International Political Economy*, Cambridge, MA: MIT Press.

   2004. Self Binding. *Harvard Magazine*, September–October: 33–36.

Mastanduno, Michael and Ethan Kapstein. 1999. Preserving the Unipolar Moment: Realist Theories and U.S. Grand Strategy after the Cold War. In Kapstein and Mastanduno, eds., *Unipolar Politics: Realism and State Strategies after the Cold War*. New York: Columbia University Press, 11–13.

Mautner, Thomas. 2005. Grotius and the Skeptics. *Journal of the History of Ideas*, 66: 577–602.

Maynard Smith, John. 1982. *Evolution and the Theory of Games*. Cambridge University Press.

Mazarr, Michael. 2000. Opportunity Seized: Preventive Diplomacy in Korea. In Druce Jentleson, ed., *Opportunities Missed, Opportunities Seized*. Lanham, MD: Rowman & Littlefield.

Mendelson, Sarah E. and Theodore P. Gerber. 2005–06. Soviet Nostalgia: An Impediment to Russian Democratization. *Washington Quarterly* 29 (1): 83–96.

Mercer, Jonathan. 1995. Anarchy and Identity. *International Organization* 49: 299–352.

1996. *Reputation and international politics*. Ithaca, NY: Cornell University Press.

Meyssonnier, Simone. 1989. *La Balance et l'Horloge. La genèse de la pensée libérale en France au XVIIIe siècle*. Paris: Editions de la passion.

Michishita, Narushiga. 2003. *Calculated Adventurism: North Korea's Military-Diplomatic Campaign 1966–2000*. Tokyo: Japan National Institute for Defense Studies.

Migranyan, Andranik. 2008. Voices from Afar: Russia Makes Partner. In Johnson. *Russia List #194*, October 24, www.cdi.org/russia/johnson/.

Miller, Benjamin. 2007. *States, Nations and the Great Powers: The Sources of Regional War and Peace*. Cambridge University Press.

Milner, Helen. 1992. International Theories of Cooperation. *World Politics*, 44: 466–96.

Minden, Karen, Nicole Galant, and Paul Irwin. 1997. *Canada's Role in APEC*. In Fen Osler Hampsen, Maureen Appel Molot and Martin Rudner, eds., *Asia Pacific Face-Off, Canada Among Nations*. Ottawa: Carleton University Press.

Mittleman, James M. 2000. *The Globalization Syndrome: Transformation and Resistance*. Princeton University Press.

Molander, Per. 1985. The Optimal Level of Generosity in a Selfish, Uncertain Environment. *Journal of Conflict Resolution*, 29: 611–18.

Montesquieu. 1951. Réflexions sur la monarchie universelle en Europe. In *Œuvres complètes*. Paris, Gallimard.

1989 [1750]. *The Spirit of the Laws*, ed. Anne M. Cohler, Basia C. Miller, and Harold S. Stone. Cambridge University Press.

1991. *Pensées*, ed. Louis Desgraves. Paris: Collection Bouquins.

1998. *Correspondance*, ed. Louis Desgraves, and Edgar Mass. *Œuvres complètes*, vol. 18. Oxford: Voltaire Foundation.

Moore, Thomas G. 2000. China and Globalization. In Samuel S. Kim, ed., *East Asia and Globalization*. Lanham, MD: Rowman & Littlefield.

Moore, Thomas G. and Dixia Yang. 2001. Empowered and Restrained: Chinese Foreign Policy in the Age of Economic Interdependence. In D. Lampton, ed. *Making of Chinese Foreign and Security Policy*. Stanford University Press.

Morgenthau, Hans J. and Kenneth W. Thompson. 1985. *Politics Among Nations: The Struggle for Power and Peace*, 6th ed. New York: Alfred A. Knopf.

Mummendey, Amelie, Andreas Klink, Rosemarie Mielke, Michael Wenzel, and Mathias Blanz. 1999. Socio-structural Characteristics of Intergroup Relations and Identity Management Strategies: Results from a Field Study in East Germany. *European Journal of Social Psychology*, 29: 259–85.

Mummendey, Amelie and Hans-Joachim Schreiber. 1984. "Different" Just Means "Better": Some Obvious and Some Hidden Pathways to In-Group Favouritism. *British Journal of Social Psychology*, 23: 363–68.

Murnigham, J. K. 1978. Models of Coalition Behavior. *Psychological Bulletin*, 85: 1130–53.

Myerson, Roger B. 1991. *Game Theory: Analysis of Conflict*. Cambridge, MA: Harvard University Press.

Nash, John F. 1950. The Bargaining Problem. *Econometrica*, 18: 155–62.

Neff, Stephen C. 1990. *Friends but No Allies: Economic Liberalism and the Law of Nations*. New York: Columbia University Press.

Neumayer, Eric. 2003. *Explaining the Pattern of Aid Giving*. London: Routledge.

Newman, Edward. 2007. *A Crisis in Global Institutions? Multilateralism and International Security*. London: Routledge.

Newman, Edward, Ramesh Thakur, and John Tirman, eds. 2006. *Multilateralism Under Challenge? International Order, and Structural Change*. Tokyo: United Nations University Press.

Nicolson, Sir Harold. 1963. *Diplomacy*. Oxford: Galaxy.

Noguez, Maria-Isabel Studer. 2002. *The Global Strategies of Multinationals and Government Policies*. London: Taylor & Francis.

Nossal, Kim Richard. 1992. A European Nation? The Life and Times of Atlanticism in Canada. In John English and Norman Hillmer, eds., *Making a Difference? Canada's Foreign Policy in a Changing World Order*. Toronto: Lester Publishing.

Nowak, Martin A. and K. Sigmund. 1992. Tit for Tat in Heterogeneous Populations. *Nature*, 355: 250–53.

    1993. A strategy of Win–Stay, Lose–Shift that Outperforms Tit-for-Tat in the Prisoner's Dilemma Game. *Nature*, 364: 56–58.

    1998. Evolution of Indirect Reciprocity by Image Scoring. *Nature*, 393: 573–77.

Nye, Joseph Jr. 2002. *The Paradox of American Power: Why the World's Only Superpower Can't Go It Alone*. New York: Oxford University Press.

    2004. *Soft Power: The Means to Success in World Politics*. New York: Public Affairs.

Office of the Secretary of Defense, United States Department of Defense. 2008. Annual Report to Congress: Military Power of the People's Republic of China 2008, available at www.defenselink.mil/pubs/pdfs/China_Military_Report_.08.pdf.

Ogata, Sadako. 1988. *Normalization with China*. Berkeley: UCB Institute of East Asian Studies.

O'Neill, Barry. 1994. A Survey of Game Theory Models on Peace and War. In R. Aumann and S. Hart, eds., *Handbook of Game Theory*, vol. 2. Amsterdam: North-Holland, 995–1053.

    1999. *Honor, Symbols, and War*. Ann Arbor: University of Michigan Press.

Organski, A. F. K. 1958. *World Politics*. New York: Knopf.

Osborne, Martin J. and Ariel Rubinstein. 1994. *A Course in Game Theory*. Cambridge, MA: MIT Press.

Osgood, Charles E. 1962. *An Alternative to War or Surrender*. Urbana: University of Illinois Press.

Ouwerkerk, Jaap W. and Naomi Ellemers. 2002. The Benefits of being Disadvantaged: Performance-Related Circumstances and Consequences of Intergroup Comparisons. *European Journal of Social Psychology*, 32: 73–91.

Overbeck, Jennifer R., John T. Jost, Cristina O. Mosso, and Agnieszka Flizik. 2004. Resistant versus Acquiescent Responses to Ingroup Inferiority as a Function of Social Dominance Orientation in the USA and Italy. *Group Processes & Intergroup Relations*, 7 (1). 35–54.

Oye, Kenneth A., ed. 1986a. *Cooperation under Anarchy*. Princeton: Princeton University Press.

1986b. *The Sterling-Dollar-Franc Triangle: Monetary Diplomacy 1929–1937*. In Oye, ed., *Cooperation under Anarchy*. Princeton: Princeton University Press, 173–99.

Pagden, Anthony. 1995. *Lords of All the World. Ideologies of Empire in Spain, Britain and France, 1500–1800*. New Haven: Yale University Press,

Pangle, Thomas L., and Peter L. Ahrensdorf. 1999. *Justice among Nations: On the Moral Basis of Power and Peace*. Laurence, KS: University Press of Kansas.

Pape, Robert A. 2005. Soft Balancing against the United States. *International Security* 30 (1): 7–45.

Patrick, Stewart. 2002. Multilateralism and Its Discontents: The Causes and Consequences of US Ambivalence. In Stewart Patrick, and Shepard Forman, *Multilateralism and US Foreign Policy*. Boulder and London: Lynne Rienner.

Patrick, Stewart and Shepard Forman, eds. 2002. *Multilateralism and US Foreign Policy: Ambivalent Engagement*. Boulder: Lynne Rienner.

Paul, T. V. 2004. Introduction: The Enduring Axioms of Balance of Power Theory and Their Contemporary Relevance. In T. V. Paul, James M. Wirtz, and Michel Fortmann, eds., *Balance of Power: Theory and Practice in the 21st Century*. Stanford University Press, 1–28.

Pauly, J. Jr. 2005. *US Foreign Policy and the Persian Gulf: Safeguarding American Interests through Selective Multilateralism*. London: Ashgate.

Pearson, Margaret M. 1999. The Major Multilateral Economic Institutions Engage China. In Alastair I. Johnston and Robert S. Ross eds. *Engaging China: The Management of an Emerging Power*. New York: Routledge.

Pekkanen, Saadia M. 2005. Bilateralism, Multilateralism, or Regionalism? Japan's Trade Forum Choices. *Journal of East Asian Studies*, 5 (1): 77–103.

Perrot, Jean-Claude. 1990. *Une Histoire intellectuelle de l'économie politique (XVIIe–XVIIIe siècle)*. Paris: Editions de l'EHESS.

Pitts, Jennifer. 2005. *A Turn to Empire. The Rise of Imperial Liberalism in Britain and France*. Princeton University Press.

Pocock, J. G. A. 1975. *The Machiavellian Moment. Florentine Political Thought and the Atlantic Republican Tradition*. Princeton University Press.

1985. *Virtue, Commerce and History*. Cambridge University Press.

ed. 1993. *The Varieties of British Political Thought, 1500–1800*. Cambridge University Press.

Porter, Tony. 2001. The Democratic Deficit in the Institutional Arrangements for Regulating Global Finance. *Global Governance: A Review of Multilateralism and International Organizations*, 7: 427–40.

Posen, Barry R. 2001–02. The Struggle against Terrorism: Grand Strategy, Strategy, and Tactics. *International Security*, 26 (3): 39–55.

Posen, Barry R. and Andrew L. Ross. 1996–97. Competing Visions for US Grand Strategy. *International Security*, 21 (3): 5–53.

Posner, Barry. 1993. The Security Dilemma and Ethnic Conflict. In Michael Brown, ed., *Ethnic Conflict and International Security*. Princeton University Press.

Powell, Colin L. 2004. A Strategy of Partnerships. *Foreign Affairs*, January/February: 32.

Powell, Robert. 1991. Absolute and Relative Gains in International Relations Theory. *American Political Science Review*, 85: 1303–20.

Pressman, Jeremy. 2008. *Warring Friends: Alliance Restraint in International Politics*. Ithaca: Cornell University Press.

Pruitt, Dean G. 1998. Social Conflict. In Daniel T. Gilbert, Susan T. Fiske, and Gardner Lindzey, eds., *The Handbook of Social Psychology*, 4th ed., vol. 2. Boston: McGraw-Hill, 470–503.

Pufendorf, Samuel. 1934 [1672]. *De Jure Naturae et Gentium*, ed. James Brown Scott, trans. C. H. and W. A. Oldfather. Classics of International Law. Oxford: Clarendon Press.

Purdum, Todd, S. 2002. NATO Strikes Deal to Accept Russia In a Partnership. *New York Times*, May 15: 1.

Pushkov, Alexander. 1998. The "Primakov Doctrine" and a New European Order. *International Affairs* (Moscow), 44 (2): 1–13.

   2000. Russia and the New World Order. *International Affairs* (Moscow) 6.

Pushkov, Alexey K. 2007. Missed Connections. *National Interest*, May–June: 53.

Putnam, Robert. 1988. Diplomacy and Domestic Politics: The Logic of Two-Level Games. *International Organization*, 42: 427–60.

Quandt, William B. 2001. *Peace Process*, rev. cd. Washington, DC: Brookings.

Rapoport, Anatol. 1960. *Fights, Games, and Debates*. Chicago: University of Michigan Press.

   1966. *Two-Person Game Theory: The Essential Ideas*. Ann Arbor: University of Michigan University Press.

Rapoport, Anatol and Albert M. Chammah (with the collaboration of Carol J. Orwant). 1965. *Prisoner's Dilemma: A Study in Conflict and Cooperation*. Ann Arbor: University of Michigan Press.

   1969. The Game of Chicken. In Ira R. Buchler, and Hugo G. Nutini, eds., *Game Theory in the Behavioral Sciences*. Pittsburgh: University of Pittsburgh Press, 151–75.

Rauch, Jonathan. 2002. Seeing Around Corners. *Atlantic Monthly*: 35–48.

Reinicke, Wolfgang H. 1999–2000. The Other World Wide Web: Global Public Policy Networks. *Foreign Policy*, 117 (Winter): 44–57.

Reinisch, August. 2001. Securing the Accountability of International Organizations. *Global Governance: A Review of Multilateralism and International Organizations*, 7: 131–50.

Reus-Smit, Christian. 2004. *American Power and World Order*. Cambridge: Polity Press.

RFE/RL Newsline. 2007. February 2, 9, 12, 20, available at www.rferl.org/archive/en-newsline/20070101/683/683.html.

RIA Novosti. 2002. June 27, http://en.rian.ru.

RIA Novosti, September 30, 2008, http://en.rian.ru.

Rieber, Alfred F. 2007. How Persistent Are Persistent Factors? In Robert Legvold, ed., *Russian Foreign Policy in the Twenty-first Century and the Shadow of the Past*. New York: Columbia University Press.

Richerson, Peter, Robert Boyd, and Joseph Henrich. 2003. Cultural Evolution of Human Cooperation. In Peter Hammerstein, ed., *The Genetic and Cultural Origins of Cooperation*. Cambridge, MA. MIT Press.

Rifkin, Jeremy. 2004. *The European Dream: How Europe's Vision of the Future is Quietly Eclipsing the American Dream*. New York: Jeremy P. Tarcher.

Riker, William H. 1962. *Theory of Political Coalitions*. New Haven: Yale University Press.

Riley, P. W. J. 1978. *The Union of England and Scotland: A Study in Anglo-Scottish Politics of the Eighteenth Century*. Manchester University Press.

Rischard, F. 2002. *High Noon: 20 Global Problems: 20 Years to Solve Them*. New York: Basic Books.

Risse, Thomas. 2000. Let's Argue! Communicative Action in World Politics. *International Organization*, 54 (1): 1–40.

Robertson, John. 2005. *The Case for the Enlightenment: Scotland and Naples 1680–1760*. Cambridge University Press.

   ed. 1995. *A Union for Empire. Political Thought and the British Union of 1707*. Cambridge University Press.

Roche, Daniel. 1993. *La France des Lumières*. Paris: Fayard.

Romberg, Alan D. 2003. *Rein In at the Brink of the Precipice: American Policy toward Taiwan and US–PRC Relations*. Washington, DC: Henry L. Stimson Center.

Rosanvallon, Pierre. 1990. *L'Etat en France de 1789 à nos jours*. Paris: Seuil.

Rosecrance, Richard, ed. 2001. *The New Great Power Coalition: Toward a World Concert of Nations*. Lanham, MD: Rowman & Littlefield.

Rosenau, James N. 1997. The Person, the Household Community, the Community, and the Globe: Notes for a Theory of Multilateralism in a Turbulent World. In Robert Cox, ed., *The New Realism: Perspectives on Multilateralism and World Order*. New York: United Nations University.

Ross, Dennis 2004. *The Missing Peace*. New York: Farrar, Straus, & Giroux.

Ross, Robert S. 1995. *Negotiating Cooperation: The United States and China, 1969–1989*. Stanford University Press.

   1999. Engagement in US–China Policy. In A. Johnston and Ross, eds., *Engaging China: The Management of an Emerging Power*. New York: Routledge, 176–206.

   2000. The 1995–1996 Taiwan Strait Confrontation: Coercion, Credibility, and the Use of Force. *International Security*, 25 (2): 87–123.

   2005. Assessing the China's Threat. *National Interest*, 81 (Fall): 81–87.

Rubenstein, Ariel, 1982. Perfect Equilibrium in a Bargaining Model. *Econometrica*, 50: 97–109.

Rubin, Jeffrey Z. and Bert R. Brown. 1975. *The Social Psychology of Bargaining and Negotiation*. New York: Academic Press.

Rubin, Jeffrey Z., Dean G. Pruitt, and Sung Hee Kim. 1994. *Social Conflict: Escalation, Stalemate, and Settlement*. New York: McGraw-Hill.

Ruggie, John Gerard. 1992. Multilateralism: The Anatomy of an Institution. *International Organization*, 46 (Summer): 569–74.

1993a. Multilateralism: The Anatomy of an Institution. In Ruggie, ed., *Multilateralism Matters: The Theory and Praxis of an Institutional Form*. New York: Columbia University Press.

ed. 1993b. *Multilateralism Matters: The Theory and Praxis of an Institutional Form*. New York: Columbia University Press.

1997. The Past as Prologue? Interests, Identity, and American Foreign Policy. *International Security*, 21 (4): 108.

2003. The United Nations and Globalization: Patterns and Limits of Institutional Adaptation. *Global Governance: A Review of Multilateralism and International Organizations*, 9: 301–22.

Sanger, David E. 2002. NATO Gives Russia a Formal Welcome. *New York Times*, May 29.

Schelling, Thomas. 1960. *The Strategy of Conflict*. Cambridge, MA: Harvard University Press.

1978. *Micromotives and Macrobehavior*. New York: W. W. Norton.

Schmitt, Carl. 1950. *Der Nomos der Erde im Völkerrecht des Jus Publicum Europaeum*. Cologne: Greven Verlag.

Schroeder, Paul W. 2004. The Nineteenth Century System: Balance of Power or Political Equilibrium? In Paul Schroeder et al., eds., *Systems, Stability, and Statecraft: Essays on the International History of Modern Europe*. New York: Palgrave Macmillan.

Schwartzman, David. 1988. *Games of Chicken: Four Decades of US Nuclear Policy*. New York: Praeger.

Schweller, Randall L. 1998. *Deadly Imbalances: Tripolarity and Hitler's Strategy of World Conquest*. New York: Columbia University Press.

1999a. Managing the Rise of Great Powers: History and Theory. In Alastair Iain Johnston, and Robert S. Ross, eds. *Engaging China: The Management of an Emerging Power*. New York: Routledge.

1999b. Realism and the Present Great Power System: Growth and Positional Conflict Over Scarce Resources. In Ethan Kapstein and Michael Mastanduno, eds., *Unipolar Politics: Realism and State Strategies After the Cold War*. New York: Columbia University Press, 28–68.

Schweller, Randall L. and Michael J. Reese. 2004. The Peculiar Absence of Balancing Against US Polarity: Delegitimation and Entrepreneurial Revisionism, paper presented at the American Political Science Association Convention, Chicago, September.

Sebenius, James K. 2002. International Negotiation Analysis. In Victor A. Kremenyuk, ed., *International Negotiations: Analysis, Approaches*, Issues, 2nd ed. San Francisco: Jossey-Bass.

Semmel, Bernard. 1993. The National Economists against Free-Trade Empire. In B. Semmel, *The Liberal Ideal and the Demons of Empire: Theories of Imperialism from Adam Smith to Lenin*. Baltimore: Johns Hopkins University Press, 57–84.

Shales, Amity. 2004. Bush Has It Right on Nuclear Proliferation. *Financial Times*, October 4: 19.

Shambaugh, David. 2005. China Engages Asia: Reshaping the Regional Order. *International Security* 29 (3): 64–99.

2006. Return to the Middle Kingdom? China and Asia in the Early Twenty-First Century. In Shambaugh, ed., *Power Shift: China and Asia's New Dynamics*. Berkeley: University of California Press, 23–47.

Shapley, L. S. and M. Shubik, 1954. A Method of Evaluating the Distribution of Power in a Committee System. *American Political Science Review*, 48 (3): 787–92.

Shlapentokh, Vladimir. 2002. Is the 'Greatness Syndrome' Eroding? *Washington Quarterly*, 25 (1): 131–46.

Sheetz, Mark S. 1997–98. Correspondence: Debating the Unipolar Moment. *International Security*, 22 (3): 168–74.

Sher, Richard B. 1985. *Church and University in the Scottish Enlightenment: The Moderate Literati of Edinburgh*. Princeton University Press.

Shevtsova, Lilia. 2003. *Putin's Russia*. Washington, DC: Carnegie Endowment.

2007. *Russia – Lost in Transition: The Yeltsin and Putin Legacies*, trans. Arch Tait. Washington, DC: Carnegie Endowment.

Sigal, Leon V. 2000. The United States and North Korean Cooperative Security on the Agreed Framework and Beyond. In Richard Haass and Meghan O'Sullivan, eds., *Honey and Vinegar: Incentives, Sanctions and Foreign Policy*. Washington, DC: Brookings.

Simai, Mihaly. 1994. *The Future of Global Governance: Managing Risk and Change in the International System*. Washington, DC: United States Institute of Peace Press.

Simes, Dimitri K. 2007. Losing Russia. *Foreign Affairs*, 86 (6): 36–52.

Simmons, P. J. and Chantal de Jonge Oudraat. 2001. From Agenda to Accord. In Simmons and de Jonge Oudraat, eds., *Managing Global Issues*. Washington, DC: Carnegie Endowment.

Sisk, Timothy. 1995. *Democratization in South Africa*. Princeton: Princeton University Press.

Skinner, Quentin. 1978. *The Foundations of Modern Political Thought*. Cambridge University Press.

Slaughter, Anne-Marie. 2004. *The New World Order*. Princeton University Press.

Smith, Adam. 1981 [1776]. *An Inquiry into the Nature and Causes of the Wealth of Nations*, ed. R. H. Campbell and A. S. Skinner. Indianapolis: Liberty Fund.

1982 [1766]. *Lectures on Jurisprudence*, ed. R. L. Meek, D. D. Raphael, and P. G. Stein. Indianapolis: Liberty Fund.

1984 [1759]. *The Theory of Moral Sentiments*, ed. D. D. Raphael and A. L. Macfie. Indianapolis: Liberty Fund.

Smith, Eric A. 2003. Human Cooperation. In Peter Hammerstein, ed., *The Genetic and Cultural Origins of Cooperation*. Cambridge, MA: MIT Press.

Snidal, Duncan. 1985a. Coordination vs. Prisoner's Dilemma: Implications for International Cooperation and Regimes. *American Political Science Review*, 79: 923–42.

1985b. The Limits of Hegemonic Stability Theory. *International Organization*, 39 (4): 207–32.

1991. Relative Gains and the Pattern of International Cooperation. *American Political Science Review*, 85: 701–26.

1993. *Relative Gains and the Pattern of International Cooperation*. In David A. Baldwin, ed., *Neorealism and Neoliberalism: The Contemporary Debate*. New York: Columbia University Press.

Snyder, Glenn H. 1971. 'Prisoner's Dilemma' and 'Chicken' Models in International Politics. *International Studies Quarterly*, 15: 66–103.

Snyder, Glenn H. and Paul Diesing. 1977. *Conflict Among Nations: Bargaining, Decision Making, and System Structure in International Crises*. Princeton: Princeton University Press.

Sober, Elliott and David Sloan Wilson. 1998. *Unto Others: The Evolution and Psychology of Unselfish Behavior*. Cambridge, MA: Harvard University Press.

Spar, Debora and James Dail. 2002. Of Measurement and Mission: Accounting for Performance in Non-governmental Organizations. *Chicago Journal of International Law*, 3: 171–81.

Spears, Russell, Bertjan Doosje, and Naomi Ellemers. 1997. Self-stereotyping in the Face of Threats to Group Status and Distinctiveness: the Role of Group Identification. *Personality and Social Psychology Bulletin*, 23, 5 May: 538–53.

Spector, Bertram I. and I. William Zartman, eds. 2003. *Getting It Done: Post-Agreement Negotiations and International Regimes*. Washington, DC: United States Institute of Peace Press.

Spiro, Peter. 2002. Accounting for NGOs. *Chicago Journal of International Law*, 3: 161–69.

Spitz, Jean-Fabien. 1995. *La Liberté politique*. Paris: PUF.

Stanger, Allison. 2004. *Replicating Cohen, Riolo, and Axelrod: A Docking Challenge*. Working Paper Series. Jena: Max-Planck Institute.

Starr, Penny. 2008. Global Governance Advocates Blame US for Economic Crisis. CNS News, November 17, available at www.cnsnews.com/public/content/article.aspx?RsrcID=39418.

Stein, Arthur. 1982. Coordination and Collaboration: Regimes in an Anarchic World. *International Organization*, 36: 294–324.

1990. *Why Nations Cooperate: Circumstance and Choice in International Relations*. Ithaca: Cornell University Press.

Stein, Janice. 1995. *Getting to the Table: The Processes of International Prenegotiation*. Baltimore: Johns Hopkins University Press.

Stein, Janice and Louis Pauly, eds. 1993. *Choosing to Cooperate*. Baltimore: Johns Hopkins University Press.

Steinberg, James, Anne-Marie Slaughter, Ivo Daalder, and Kurt Campbell. 2008. Strategic Leadership: Framework for a 21st Century National Security Strategy, available at www.brookings.edu/~/media/Files/rc/reports/2008/07_national_security_brainard/07_national_security_brainard.pdf.

Steinberg, Richard H. 2002. In the Shadow of Law or Power? Consensus Based Bargaining and Outcomes in the GATT/WTO. *International Organization*, 56 (2): 339–74.

Strange, Susan. 1999. The Westfailure System. *Review of International Studies*, 25: 345–54.

Surkov, Vladislav. 2006. Sovereignty – Political Synonym of Competitiveness. address to the students of the United Russia party study center, *Moskovskie Novosti*, 8, March 10–16: 10–11.

Swaine, Michael D. 2004. China: Exploiting a Strategic Opening. In Ashley J. Tellis, and Michael Wills, eds., *Strategic Asia 2004–2005: Confronting Terrorism in the Pursuit of Power*. Seattle: National Bureau of Asian Research.

Swaine, Michael D. and Ashley J. Tellis. 2000. *Interpreting China's Grand Strategy: Past, Present and Future*. Santa Monica: Rand.

Tajfel, Henri, ed. 1978. *Differentiation between Social Groups: Studies in the Social Psychology of Intergroup Relations*. London: Academic Press.

Tajfel, Henri. 1981. *Human Groups and Social Categories*. Cambridge University Press.

Tajfel, Henri and John C. Turner. 1979. An Integrative Theory of Intergroup Conflict. In William G. Austin and Stephen Worchel, eds., *The Social Psychology of Intergroup Relations*. Monterey, CA: Brooks/Cole, 33–47.

1986. The Social Identity Theory of InterGroup Behavior. In S. Worchel and W. G. Austin, eds., *Psychology of Inter-group Relations*. Chicago: Nelson-Hall.

Tarp, Finn, et al. 1999. Danish Aid Policy: Theory and Empirical Evidence. In Kanhaya L. Gupta, ed., *Foreign Aid: New Perspectives*. Boston: Kluwer Academic Publishers, 149–69.

Taverniese, Sabrina. 2002. Western Companies Warm to Russia. *New York Times*, May 30: W1.

Taylor, Brendan. 2008. The Bush Administration and Asia Pacific Multilateralism: Unrequited Love? *Australian Journal of International Affairs*, 62 (1): 1–15.

Taylor, Michael. 1976. *Anarchy and Cooperation*. New York: Wiley.

1987. *The Possibility of Cooperation*. Cambridge University Press.

Tepperman, Jonathan D. 2004. Some Hard Truths about Multilateralism. *World Policy Journal*, June.

Tesfatsion, Leigh. 2002. Agent-Based Computational Economics: Growing Economies from the Bottom Up. *Artificial Life*, 8 (1): 55–82.

Tessman, Brock F. and Steve Chan. 2004. Power Cycles, Risk Propensity, and Great-Power Deterrence. *Journal of Conflict Resolution*, 48 (2): 131–53.

Thakur, Ramesh. 2001. Global Norms and International Humanitarian Law. *International Review of the Red Cross*, 841: 19–44.

Torkunov, Anatolii. 2000. International Relations in the Post-Kosovo Context. *International Affairs* (Moscow), 46 (1): 74–81.

Touval, Saadia. 1982. *The Peace Brokers*. Princeton: Princeton University Press.

1989. Multilateral Negotiation: An Analytic Approach. *Negotiation Journal*, 5 (2): 159–73.

1994. Why the UN Fails: It Cannot Mediate. *Foreign Affairs*, 73 (5): 44–57.

2002. *Mediation in the Yugoslav Wars: The Critical Years, 1990–1995*. New York: Palgrave.

Touval, Saadia, and I. William Zartman. 2001. International Mediation in the Post-Cold War Era. In C. A. Crocker, F. O. Hampson, and P. Aall, eds., *Turbulent Peace: The Challenges of Managing International Conflict*, Washington, DC: United States Institute of Peace Press.

Toynbee, Arnold J. 1954. *A Study of History*, vol. 9. London: Oxford University Press.

Traulsen, A. and Martin Nowak, 2006. *Proceedings of the National Academy of Science*, 103: 13367.

Trenin, Dmitri. 2002. *The End of Eurasia: Russia on the Border Between Geopolitics and Globalization*. Washington, DC: Carnegie Endowment for International Peace.

2003–04. Pirouettes and Priorities: Distilling a Putin Doctrine. *National Interest* (Winter): 76–83.

2006. Russia Leaves the West. *Foreign Affairs*, 85 (4): 88–89.

2007. Russia Redefines Itself and Its Relations with the West. *Washington Quarterly*, 30 (2): 95–105.

Trivers, R. 1971. The Evolution of Reciprocal Altruism. *Quarterly Review of Biology*, 46 (1): 35–57.

Tsygankov, Andrei. 2006. *Russia's Foreign Policy: Change and Continuity in National Identity*. Lanham, MD: Rowman & Littlefield.

Tuck, Richard. 1977. *Natural Rights Theories: Their Origin and Development*. Cambridge University Press.

1983. Grotius, Carneades and Hobbes. *Grotiana*, 4: 43–61.

1987. The Modern Theory of Natural Law. In Anthony Pagden, ed., *The Languages of Political Theory in Early-Modern Europe*, Cambridge University Press.

1999. *The Rights of War and Peace: Political Thought and the International Order from Grotius to Kant*. Oxford University Press.

Tully, James, 1993a. *An Approach to Political Philosophy: Locke in Contexts*. Cambridge University Press.

1993b. Placing the Two Treatises. In Nicolas Phillipson and Quentin Skinner, eds., *Political Discourse in Early Modern Britain*. Cambridge University Press, 253–82.

Turner, J. and R. Brown. 1978. Social Status, Cognitive Alternatives, and Intergroup Relations. In Henri Tajfel, ed., *Differentiation between Social Groups*. New York: Academic Press, in cooperation with European Association of Experimental Social Psychology, 201–34.

Udalov, Vadim. 1995. National Interests and Conflict Resolution. In I. William Zartman and Victor Kremenyuk, eds., *Cooperative Security: Reducing Third World Wars*. Syracuse University Press.

Underdal, Arild. 1994. Leadership Theory: Rediscovering the Arts of Management. In I. William Zartman, ed., *International Multilateral Negotiation*. San Francisco: Jossey-Bass.

USInfo. 2005. US Academic Experts Advise Against Security Council Expansion, available at www.usinfo.state.gov/is/Archive/2005/Aug/11–509220.html.

Valdez, Jonathan. 1995. *The Near Abroad, the West, and National Identity in Russian Foreign Policy*. In Adeed Dawisha and Karen Dawisha, eds., *The Making of Foreign Policy in Russia and the New States of Eurasia*. Armonk, NY: M. E. Sharpe.

Vasquez, John A. 1993. *The War Puzzle*. Cambridge University Press.

Vennstra, Kristine and S. Alexander Haslam. 2000. Willingness to Participate in Industrial Protest: Exploring Social Identification in Context. *British Journal of Social Psychology*, 39: 153–72.

Vladislav Surkov's Secret Speech: How Russia Should Fight International Conspiracies. 2005. July 11, available at www.rferl.org.

Vogel, Gretchen. 2004. The Evolution of the Golden Rule. *Science*, 303 (February 20): 1131.

Waever, Ole. 1998. Insecurity, Security, and Asecurity in the West European Non-war Community. In Emanuel Adler and Michael Barnett, eds., *Security Communities*. Cambridge University Press, 81–93.

Wallace, Michael D. 1973. *War and Ranks Among Nations*. Lexington: Heath.

Wallander, Celeste A. 1996. Ideas, Interests, and Institutions in Russian Foreign Policy. In Wallander, ed. *The Sources of Russian Foreign Policy After the Cold War*. Boulder, CO: Westview.

Walt, Stephen M. 1987. *The Origin of Alliances*. Ithaca: Cornell University Press.
2001–02. Beyond bin Laden: Reshaping US Foreign Policy. *International Security*, 26 (3): 56–78.
2002. Keeping the World "Off Balance": Self Restraint and US Foreign Policy. In G. John Ikenberry, ed., *America Unrivaled: The Future of the Balance of Power*. Ithaca: Cornell University Press, 121–54.
2005. *Taming American Power: The Global Response to US Primacy*. New York: W. W. Norton.
Waltz, Kenneth N. 1979. *Theory of International Politics*. New York and St. Louis: McGraw-Hill.
Wapner, Paul. 2002. Defending Accountability in NGOs. *Chicago Journal of International Law*, 3: 197–205.
Ward, Hugh. 1990. Three Men in a Boat, Two Must Row: An Analysis of a Three-Person Chicken Pregame. *Journal of Conflict Resolution*, 34: 371–400.
Warkentin, Craig and Karen Mingst. 2000. International Institutions, the State, and Global Civil Society in the Age of the World Wide Web. *Global Governance: A Review of Multilateralism and International Organizations*, 6 (2): 237–58.
Washburn, John L. 2001. The United Nations' Relations with the United States: The UN Must Look Out for Itself. In Paul F. Diehl, ed., *The Politics of Global Governance*, 2nd ed. Boulder: Lynne Rienner: 467–82.
Watkins, Kevin and Ngaire Woods. 2004. Africa Must Be Heard in the Councils of the Rich. *International Herald Tribune*, October 2–3: 8.
Weber, Steve. 1992. Shaping the Postwar Balance of Power: Multilateralism in NATO. *International Organization*, 46 (3): 633.
Wehberg, Hans. 1959. Pacta sunt Servanda. *American Journal of International Law*, 53: 775–86.
Weiss, Thomas G. 2003. The Illusion of UN Security Council Reform. *Washington Quarterly*, 26 (4): 147–61.
Weiss, Thomas G. and Don Hubert. 2001. *The Responsibility to Protect: Research, Bibliography, and Background*. Ottawa: International Development Research Centre.
Wells, Clare. 1987. *The UN, UNESCO, and the Politics of Knowledge*. New York: St. Martin's Press.
Wendt, Alexander. 1999. *Social Theory of International Politics*. Cambridge University Press.
Whiting, Allen S. 1997. ASEAN Eyes China: The Security Dimension. *Asian Survey*, 37 (4): 292–322.
Wight, Martin. 1991. *International Theory. The Three Traditions*. Leicester University Press.
Willetts, Peter. 2000. From "Consultative Arrangements" to "Partnership": The Changing Status of NGOs in Diplomacy at the UN. *Global Governance: A Review of Multilateralism and International Organizations*, 6: 191–212.
Williams, Frances. 2004. WIPO to Head Concerns of Poor. *Financial Times*, October 4: 8.
Winch, Donald. 1978. *Adam Smith's Politics*. Cambridge University Press.

1983. Adam Smith's Enduring Particular Result: A Political and Cosmopolitan Perspective. In Istvan Hont and Michael Ignatieff, eds., *Wealth and Virtue: The Shaping of Political Economy in the Scottish Enlightenment*. Cambridge University Press, 253–69.

1991. Adam Smith's Politics Revisited. *Quaderni di Storia dell'Economica Politica*, 9: 3–27.

1992. Adam Smith: Scottish Moral Philosopher as Political Economist. *Historical Journal*, 35: 91–113.

1996. *Riches and Poverty. An Intellectual History of Political Economy in Britain, 1750–1834*. Cambridge University Press.

Winham, Gilbert and Elizabeth DeBoer-Ashworth. 2000. Asymmetry in Negotiating the Canada–US Free Trade Agreement. In I. William Zartman and Jeffrey Z. Rubin, eds., *Power and Negotiation*. Ann Arbor: University of Michigan Press.

Wohlforth, William C. 1999. The Stability of a Unipolar World. *International Security*, 24 (1): 5–42.

Wong, John and Sarah Chang. 2003. China–ASEAN Free Trade Agreement: Shaping Future Economic Relations. *Asian Survey*, 43: 507–26.

Woods, Ngaire. 2001. Making the IMF More Accountable. *International Affairs*, 77 (1): 83–100.

Wootton, David. 1986. *Divine Right and Democracy: An Anthology of Political Writing in Stuart England*. Harmondsworth: Penguin.

Wright, Quincy. 1965. *A Study of War*, 2nd ed. Chicago: University of Chicago Press.

Wu, Anne. 2005. What China Whispers to North Korea. *Washington Quarterly* 28 (2): 35–48.

Xinbo, Wu. 2005–2006. The End of the Silver Lining: A Chinese View of the US–Japanese Alliance. *Washington Quarterly*, 29 (1): 119–30.

Xinhua. 1996. 30 December in *FBIS-CHI*-1996–251.

Yang, Dali L. 2002. China in 2001: Economic Liberalization and Its Political Discontents. *Asian Survey*, 42 (1): 14–29.

Young, Oran. 1989. *International Cooperation*. Cornell University Press.

Zagoria, Donald S. 2006. The US–China–Taiwan Triangle: Towards Equilibrium. May 23, available at www.nautilus.org/fora/security/0640Zagoria.html.

Zakaria, Fareed. 2004. Bush's Quiet Multilateralism. *Newsweek*, May 10, available at http://msnbc.msn.com/id/4880290/.

Zartman, I. William. 1989. *Ripe for Resolution*. Oxford University Press.

ed. 1994a. *International Multilateral Negotiation: Approaches to the Management of Complexity*. San Francisco: Josey-Bass Publishers.

1994b. *Introduction*. In I. William Zartman, ed. *International Multilateral Negotiation*. San Francisco: Jossey-Bass.

1995. Negotiations in South Africa. In I. William Zartman, ed. *Elusive Peace: Negotiating an End to Civil Wars*. Brookings Institute.

1997a. Ripeness. *PINPoints*, 11: 2–3.

1997b. The Structuralist Dilemma in Negotiation. *Research on Negotiation in Organizations*, 6: 227–45.

2000. Beyond the Hurting Stalemate: Ripeness Revisited. In Paul Stern and Daniel Druckman, eds, *International Conflict Resolution after the Cold War*. Washington, DC: National Academies Press.

ed. 2001. *Preventive Negotiation: Avoiding Conflict Escalation*. Lanham: Rowman & Littlefield.

2005a. Comparative Case Studies. *International Negotiation*, 10 (1): 3–15.

2005b. *Cowardly Lions: Missed Opportunities to Prevent State Collapse and Deadly Conflict*. Boulder, CO: Lynne Rienner.

2005c. Resolving the Toughness Dilemma. In Guy Olivier Faure, ed., *La Negociation: regards sur sa diversité*. Paris: Publibook.

ed. 2008. *Imbalance of Power: The Post-bipolar System of World Order*. Boulder: Lynne Rienner.

Zartman, I. William and Maureen Berman. 1982. *The Practical Negotiator*. New Haven: Yale University Press.

Zartman, I. William and Rubin, Jeffrey Z., eds. 2000. *Power and Negotiation*. Ann Arbor: University of Michigan Press.

Zartman, I. William et al. 1996. Negotiation as a Search for Justice. *International Negotiation*, 1 (1): 79–98.

Zhang, Yunling and Shiping Tang. 2005. China's Regional Strategy. In David Shambaugh, ed., *Power Shift: China and Asia's New Dynamics*. Berkeley: University of California Press.

Zimmermann, Reinhard. 1990. *The Law of Obligations. Roman Foundations of the Civilian Tradition*. Wynberg, Cape: Rustica Press.

Index